PSYCHOLOGICAL ISSUES

VOL. VI, NO. 2 MONOGRAPH 22

TOWARD A UNITY OF KNOWLEDGE

Edited by

MARJORIE GRENE

INTERNATIONAL UNIVERSITIES PRESS, INC.
239 Park Avenue South • New York, N. Y. 10003

Library of Congress Catalog Card Number: 69-17280

PSYCHOLOGICAL ISSUES

Subscription per Volume, $10.00
Single Copies of This Number, $5.00

CONTENTS

EDITOR'S INTRODUCTION

A new experimental group may hesitate to publish its proceedings; yet such a group can clarify its own aims, and gain impetus and support to carry them through, only if it in some form consolidates and gives to the public the fruits of its experiment. The present volume is meant to perform this service for the first meeting of the Study Group on Foundations of Cultural Unity, held at Bowdoin College, Brunswick, Maine from August 23 to August 28, 1965, under the sponsorship of the College and with the support of a grant from the Ford Foundation.

In planning the meeting, the organizing committee stated our interests and aims as follows:

> Since the 17th century the kind of knowledge afforded by mathematical physics has come more and more to furnish mankind with an ideal for all knowledge. This ideal also carries with it a new conception of the nature of things: all things whatsoever are held to be intelligible ultimately in terms of the laws of inanimate nature. In the light of such a reductionist program, the finalistic nature of living beings, the sentience of animals and their intelligence, the responsible choices of man, his moral and aesthetic ideals, the fact of human greatness seem all of them anomalies that will be removed eventually by further progress. Their existence—even the existence of science itself—has no legitimate grounds; our deepest convictions lack all theoretical foundation.
>
> This movement claims to unify science and to comprehend in it all subjects of study. But, since its ideal is fundamentally mistaken, the result has been to debase the conception of man entertained by the psychological and social sciences and at the same time to isolate from science the humanistic core of history and criticism. It has displaced the traditional endeavor of philosophy to comprehend the whole domain of human thought and produced instead distortion and fragmentation. Although these views have been developing since the

Copernican revolution, they have gained the power to shake the foundations of our culture only in the last hundred years. There have been countermovements: attempts to restore metaphysics, attempts to reformulate our conception of knowledge. In our own time, existentialism, supported by the ideas of phenomenology, has been perhaps the most potent countermovement. Movements of this sort are strongholds defying the current scientific outlook; but they do not appear to be equipped for overthrowing and replacing it. Today, however, there are signs of new centers of resistance among scholars, scientists, and writers in almost every region of knowledge. Many share the conviction that a deep-seated philosophical reform is needed—one that would radically alter prevailing conceptions, not only of the nature of knowledge and of creative achievements in general, but of the human agent who inquires and creates, and of the entire fabric of the culture formed by such activities. Of these thinkers, some have thus far confined their efforts to the critique of scientism; others are interested in the bearing of empirical investigations on the gradual clarification of epistemological problems; still others have embarked upon comprehensive philosophical reorientations.

Convinced that there is an unsuspected convergence of ideas separately developed in various fields, we propose a meeting of a number of persons who actively oppose in their work the scientism, and the related methodological and ontological oversimplifications, which in one or another form are ascendant in every field of scholarly endeavor. The realization on the part of those attending this meeting that they are participating in one common movement of thought could strengthen each of them. It would help any attempts at systematizing the principles they perhaps unwittingly share and would make it possible for the general ideas that emerge to receive criticism from workers in widely different fields.

We tried, then, to bring together 25 people whose work converged on a common problem: essentially a philosophical problem, but one which arises, if in somewhat different forms, at the boundary of a number of widely separated disciplines: painting or psychology, physics or poetry. Indeed, as those of us who work in philosophy already know, it is a whole nest of related problems that are in question, whether the crux of the matter be put as "the crisis of man's self-knowledge," as "the alienation of the modern mind," as "the fragmentation of our culture." In short, however one puts the core question, and from whatever specialized perspective one approaches it, there is not only a common question, and a common interest, but a spectrum of common questions and common interests in which, we believed, we could all assist one another. Clearly this was a gamble. Clearly, we concluded at the close of the week's discussion, it had been a gamble that paid off. Not wholly unequivocally, of course: the week had its ups and downs, its encounters and its failures to communicate. Yet as the week went on there was an increasing and palpable sense, not so much just of agreement, as of something very important that the whole procedure was building up to. This can be specified, perhaps, along a number of lines. First, there was the impression of a new and exciting opening of windows through interdisciplinary contacts. Second, the occasion was enriched by the presence of men of distinguished achievement in differing fields, whose insights contributed to the discussion and who brought, as personalities, something unique to the human quality of the meeting. Third, the kinship of philosophical, scientific, and artistic problems was strikingly displayed, so that the week's program led organically up to its culmination in the arts. The contribution of Donald Weismann's collages and Elizabeth Sewell's reading was of especial importance in this connection. But fourth, the conference seemed most of all to be a beginning: to have laid the foundation for continued contact and collaboration on a number of particular problems which had opened up as material for further discussion. The problem of the nature and role of the imagination, from scientific discovery in general, through biology (in particular, taxonomy), to the arts, was one such theme. Another which kept recurring was the question of levels of explanation and levels of reality: a central question not only for philosophy, but for the relation between the sciences of life—man, on the one hand, and physics, on the other—and indeed for the interpretation of the art object as well—the problem of its reality and its capacity to teach us about ourselves and our world.

It is the last point—the range of problems opened up by the meeting—around which I had hoped to organize the present volume. Unfortunately, considerations of space have necessitated cutting a number of papers as well as a very great deal of the discussion. In the circumstances, I have chosen those topics of study which seemed to be most germane to the interests of readers of the present monograph. We have tried to rectify the omissions resulting from this policy by publishing, in a more permanent form, with a more explicitly philosophical emphasis, a collection of selected papers from the first two years of our Study Group—that is, 1965 and

1966. That volume includes, as I have regretfully been unable to do here, both Edward Pols's paper on the "Philosophical Knowledge of the Person," which set the direction of our major metaphysical interests, and Elizabeth Sewell's poem, "Cosmos and Kingdom," which put, more persuasively than philosophers are able, our sense of the past and our hope for the future.[1]

The Study Group's minimal hope was for a convergence of problems: we hoped for mutual encouragement from a sharing of common difficulties in a shared intellectual crisis. More than this, however, we hoped to assist one another, from the points of view of our different disciplines, in carving out paths along which these shared problems might be solved. Part I introduces our problem, and Parts II to IV indicate some of the lines along which such undertakings were projected. Although there are crisscrossings, the sequences of papers and discussions should, on the whole, exhibit the variety as well as the unity of our work-in-progress.

ORIGINAL PROGRAM OF THE 1965 MEETING OF THE STUDY GROUP ON FOUNDATIONS OF CULTURAL UNITY

Philosophical Introduction (A)

Chairman: Edward Pols
Paper: Michael Polanyi: "The Creative Imagination"
Comments, informal, by other participants

Philosophical Introduction (B)

Chairman: John Lucas
Papers: (1) Edward Pols: "Philosophical Knowledge of the Person"
(2) Richard Tansey: "Agency, Abstraction, and Control: Outline of a Theory of the Artificial"
Comments, informal, by other participants

Physics and Reality

Chairman: William H. Poteat
Paper: Eugene P. Wigner: "Epistemology of Quantum Mechanics—Its Appraisal and Demand"
Comments: (1) John Lucas
(2) Jerald C. Kindred

[1] See *The Anatomy of Knowledge*, London: Routledge and Kegan Paul; and Amherst: University of Massachusetts Press, 1968.

Philosophical Foundations of Biology (A)

Chairman: Marjorie Grene
Paper: Helmuth Plessner: "A Newton of a Blade of Grass"?
Comments, informal, by other participants

Philosophical Foundations of Biology (B)

Chairman: William T. Scott
Paper: (1) C.F.A. Pantin: "Organism and Environment"
Comment: M.R.A. Chance
Paper: (2) M.R.A. Chance: "Man in Biology"
Comment: Marjorie Grene

The Predicament of Psychology (A)

Chairman: George S. Klein
Papers: (1) Sigmund Koch: "Value Properties: Their Significance for Psychology, Axiology, and Science"
(2) Henry A. Murray: "A Myth about the Study Group"
Comments, informal, by other participants

The Predicament of Psychology (B)

Chairman: John R. Silber
Paper: Erwin Straus: "Embodiment and Excarnation"
Comment: (1) Frederick Crosson
(2) George S. Klein

Linguistics; Perception of Paintings

Chairman: Henry A. Murray
Papers: (1) W. Haas: "The Science of Language"
(2) M.H. Pirenne: "Perception of Paintings"
Comment, informal, by other participants

Art and Creativity (A): *The Visual Arts*

Chairman: Marjorie Grene
Paper: Donald L. Weismann: "The Collage as Model"
Comment: Richard G. Tansey

Art and Creativity (B): *Literature*

Chairman: Richard G. Tansey
Paper: Herbert Gold: "The Life Contained in Novels and the Novelist's Life"
Comment: Elizabeth Sewell
Poem: Elizabeth Sewell: "Cosmos and Kingdom"

Visitors to the meeting who participated in discussions:

Professor Kenneth Freeman, Department of Philosophy, Bowdoin College
Professor Fritz Koelln, Department of German, Bowdoin College
Professor C. Douglas McGee, Department of Philosophy, Bowdoin College
Mrs. Helmuth Plessner

PART I

THE TASK BEFORE US

Professor Stallknecht's paper puts in less condensed form than our manifesto the central purpose of the Study Group: to restore man as a conscious and responsible being to a stable place in the natural world. As a physicist, Professor Wigner stands at a vantage point from which he sees this issue sharpened to paradox. His paper therefore sets dramatically the nub of our common problem.

1

PHILOSOPHY AND CIVILIZATION

NEWTON P. STALLKNECHT

This paper is written in defense of a few platitudes, the basic platitudes of our civilization. These platitudes are harder to accept and to defend than many of their sincere supporters have recognized. They are thus not really platitudes at all, but—shall we say?—"plongitudes" disguised by their own prestige. As this becomes obvious they may regain their rightful place at the heart of philosophical discussion.

The sense of value that supports the ideology of our Western world has long centered upon the idea of the autonomous and responsible individual. This notion, as a regulative idea, never completely realized, characterizes our civilization, and its reflection in religion, social policy, and the arts is often considered an index of our cultural maturity. From this point of view, such an institution as school, church, or state, indeed any corporate entity, can ultimately justify itself only in so far as it enriches the lives of its members, and of those who come in one way or another under its influence, by granting and encouraging freedom of self-development.

Furthermore, we have come to recognize that the quality of these organizations depends upon the contributions of individual human beings whose thinking and overt action revitalize and redirect the cultural movements upon which their effectiveness depends. It is from the insight, decisions, and commitments of its individual members—both of those who attain leadership and those who support the leadership of others with sympathy and understanding—that the health of our community is maintained. As Wordsworth once put it, the true wealth of nations lies in the character of its citizens.

Before such a way of life can approach its full realization, the notion of the individual both as an effective agent and as an end in himself must be clearly envisaged. Such vision is a considerable achievement. In many primitive cultures, even in that reflected in the Homeric poems, this notion is not fully developed. In Homer the gods, symbolizing or accepted as identical with forces of nature or deeply rooted tendencies of human nature, are often said to overwhelm the individual in moments of great crisis, when his decision can hardly be described as his own. In more primitive cultures, social attitudes and patterns of approved behavior actually leave the individual a very minimum of freedom. The fear of violating firmly established folkways and prohibitions stands as the primary source of motivation, and the individual, rather than being recognized as an end in himself and as a source of evaluation and decision, is held, so to speak, in solution within the life of the community. In contrast, the discovery—we might almost say the creation—of the individual, recognized both as an agent and as an ultimate value, stands as a revolution of enormous significance. Such a revolution is not a matter of a decade, a generation, or even a century. It moves slowly between remote extremes, between, say, the unchallenged expulsion of a native who has, perhaps unwittingly, violated a tribal taboo and, on the other hand, the meeting of minds achieved by a group of voluntary fellow workers committed to a common objective, who have learned to share and mutually profit by one another's experience and insight.

We cannot here trace the notion of the individual, as an idea and as an ideal, to its historical origin. Let us point, however, to its early development in classical civilization, in the imagination and the thinking of the Greeks, where human consciousness came gradually to recognize itself as a source of self-determination. This notion is present, at least by anticipation, in ancient tragedy, and it takes on an intellectual form during the lively disputes between Socrates and the Sophists. It is often central in Plato's thought, as in the beautiful myth of Er, and again in Aristotle's sober consideration of moral decision. It is dominant in the thinking of the Stoics. Against a different background, it becomes increasingly clear in the development of Hebrew-Christian thought, gradually overcoming the heavy resistance offered by the institutionalism of religious establishments and the vested interests of powerful minorities.

Springing from the heart of Christian belief, supplemented by Greek wisdom, this notion has in modern times inspired the internal organization of the Christian community, reforming ecclesiastical policy and reorienting political theory and practice. It has also appeared in the arts and in education as the ideal of creation has gradually superseded that of imitation. One can hardly overemphasize the far-flung influence of the Socratic "Know thyself," of the Christian "As a man thinketh in his heart so is he," and of the equally important "The Sabbath was made for man, not man for the Sabbath." In sympathy with these insights, we all respect the ideal of a kingdom of ends, that furthers the realization of human individuals in a life of self-expression carried on in a spirit of cooperation and mutual responsibility. We are all ready to accept the ideal of such responsible freedom shared in community. For Western thought this freedom is often accepted as the very quality of man. In this sense we are all humanists. Even the Marxians have recognized such an ideal as justifying the rigorous restrictions of a prolonged period of social transition. Indeed, so widespread and so authoritative has this ideal become that its statement is now little more than an obvious platitude and there is always the danger that we will take it too readily for granted as a background that we need not examine very carefully. As a result, this noblest of ideals is often caricatured by hasty, if sincere, thinking. Thus the notion of responsible individualism has at times been distorted to justify an economy of unrestrained competition, including the unrestricted freedom of an employer in his relations with his workers.

There are, however, difficulties of another sort that arise when we concentrate our attention upon the idea of the free individual. It has not been easy for modern philosophy to come to terms with this way of thinking. As a result, academic philosophy and what we might call the traditional common sense of our civilization have often been at odds. It is an irony of history that as the ideal of the responsible individual gathers prestige in the political and religious thought of modern times, the concept of nature that emerges with the beginnings of modern science renders this ideal increasingly difficult to formulate in philosophical terms. Thus, when considered conscientiously by the theorist, the freedom of the individual becomes difficult to define and especially difficult to reconcile with other concepts that the philosopher is often reluctant to dismiss.

As a physical organism, even an organism of extraordinary development, man remains a part of nature. Nature is interpreted as an interplay of events that manifest, at least on the level of molar masses and living things, a system of predictable patterns, including cyclical routines, so that the structure of the present appears as an extrapolation of the structure of the past. This would seem to leave no room for conscious initiative, for self-motivated control or telic orientation. Modern science, especially in the form taken by early developments in physics and astronomy, that is, by those very developments which in the 18th and 19th centuries appealed most vividly to the popular imagination, has often been inclined to identify the intelligible with the predictable and to insist that any genuine aspect of nature will in time be so understood. Human conduct is often included under this assumption. Many philosophers have accepted this bold postulate and have offered the layman an image of human nature that he has been reluctant to accept, preferring rather to view the philosophical enterprise itself as suspect.

The layman often stands closer to the spirit of Western civilization than the modern philosopher, and he is not ready to accept a theory of selfhood that renders our conscious motivation primarily an outcome of previous events, and therefore, ideally speaking, essentially predictable. For the layman, as for certain Greek philosophers, the psyche initiates motion, the human self stands as a center of choice that directs commitment. Sentences such as "I changed my mind" or "I kept my temper" must be interpreted in the light of these assumptions. This attitude of the layman is not a matter of sheer sentimentality. His opposition to a determinist interpretation of human behavior deserves more attention than many a philosopher is likely to bestow upon it.

Determinism can have grave consequences for human relations, consequences that may undermine the traditional respect for the individual that the layman finds so important. After all, if we consider the consciousness of our fellow man as the outcome of external conditioning, we may well come to follow the strategy and techniques so often employed by the advertising expert rather than those of the Socratic teacher. We may well be tempted to control behavior rather than to share experience and exchange points of view. Once we have finally accepted a philosophy of determinism, we will not seek to awaken our fellows to problematic situations, inviting them to answer our questions in their own way and to offer suggestions that occur to them as they survey the situation from their own points of view. As teachers, we will be more interested in the formation of habits, perhaps primarily habits of speech, than in awakening a sense of responsibility. We will not be eager to share problems but to press toward the propagation of ready-made attitudes. In such a situation, the teacher becomes a trainer, and the politician a salesman.

On the other hand, just in so far as we scorn, as the good teacher so often does, to employ such methods, we will find ourselves acting on assumptions that commit us to a very different concept of human nature. It is interesting to notice that the spirit of common courtesy, which reflects a genuine respect for the autonomy and responsibility of our fellows, renders distasteful any effort to press them toward practical commitments and overt statements of opinion that they have not made their own. In this respect we are all laymen and resent the slightest hint that our thinking is to be conditioned by expert technicians, whether they be salesmen, political or religious, propagandists, or aggressive educators. The essence of courtesy lies in a willingness to respect the experience and insights of other people. This respect for others goes hand in hand with our own self-respect, for if we treat the thinking of others as the outcome of external conditioning, we can hardly make an exception of ourselves. Our own thought has been conditioned too, even if we know not how. It is perhaps only in a community where the ideal of individual responsibility and autonomy is kept constantly in mind, both in theory and practice, that genuine thinking and sincere expression can flourish and be taken seriously.

The delight that we take in the arts and the respect that we pay the achievements of science include at least a tacit recognition of the freedom or responsible autonomy that is manifest in their production. This freedom often has to resist early conditioning rather than profiting by it. The poet or any serious writer must free himself from the use of clichés. Thus, he must resist some of the most powerful associations established by listening to the speech around him. He must even take care not to imitate his favorite authors. And the scientific thinker must be capable of surveying his data from many points of view, resisting at least temporarily the pressure of dominant opinion, as he explores unfashionable possibilities of interpretation. Successful work in art and in science requires an integration of detail that is possible only to a mind capable of resisting distraction of all sorts, a mind capable of reconditioning itself as it enters new situations and accepts new objectives.

But freedom is by no means negative in spirit. The ability to resist fashionable patterns of thought and commonplace modes of expression must be supplemented by the responsibility that underwrites or answers for (*respondeo*) those patterns and modes actually accepted and embodied in action. We all accept the proposition that such responsibility is possible. To deny it would be to consider the words *true* and *false* as uttered by human beings to be virtually meaningless.

The above seems, I think, to indicate that the layman, the artist, and the scientist have, all three, reason to respect the ideal of the autonomous and responsible individual, in whose conscious activity freedom of action, of expression, and of thought may be realized. From this point of view the nature of consciousness and its relation to its world assumes great importance, and it is to such inquiry that the philosopher should turn his attention. In studying consciousness, we find ourselves reminded of Plato's attitude in the famous Seventh Letter. We can often do little more than invite our readers to look for themselves. Verification will be in the self-examination of each one of us. At times a few steps of deductive argument will be possible. But in general we are appealing to the experience of the reader and urging him to report on certain features of his own conscious life.

Our consciousness presents itself as activity—not a Cartesian *res cogitans* or *chose qui pense,* but an activity that shapes itself so that it is difficult to tell the "dancer from the dance." And yet the dance offers a better metaphor than William James's famous "stream of consciousness." This is because in consciousness there seems always to be not only some sense of continuity with the past but some sense of direction or expectation and some sense of selective choice. We do not, to be sure, perceive an agent imposing direction upon our thinking. Rather some sense of continuity, some degree of choice and intention, seem to characterize each moment of consciousness and to distinguish it from sheer feeling. These features vary with the intensity of consciousness. Together they afford a context within which the first-person pronoun acquires meaning.

The basic activity of consciousness has to do with attention. We pay attention and we shift attention. Even a voluntary decision centers, as William James used to teach, upon a concentration of attention that initiates overt action. It is important to notice that attention is always both objectively and subjectively oriented. In the first place, consciousness, as both Kant and Husserl would insist, is always consciousness *of*. There is always reference to something, not to be considered as identical with consciousness itself. But at the same time we must recognize that the structure of consciousness justifies our use of the first-person pronoun. Whatever object we apprehend, there is always some felt continuity of our present activity with our past and some sense of some further activity to follow. Acts of attention appear as *our* acts just in so far as they are not isolated from one another. Indeed the subjective orientation of consciousness lies precisely in overcoming or avoiding this isolation. "*I am*" seems usually to be an elliptical expression. It seems to mean something as follows: *Here I am* doing thus and so, involved in such and such an undertaking begun in the past and opening upon a future still indeterminate in detail. In moments of reflection this time span referred to may be a very long one, half a lifetime or more, and still open to the future. This subjective continuity is maintained only so far as we recognize some relevance of present things and events to those things and events that preceded them and with which we were previously concerned. The trans-temporal relevance is apprehended through our ability to interpret our situation as in some way continuing features of the past. This primary interpretation is basic to perception itself, which entertains objects and continued events by recognizing their appearance and reappearance over considerable lapses of time. When we remember that these appearances do not necessarily resemble each other, the importance of this primary interpretation becomes clear.

Consciousness is, however, not merely a matter of seeing our present as in one way or another a continuation of our past. We are always concerned in some degree with the future. There is something ever more about to be with the shaping of which we find ourselves involved; for consciousness is not purely cognitive: it has always a conative aspect. *I was, I will be,* and *I want to be* or *I intend to be* qualify the *I am* which is no mere punctual presence. We can be misled by the neatness of the grammarian who finds *I am* and *it is* belonging to the same tense. In this respect *am,* along with the experience that justifies its use, stands in sharp contrast with *is. Am* straddles all three major tenses. From this point of view *am* and *is* should not be considered forms of the same verb. *Am,* so to speak, always projects itself into an unfinished and partially indeterminate future and carries its past along with it. Consciousness overlaps past and future. This is especially obvious in any activity that requires the employment of a language or a system of symbols. The construction of an intelligible sentence, to say nothing of a sustained argument, calls for many decisions and adjustments over which presides our conscious intention to communicate or to persuade. Here we must keep ahead of ourselves, sensing the direction or intent of statements still in the making. This unrealized intention constitutes our hold upon the future. This future may actually come to be in the decision that we are making, as we move from a scheme of alternative possibilities toward a texture of fully detailed and concrete events. While the alternatives are still open, consciousness is engaged in shaping an outcome. Thus a conscious individual lives largely in his own future, what we might call his future concrescent.

It is most important to recognize that this future concrescent is not a mere idea of ours. It has a reality of its own. It is not to be identified with our thinking. It is something about which we think and with which we work. Our thinking concerning this future may be true or false—false when in confusion we commit ourselves to an impossibility, as when we become circle-squarers or dream of constructing a perpetual motion machine—again false when we envisage a genuine possibility but fail to notice that we have no facilities at *our* disposal to assure *our* realization thereof. When, however, our thinking is free from any such confusion the possibility envisaged is a genuine component of our open future, even if at last we renounce it or fail to realize it. Of course, such an entity is not to be confused with a concrete object, but it remains a genuine object of responsible thinking, in this one respect similar to a Platonic form. Consciousness operates between what is and what may be, somewhat as the soul in Plato's philosophy apprehends both things and the forms. Consciousness is neither an actual concretion nor an unrealized possibility but a productive interplay of the two. Thus consciousness is an ontological amphibian. It qualifies and in a sense criticizes the concrete by setting it in a context of nonexistent possibility. This is supported by that triumph of conscious activity, the negative judgment, through which consciousness may invite the realization of what would otherwise never take place.

So conceived, consciousness, and with consciousness the individual selfhood that characterizes its higher development, cannot be identified with or located in the spatial layout of an organism as it exists at any one moment of observation. In this Leibniz was right. If the human brain and nervous system were expanded in size to equal that of a mill or factory and we were allowed to walk within it, we would observe nothing but moving parts, of one kind or another, in their intricate relationship. We would not come face to face with feelings, perceptions, and ideas. This is consistent with the notion that consciousness is not limited to the concrete.

It does not exist as an actual event with a concrete tissue of other actual events. A pronounced syllable or word may so exist but not the consciousness that expresses itself through that word with reference to the meaning that is taking shape as the word is chosen. Here we are tempted to borrow a phrase from the idealists of an earlier generation. Consciousness, while in contact with the spoken word, *transcends* it. The meaning of *transcends* may be discerned through an examination of the conscious situation as a whole. A word, considered not as the beating of the air with the tongue but as enjoyed by consciousness, participates in a meaning, still incompletely formulated, with whose final formulation consciousness is concerned. The pronounced word may perhaps be likened to a point at which activity of consciousness contributes to the concrete but does not identify itself with it.

Fully alerted and active consciousness, indeed any activity over which such consciousness presides, is not, like certain phenomena in the physical order, a system or series of events whose most prominent features may be considered as fully predictable. Consider a moment of choice—perhaps we should say of creative choice—when a poet adds a final phrase to a stanza, or corrects the ending of a line already in context, a moment in the growth of an unfinished poem. To some slight degree the new phrase has been predictable—by the poet himself or by a friend who has heard the lines already composed. This prediction may be based on the fact that the metrical scheme of the phrase and the rhyme tone of its last syllable must fit into patterns already established, and syntactically the phrase must conform with a sentence structure already in being. In other words, the new phrase must be reconciled with certain features of past composition, and hence its character is in some degree predictable. Yet the phrase itself considered as a fully concrete achievement, the phrase with the final wording that supports its imagery and metaphorical significance, has not been predictable. To predict to this extent would have been to complete the phrase and to have enjoyed its aesthetic relation to the poem as it took shape. Such prediction would coincide with creation. The predicting observer would have taken over the writing of the poem for himself. The first author, while perhaps admiring his observer's contribution, would in all probability not accept it as his own—unless he stood in deepest sympathy with the observer and was willing to accept him as a collaborator.

What is so obviously true of artistic creation should be true also of any act of fully alert consciousness that carries constructive choice beyond the consideration of familiar generalities. Prediction cannot reach the full detail with which the conscious individual realizes a long-term objective of recognized importance. To be sure, certain very general anticipations of human decision often take place. Thus we may be very sure that certain people will not choose to travel by air, and we may be well aware of the circumstances that have conditioned this decision. But just how these people will choose to travel as they plan and enjoy their vacations soon surpasses the scope of our foresight. What transport they will prefer from time to time, what will be their routes, their stopping places, when they will be willing to exceed their budgets, etc., etc.—all this is not a matter of close prediction.

After all, to understand the activity of a conscious individual does not depend upon an effort to reduce its pattern to a trajectory. In so far as such understanding is possible, it calls for the methods of the historian and the biographer, even of the literary critic, and it is to their methods rather than to those of the physicist or the astronomer that we should turn in trying to comprehend the action and utterance of a human individual. What we seek is an intellectual sympathy through which we reproduce the orientation including the evaluation of circumstances, available alternatives, and objectives within which the individual has lived, has taken action, and has tried to justify it. We need, more than anything else, some glimpse of the individual's image of himself or of his work and his sense of what he would achieve. Such understanding can complete itself only in retrospect. This is very clear in the work of the great artist whose new departures often for a time baffle his most friendly critics.

It is, I submit, one of the chief tasks of the philosopher to explore the presuppositions of such inquiry. With such a philosophy human consciousness must occupy the central, indeed a privileged, position. But there is a danger that we will so emphasize its importance that we will isolate it by interpreting it as a miracle that terminates all further inquiry. Here we may profit by the wisdom of that master of speculative philosophy, the late A. N. Whitehead, whose contribution is today all too likely to be overlooked. Consider the following passage from Whitehead's *Modes of Thought:*

> Human nature has been described in terms of its vivid accidents, and not of its existential essence. The description of its essence must apply to the unborn child, to the baby in its cradle, to the state of sleep, and to that vast background of feeling hardly touched by consciousness. Clear, conscious discrimination [including the entertainment of alternatives] is an accident of human existence. It makes us human. But it does not make us exist. It is of the essence of our humanity. But it is an accident of our existence [Whitehead, 1938, p. 158].

Here, I think, a slight qualification is in order. Clear conscious discrimination is an accident of our *existence,* an accident, of course, in the Aristotelian sense. But it may become, even so, the heart of *our* individual existence—of the existence of a human being who achieves a responsible autonomy. This autonomy or mature individuality is not forced upon us. It is made possible but not guaranteed by our intricate biological and physical substructure and by a welter of feeling and unenlightened emotion. Without this substructure there could be no conscious *life*—nor would consciousness be in contact with its world. Here perhaps another quotation from Whitehead's book is in order:

> I find myself as essentially a unity of emotions, enjoyments, hopes, fears, regrets, valuations of alternatives, decisions—all of them sub-

jective reactions to the environment as active in my nature. My unity —which is Descartes' 'I am'—is my process of shaping this welter of material into a consistent pattern of feelings. The individual enjoyment is what I am in my role of a natural activity, as I shape the activities of the environment into a new creation, which is myself at this moment; and yet, as being myself, it is a continuation of the antecedent world. If we stress the role of the environment, this process is causation. If we stress the role of my immediate pattern of active enjoyment, this process is self-creation. If we stress the role of the conceptual anticipation of the future whose existence is a necessity in the nature of the present, this process is the teleological aim at some ideal in the future. This aim, however, is not really beyond the present process. For the aim at the future is an enjoyment in the present. It thus effectively conditions the immediate self-creation of the new creature [p. 228].

For Whitehead, we must remember, the "present process" is not a static instant but an invasion of the future. Whitehead has boldly spoken of this process as a self-creation emerging from our "subjective reaction to the environment." He has even dared to use Spinoza's phrase *causa sui*. A finite *causa sui* is an even more difficult concept than that of Spinoza's *deus sive natura*. The interplay of mutual adjustment constantly taking place in what is sometimes called the concert of the living organism gives us some inkling of what is meant. Enlightened consciousness perfecting such an organism presents a more spectacular example. Here we have not so much an adaptation to environmental circumstance as a control, within limits, of the environment itself—an imposing of an intricate and very specific order, which may be revised and redirected almost indefinitely. Such activity is subject to the conditioning and limitations arising from its substructure, but on its own level it may condition itself having in view the achievement of chosen objectives.

Perhaps the best way further to understand the autonomous responsibility of which consciousness is capable is to consider those moments in which consciousness, so to speak, "loses its grip" on past and future so that our conduct becomes less and less our own. This can happen in moments of extreme pain, fear, anger, acute embarrassment, or when we are subjected to a rigid routine of behavior like that imposed on a parade ground. Under such pressures, we lose sight of what the past might have taught us and we fail to entertain any detailed anticipation of the future. We are not then active beyond the prospect of a very narrow present, as in the experience of "losing our temper." When we regret our angry outburst we return toward a wider consciousness and "become ourselves" once more. Thus when I ask forgiveness for impulsive thoughtlessness I may say "I was not myself," although of course I admit that I should have been. This admission stands at the threshold of moral philosophy. The selfhood of the individual, as it attains and surpasses the minimal continuity of personal identity, seems to have a normative or axiological dimension. We may come to recognize that to be oneself, that is, to possess a past and a future of one's own, is an achievement. It is this achievement that we may come most to respect in our evaluation of things human and it is toward the furthering of this achievement that our way of life should be oriented. This is the task of practical philosophy.

The physical and biological substructure of consciousness affords the background and the possibility of such a way of life. It is in this light that the philosopher should study them, if he is to contribute significant support to the basic ideology of our civilization. This task is not an easy one, and the student who accepts may often find himself discouraged. We must remember, however, that we have as much right to begin with the presence of consciousness in our world as with any other point of departure. By doing so we are more likely to keep in contact with the sense of value and moral common sense of our civilization. We should look forward to such a *rapprochement* and encourage its development in every way possible.

Bibliography

Whitehead, A. N. (1938), *Modes of Thought.* New York: Macmillan.

2

EPISTEMOLOGY OF QUANTUM MECHANICS—ITS APPRAISAL AND DEMANDS

EUGENE P. WIGNER

INTRODUCTION AND PREVIEW

I believe that in a conference such as ours every participant should contribute some of his specialized knowledge which has a bearing on the main subject of the conference. However, he should also give his thoughts on the main subject even if this is outside his specialized competence, and he should do this freely, not restricting himself to the areas of impact of his specialty. This may give a dilettantish taste to some of his remarks, and I wish to apologize in advance for my own. The specialty which I wish to contribute lies in the area of the epistemology suggested by our present picture of the conceptual limitations of physical theory. However, I would like to come to this subject, and its place in our subject of inquiry, from a more general discussion of cultural unity and the role of science in general therein.

THE EXPANDED ROLE AND GOAL OF SCIENCE

Forty years is not a very short period in human affairs, and it is likely that some aspect of man's world has undergone important changes in almost any period of forty years. Our attention is, naturally, focused on those aspects of our world which are changing, and I believe that the changes in the role and also in the goals of science are as characteristic of our times as any.

Forty years ago most people knew about science only as something esoteric. When I was a child there was only one scientist in the circle of acquaintances of my family, and he was considered to be somewhat odd. Today in the U. S. one person in 30 works directly or indirectly either on improving our understanding of nature or to make better use of the understanding which we possess. Forty years ago, the demands of science on our economy were negligible—the most spectacular ones being for astronomical equipment. Today the U. S. spends $20 billion a year on research and development. This is 3½% of the gross national product.

Forty years ago few people paid much attention to what scientists thought or said; today their voice carries great weight in national as well as international affairs—often uncomfortably great weight. The attention, also, which the world pays to scientific discoveries or observations has grown to an almost disagreeable extent, and a significant scientific error could, in fact occasionally does, cause embarrassment to its country of origin.

Hand in hand with this expanding role of science went an expansion of its goals. Forty years ago science was happy to provide increased insights into very limited areas—the motion of celestial bodies being a prime example. Today science seems to strive for an encompassing view of the whole universe in all of its manifestations, both in the large and in the small.

As I hope to explain on some other occasion, the expanded role and the expansion of the goals of science hold great promises for the future of man but also bring a new and more subtle type of danger thereto. The promise is, of course, that men, instead of fighting with each other for power and influence, will fight together for an increase of our knowledge and understanding. If there is to be a cultural unity among men, science will have to provide most of the pillars thereto.

The Present Schism in Science

What is the most important gap in present science? Evidently, the separation of the physical sciences from the sciences of the mind. There is virtually nothing in common between a physicist and a psychologist—except perhaps that the physicist has furnished some tools for the study of the more superficial aspects of psychology, and the psychologist has warned the physicist to be alert lest his hidden desires influence his thinking and findings.

Yet psychological schools have maintained that they wish to explain, eventually, all "processes of the mind" by known laws of physics and chemistry and, as I will enlarge upon later, physicists came to conclude that, in ultimate analysis, the laws of physics give only probability connections between the outcomes of subsequent observations or contents of consciousness. Hence, there is a striving, on the part of both the psychological and the physical sciences, to consider the reality of the subject of the other one the more basic. Perhaps I should interject here that it is my belief that the endeavor to understand the functioning of the mind in terms of the laws of physics is doomed to have no more than temporary and very partial success, whereas the direction into which modern physical theories point appears to me to be more fertile. Fundamentally, however, I believe that physics and chemistry, the disciplines of inanimate matter, will prove a limiting case of something more general, and that the fault of our ancestors in having thought of body and mind as separate was not of having thought of both of them but of having thought of them as separate. They form a unit, and both of them will be understood better if they are considered jointly.

This is, of course, only an opinion and a belief which may not be fully appropriate to our subject. What I feel sure of, however, is that there is a vast area of interesting knowledge here, waiting for a great mind to start its uncovering. To have such a large area may be very important if science is to become a unifying force for men, diverting them from their preoccupation with power.

Two Types of Science

The hope that man can fill the gap between the physical sciences and those of the mind is inspiring. It can be put into proper perspective, however, only if we also discuss what "filling the gap" means, i.e., what it is that science accomplishes when it pervades a subject. Before that, a distinction between two kinds of science should be drawn which is surely neither new nor precise but which is nevertheless useful. Some of our sciences, among which physics is foremost, are concerned solely with regularities. The typical statement it makes is something as follows: If two macroscopic bodies are far from each other and all other bodies, the component of their separation in any fixed direction is a linear function of time. This is, evidently, a rule of very great generality (even though it is a special case of even more general "laws"). It is, however, a highly conditional statement and leaves unanswered many questions, such as the character of the bodies which are widely separated, whether there are such bodies, and how many such bodies exist. There are other sciences which are concerned with just these questions, not with regularities. Geography, astronomy, botanics, zoology, and at present also psychology, are such sciences. They are descriptive rather than searching for regularities even though, as they develop, they may discover regularities—as did astronomy. However, these regularities then seem to become parts of another discipline.

Limitations of the Two Types

Several years ago I discussed the limits of the sciences concerned with regularities. My conclusion was that the limits are given by the finite capacity of the human mind for assimilating knowledge, by its finite interest for increasingly subtle and sophisticated theories. Some of these limitations can be overcome by cooperative science, and there is a great deal of temptation to discuss that. The limitations of the descriptive sciences evidently have the same source. Even if we could catalogue the exact locations of all houses and trees all over the earth, we would have little interest in such a catalogue. It surely would be interesting to know how the plants look on another planet on which the conditions, such as temperature, gravitational acceleration, etc., are different from ours; it would be even more interesting to know how they look on a planet which is very similar to ours. But, unless comparisons of plants on different planets suggest new regularities, interest in such comparisons would soon be exhausted. It seems to me, therefore, that if the sciences are to provide the pivot for cultural unity, we must rely in the long run principally on the sciences which discover regularities, or, as is said commonly, provide explanations.

Even the regularity-seeking sciences may become stale one day; even they may cease one day to fire man's imagination. The ideals of Arthur's Round Table did. Man may then turn to other ideals. However, the fascination of the regularity-seeking sciences should suffice to give man a taste of cultural unity; it should start him on that path.

WHAT DO THE REGULARITY-SEEKING SCIENCES FURNISH?

It is often said that physics explains the behavior of inanimate objects. This sounds somewhat like an advertisement; no ultimate explanation can be given for anything on rational grounds. As I have said elsewhere, what we call scientific explanation of a phenomenon is an exploration of the circumstances, properties, and conditions thereof, its coordination into a larger group of similar phenomena, and, above all, the ensuing discovery of a more encompassing point of view. Or, as David Bohm (1965) said a short time ago, "Science may be regarded as a means of establishing new kinds of contacts with the world, in new domains, on new levels . . ." One of the greatest accomplishments of physics in this regard is also one of its oldest accomplishments: the recognition that the motion of an object thrown into the air, the motion of the moon around the earth, and the motion of the planets around the sun follow the same regularities. The paths are all ellipses, obeying Kepler's laws. The more encompassing point of view was provided in this case by the gravitational law of Newton which permitted the coordination not only of the three phenomena enumerated but also of several other less striking phenomena.

The regularity-seeking sciences have another function: the discovery and creation of new phenomena. The phenomenon of electric induction is a case in point. Its coordination with magnetic phenomena, with the forces exerted by currents, was possible under the point of view of the Faraday-Maxwell electrodynamics.

These examples are brought forward to indicate what "filling the gap" between the physical sciences and the sciences of the mind should mean. We have at present, of course, a rather sophisticated and well-developed regularity-seeking science of inanimate objects. We also have the beginnings of a similar science of the mind. Surely, the concept of the subconscious has permitted us to see many phenomena from a common point of view, and the theory of the subconscious has been much enriched by phenomena discovered more recently. Dr. Polanyi in his paper alludes to these. However, the link between the two, the phenomena of the mind and of physics, is missing now, just as the link between gravitation and mechanics on the one hand and electromagnetism on the other was missing for a long time. The creation of the missing link is a sufficiently challenging task to form a pivot for the cultural unity which we dream about.

Before turning to the subject about which I am believed to know something, the epistemology of modern physics, I would like to make one more general remark supporting a point made by Dr. Polanyi.[1] It has little to do with cultural unity but much with the epistemology which I want to discuss.

Science Is an Extension of Primitive Knowledge; It Is Impossible Without the Latter

In order to appreciate this point we have only to imagine a mind which knows all that we know of physics but knows nothing else. Such a mind would be like that of a person who floats in dark empty space and is not subject to any outside influence. Such a mind would have no use for its abstract knowledge of physics because there would be no sensory data to be correlated, no events to be understood. In fact, the laws of physics would be meaningless for him because these give correlations between sensory data and he would receive no sensory data that he could interpret.

This is very abstract discussion, but it does show that science cannot be a replacement for our common ability to accept sensory data, an ability mostly born with us but also partly learned during our babyhood. Rather, science gives us only a different view of these sensory data; it creates pictures which permit them to be correlated in novel fashions. The primitive sensory data are the material with which science deals, which it orders and illuminates. Science does not furnish data, neither does it offer a substitute for the data—it is only interested in them.

One could object that our knowledge of nature permits us to use substitutes for sensory data, to photograph the stars rather than to look at them. This, however, is only appearance. Even if we photograph the stars, we must eventually "take in" by our senses what the photograph shows. Furthermore, without our senses we could not handle a photographic camera. Clearly, all knowledge comes to us ultimately through our senses; science only correlates this knowledge.

I make these remarks for two reasons—neither of which is di-

[1] See Professor Polanyi's paper in this volume.

rectly related to "cultural unity." First, because I believe that they are a paraphrase of Dr. Polanyi's insistence on the significance of tacit knowledge; in fact, they are perhaps somewhat more. They are an insistence that something even more primitive than tacit knowledge is the subject of science, the material it deals with, without which it would be empty and meaningless.

The second reason for my remarks is that the same conclusion at which we have arrived here abstractly will be forced on us later when we consider the epistemology of modern physics. This is not surprising; in fact, obstacles which can be understood abstractly only with foresight and imagination become obvious if one tries to travel down the road on which they stand.

The Trend in Physics in Our Century; The Conceptual Framework of Quantum Theory

Physics in our century has been under the spell of two conceptual innovations and an experimental discovery. The two conceptual innovations are the relativity and quantum theories; the experimental discovery is the realization that the structure of matter is atomic, that it can be explored with tools developed for this purpose; pictures of its constitution, enlarged to macroscopic scale, can be obtained rather directly.

Let us first look at an element that is common to relativity theory, as it was originated by Einstein, and quantum theory as it developed, often against the better wishes of its disciples. The common element—an element which is very important from the epistemological point of view—is the rejection of certain concepts which have no primitive observational basis. These concepts are very different for the two theories, and I prefer to discuss quantum theory principally because its rejection of concepts not based on direct apperception is much more radical. Let me therefore describe present quantum theory's critique of the earlier, very natural, concepts.

The quantities which characterize the state of a system of point particles were considered, in analogy to macroscopic objects, the positions and velocities of these particles. An analysis of the experimental processes available for determining atomic structures—the processes which were mentioned before as constituting the most important experimental discovery of our century—shows, however, that there is little reason to believe that these can be determined accurately on the atomic scale. Hence, quantum theory wishes to adopt an attitude which is free of preconceptions. It considers the observations themselves.

An observation implies the interaction of some "measuring apparatus" with the "object" on which the observation is to be undertaken. One can think of such an interaction as a collision between the apparatus and the object. Just as in the case of a collision, there is practically no interaction before or after the process; before and after the observation, apparatus and object are isolated from each other. The duration of the interaction is finite; it is often idealized as infinitely short. It results in a statistical correlation between the states of apparatus and object.

Since the concept of observation (also called "measurement") plays a basic role in the epistemology of physics, it may be useful to furnish an example of the kind of interaction that we have in mind. The example to be given assumes the validity of classical mechanics which will be more familiar to most people than its quantum counterpart. Since the purpose is only to illustrate the role and general character of observations or measurements, this should not matter. Although it is true that the analysis of the role of observations is not necessary in classical theory, such an analysis is valid, and it is hoped that the absence of quantum effects will render the discussion more visualizable.

As "object" let us consider a ball which can move in a horizontal trough; this is our object. We do not know where it is or what velocity it has. In order to measure or observe its position we may use, as apparatus, another ball which is moving in the same trough. This we can roll at a known speed toward our object ball. It will collide with it, return to us, and if we obtain its speed again and the time of its return we can calculate when and where it collided with our object ball. Even before it returned to us, its position depended on the position of the object ball—there was a statistical correlation between the two.

It would have been, perhaps, a bit more appropriate to use a light or radar signal for measuring the position of our ball in the trough. Light or radar signals are not so close to direct experience, but they do have the advantage that their speed need not be determined—it is light velocity. Hence, only the time of return needs to be ascertained in order to obtain the position of the ball at the time just midway between firing and receiving the light or radar signal.

This is, of course, a very primitive example. It does show, however, all the essential elements of an observation as conceived in present quantum theory. One needs an apparatus—the second ball or the radar-signal emitter—and one has to read the apparatus in the same sense as one reads a voltmeter or ammeter. In the case considered, one has to ascertain the time of return of the ball or radar pulse. The example also shows all the weaknesses of the theory. The first one is connected with the "reading" of the apparatus, that is, ascertaining the time of return. If I could not directly ascertain the position of the object ball, why should I be able to ascertain the return time of a signal? How about the apparatus? How did I send out a signal at a sharply defined time?

These are two difficult questions which relate very closely to the theme which I discussed under the heading "Science Is an Extension of Primitive Knowledge." Before turning to this connection, I would like to describe the language in which the laws of physics should be formulated—and actually are formulated in quantum theory—if we adopt as general a view on the nature of observation as indicated above.

The Language for the Laws of Nature

We shall now seek to determine what kind of use can be made of the results of observations, how they permit us to foresee the future, at least partially. Let us turn to the example of the determination of the position of the ball in the trough. The answer is that having any three such determinations, finding the positions x_1, x_2, x_3, with the corresponding times t_1, t_2, t_3, there is a linear relation between these so that

$$x_1 = vt_1 + a \qquad x_2 = vt_2 + a \qquad x_3 = vt_3 + a$$

is valid for all three pairs x, t with the same v and a. These equations simply express Newton's law for the ball in the trough: that it persists in its uniform motion. This assumes, of course, that the reflection of the radar signal did not influence the motion of the ball—

an assumption that is possible in classical theory, which deals with macroscopic objects, but would not be permissible in quantum theory, which deals with atomic particles, the motions of which are significantly influenced by the reflection of a signal.

The fact that all three equations between x, t pairs are valid with the same v, a can also be expressed by the statement that the determinant

$$\begin{vmatrix} 1 & 1 & 1 \\ x_1 & x_2 & x_3 \\ t_1 & t_2 & t_3 \end{vmatrix} = x_2t_3 - x_3t_2 + x_3t_1 - x_1t_3 + x_1t_2 - x_2t_1 = 0$$

vanishes. This is then the formulation of the law of nature (in this case of Newton's first law) which contains only observed quantities; it gives a correlation between the results of several observations. One can, perhaps, even further emphasize the observational character of the quantities appearing in the last equation by writing for each x the difference between the time of emission t_e and time of return t_r of the radar signal, divided by c. Similarly, each time t can be replaced by the average $\frac{1}{2}(t_r + t_e)$ of the time of emission and return. This gives, after some calculation,

$$t_{e2}t_{r3} - t_{e3}t_{r2} + t_{e3}t_{r1} - t_{e1}t_{r3} + t_{e1}t_{r2} - t_{e2}t_{r1} = 0,$$

where t_{e1} is the time of the emission of the first signal, t_{r1} the time it returned, and so on. The last equation contains only quantities which have a simple observational significance, at least as long as we suppose that the times of the emission and receipt of radar signals can be directly measured.

Whereas the formulation of Newton's first law, given in the last equation, may not be the most natural one, the laws of quantum physics can very naturally be formulated in terms of observations. This seems to me to be a distinct epistemological advance; after all, a law of nature is, as its name indicates, an expression of correlations, of correlations between observations or results of observations. The observations considered in quantum theory are of much, in fact infinitely, greater variety than the single, rather primitive type of observation which we considered: the emission and return of a radar signal and the measurement of the corresponding time.

If we accept the principles of quantum mechanics, it can be shown that each observation can be characterized by a self-adjoint operator in a suitable Hilbert space—the characterization Von Neumann (1943) gave to his "physical quantities." It can also be shown that the inference which past observations permit one to draw about the outcomes of future observations can be fully characterized by a vector in said Hilbert space, that is, a "wave function." However, it is dangerous to attribute physical reality to this vector, first, because it is not quite clear what physical reality means, and second, because it changes as a result of observations in a way not given by its equations of motion. This is called, in the jargon of quantum theory, the collapse of the wave function. In fact, as a result of the possibility of statistical correlations between isolated systems (such as the correlation between measuring apparatus and object), components of the wave function which refer to one system can change as a result of observations carried out on another system.

The remarks of the last paragraph were meant to establish the connection with other terminologies of the literature for those who are familiar with that literature. We now proceed to a critique of the epistemology just outlined.

The Physicist's Critique of the Conceptual Framework of Quantum Physics

The observation described in the preceding section has two elements outside the observer—the apparatus, which was the radar emitter in our example, and the "reading" of this apparatus. This was the measurement of the time of return of the radar signal.

Clearly, neither of these elements is outside the scope of physics. In fact, apparatuses for the physicist are made according to prescriptions furnished by the physicist, if not by the physicist himself. Similarly, we teach the physics student how to read the apparatuses. Neither of these two processes can be considered as truly primitive, unanalyzable, in a realistic theory.

The answer to the preceding objections is that it is possible to reduce both processes, that of the use of the apparatus and that of its reading, to simpler ones. Let us consider the reading first. This is, essentially, an observation of the state of the apparatus after its interaction with the object. Such an observation can be carried out in a way similar to the original observation by considering the apparatus used for the original observation as the *object* to be observed by a second apparatus. This second apparatus can be made to enter into a temporary interaction with the first apparatus, the result being a statistical correlation between their states. Instead of reading the first apparatus, the time of return of the signal in our case, one can read the second apparatus, perhaps the position of a dark spot on a photographic plate. If this is not yet considered as a primitive observation, one can go further and consider the eye of the observer as a third apparatus with which the second one is "read," i.e., its state observed. This is a consistent scheme as far as it goes: the statistical correlations between object and first apparatus, and between first and second apparatuses, entail a statistical correlation between object and second apparatus, so that reading the latter is equivalent to reading the first. This is very satisfactory. It should not obscure the fact that, nevertheless, an ultimate reading is unavoidable: there must be something that is *directly apparent* to the observer, though it is not necessary to specify what this is. It may be the state of his retina, it may be the position of the spot on the photographic plate, and so on.

This transferability of the dividing line between observer and apparatus was recognized by Von Neumann. It has attractive as well as perturbing aspects. It is satisfactory that the whole scheme is consistent, that the expression given by quantum theory for the probabilities of the outcomes of observations guarantees that the same results are obtained no matter what method, or how direct or indirect a method, one uses for the observation. It is perturbing that there is no definite limit to which one can and should follow the transference of the information of the state of the object. Toward the end, when looking for instance at the photographic plate, one makes use of the tacit knowledge of Dr. Polanyi. This could be seen to begin with as being ultimately unavoidable. It is nevertheless an element which is foreign to the otherwise precise and clearly articulated framework of the theory.

The situation with the apparatus is similar but perhaps even more striking. Naturally, we cannot use an apparatus unless we know its properties, whether it is a voltmeter or an ammeter. This knowledge is not born with us. To many of us it does not even come very naturally. The orthodox answer of the quantum theorist is that we should subject the apparatuses to observations which will tell us their properties. This again leads us to a chain, because in order to observe the properties of one apparatus, one must use other apparatuses, the properties of which are also unknown to begin with. In fact, the chain is not a simple one in this case but will have increasingly many branches. And in fact this is not the way one proceeds—one trusts a colleague who tells us what equipment to use and whether it is in good order. This method of ascertaining the properties of the apparatus is, however, clearly outside the framework of physical theory and illustrates even more strikingly than the situation encountered with the reading of the apparatus that present physical theory is not self-contained, that it constantly relies on everyday knowledge and is only an extension thereof.

The physicist has a few more, rather technical, points of concern with the details of the theory of observation. I mention this only in order to avoid the impression that I consider those difficulties to be solved. These difficulties concern the assumption of the instantaneous nature of the measurements and the determination of the class of measurable quantities. In my opinion these difficulties are of no concern to us now.

The present section dealt with the difficulties which one experiences as a physicist with the conceptual framework of present physical theory. Briefly, the boundaries of physics become indeterminate, and the extent of reliance on common experience is unclear. The early days of lack of concern with the conceptual foundations are gone. This may give us some nostalgia for bygone days, as does all change and progress. However, progress is also refreshing, and the evident need to be concerned with the foundations of physics, which lie partly outside of physics, may be a harbinger of more intimate connections with other sciences.

The Nonphysicist's Critique of the Conceptual Framework of Quantum Physics

The laws of nature are formulated by the quantum physicist as probability connections between outcomes of observations. Some of these observations may be simultaneous; others will take place in succession. There is a relatively simple formula for the probability that observation Q_1 yield the value q_1, that Q_2 yield q_2, . . . and so on. This probability is expressed in terms of q_1, q_2, . . . and the self-adjoint operators of Hilbert space which correspond to the measurements Q_1, Q_2, . . . and the times t_1, t_2, . . . at which they are undertaken. Hence, all that remains to perfect is the coordination of proper self-adjoint operators to suitably defined measurements!

The difficulty which the nonphysicist and the physicist alike find with the preceding picture is that it "idealizes" the observer, who is a man of flesh and blood, as a data-taking automaton, never forgetting anything, having no other knowledge but that obtained from his observations.

Obviously, this is too schematic a picture. Even as thinking men, we usually think in terms of everyday concepts, in fact mostly tacitly, as Dr. Polanyi explains. Without any mathematical support, there is an amazing consistency in simple everyday observations. As I once remarked, if our keys are not in the pocket where they should be, we do not suspect a new phenomenon, but go to look for them where we may have forgotten them. Furthermore, we stop looking for them on the second floor if our wife tells us that she found them on the first. Clearly, most correlations between observations are not obtained by the formulae of quantum physics.

Even more important, it seems to me, is the fact that we are not only cognitive beings, that correlations between cognitive functions give only a very small part of the life of our minds. The other parts will interfere with the cognitive functions so that these cannot be considered independently and in separation from the others. This is where I return to the general discussion of the schism between the physical sciences and those of the mind for which I had expressed the hope that it would become less deep than it now is.

One of the most important past accomplishments of physics is that it specified the realm of the explainable. This comprises the second and higher derivatives of the positions with respect to time, not the values and first derivatives. No abstract insight could have given this information. Similarly, the realm of the explainable in the generalized science will have to be discovered—we are far from knowing it now. The knowledge of this realm would tell us in which areas we can hope to find new and interesting illuminations. Finally, we will have to draw some limits of how much we want to know, how much we consider to be interesting. These are formidable tasks, and we can only hope that the human mind is equal to them.

Bibliography

Bohm, D. (1965), *Special Theory of Relativity*. New York: Benjamin.

Von Neumann, J. (1943), *Mathematical Foundations of Quantum Mechanics*, tr. R. T. Beyer. Princeton: Princeton University Press, 1955.

DISCUSSION

MR. J. R. LUCAS:

I want to start by taking issue with Dr. Wigner on two points. The first is his specification of what psychology, ideally, ought to be like. He says it should be a regularity science. The gap between physics and psychology is to be filled, as that between theories of electricity and magnetism was filled by Faraday-Maxwell electrodynamics, by a theory which describes regularities of mental phenomena. I disagree. We seek *rational* rather than *regularity* explanations of human conduct. Repetitive action is very boring—it is just what we are *not* interested in. What we are interested in is the action which is unique, spontaneous, not in accordance with some rule. We can still understand such action. Indeed, this is the paradigm of explanation. As Professor Pols said in his paper, "The causal efficacy of a rolling billiard ball . . . is regressive for common sense in a way in which the action of a friend in a crisis . . . is not."[1] This, surely, is right. Any "filling of the gap" between the physical sciences and the sciences of the mind must leave the sciences of the mind free to give rational rather than regularity explanations.

I am not sure if Dr. Wigner really disagrees about this. We may use "regularity" in an extended sense, so as to include what I would call "rational." Certainly the two concepts are linked. They both are contrasted with "random." Under certain conditions, rationality implies regularity, but not always; not when we are explaining mental phenomena.

My second disagreement with Dr. Wigner concerns his claim that physics does not really explain phenomena other than by stating certain regularities and that there can be no further explanation of why one sort of regularity is to be chosen rather than another. He

[1] See Program of the 1965 meeting, this volume, p. 4.

gives as an example Newtonian mechanics, which could standardize the second and higher time-derivatives of position, not the position or the first derivative. "No abstract insight could have given this information." I do not see why not. I think Dr. Wigner is arguing from the true point that we cannot give a logically complete explanation of a physical law—for then it would be analytic, it would not be empirical at all—to the conclusion that we cannot give any explanation whatever. But this does not follow. Indeed, I think we ought to seek some rationale of physical laws, although always remembering that it cannot be complete and may not seem explanatory at all to some people. Let me take Newtonian mechanics as an example and offer a tentative explanation of why Newtonian mechanics is formulated in terms of second-order differentials with respect to time, not of first-order differentials or positions themselves. First consider the positions. If mechanics were in terms of positions, then they would not express laws which are valid here, there, and everywhere. It is part of our concept of a natural law that it should apply everywhere, irrespective of where that to which it is being applied is. Hence position coordinates cannot enter into the formulation of the law itself. They must enter only as "initial conditions." Therefore the natural law *must* be expressed in terms of a differential equation, with particular position coordinates occurring *only* as constants of integration.

But why second-order differential equations? Why not allow velocities to enter into the formulation of laws of mechanics? After all, Aristotle thought so. To abbreviate a complicated (and necessarily not watertight) argument to the point of implausibility, the trouble with the Aristotle-Spinoza view of the world is that it does not allow for the possibility of *intervention*. If we are to have a world of Newtonian point particles, their criterion of identity is necessarily given by their position, which must vary only continuously in time. We cannot alter the *positions* of Newtonian particles discontinuously without their ceasing to be the *same* particles. If the phase space is no larger than the configuration space, no intervention is possible. If it is to be larger, then it could be of the form $(x_1 x_2 x_3 \ldots x_{3n} \ddot{x}_1 \ddot{x}_2 \ddot{x}_3 \ldots \ddot{x}_{3n})$. But—obviously—the form $(x_1 x_2 x_3 \ldots x_{3n} \dot{x}_1 \dot{x}_2 \dot{x}_3 \ldots \dot{x}_{3n})$ is more natural. And this is the form Newtonian mechanics has. It is a mechanics suitable for accounting for things (point particles are idealized things), things we can manipulate. To this extent, Newtonian mechanics is rational. Of course our mechanics might have been different—material bodies could have obeyed different laws of motion. But if they did, the laws would either have been more complicated, or we should not be able to regard the things that obeyed them as material bodies in terms of which all the rest of physics might be explained. Newtonian mechanics fills the bill better than any other available candidate, and we naturally concentrate our attention, for as long as possible, on those bodies which do obey its laws, those phenomena which it can explain, before going on to consider cases which are recalcitrant to Newtonian explanations.

We pay a price for the merits of Newtonian mechanics. Because it is in terms of second-order differential equations, it is reversible, independent of the direction of time. Therefore, it seems meaningless, indifferent to values; since a Newtonian world could just as well run backwards as forwards, we cannot ever feel that as it proceeds from one state to another it is redeeming the time. But what else should we expect? We made it a science of things, which man is master of, of course. Therefore, it is value free and without sense of progress. What man does he can undo, and the purposes are imposed by him, not given by his materials.

These are peripheral criticisms. With Dr. Wigner's main contentions I neither have, nor would be competent to have, a quarrel. Let me only emphasize the relation of what he has said to the central theme of our conference. First of all, he lays the Laplacean ghost, not by invoking the principle of indeterminism as often is done, but by showing the insubstantiality of the entities of physics. There is not a physical reality, independent of us, developing inexorably whether we will it or not, whether we know it or not. Rather, as the title of the paper indicates, the ontology of quantum mechanics is constituted by its epistemology. Whereas classical mechanics was not concerned with observation, but took it for granted and gave no account of it, quantum mechanics is centrally concerned with observation. (We should note that the word "observation" has two senses. It can refer to the operation of observing—the self-adjoint operators of quantum mechanics—or it can refer to the result observed—the particular *eigenvalue* that actually occurs. Quantum mechanics is concerned with both. But it is important not to confuse the operation with the result.) I am not sure if we can go as far as Dr. Wigner does and eliminate everything else—there seems then to be a loss of explanatory power, in some sense of "explanatory," and physicists often feel impelled, in spite of Von Neumann's proof (1943) of the impossibility of a hidden variable, to reintroduce some sort of unobservable, explanatory entities. But, whatever these may be, they cannot be substances in the classical sense, if only because, as London and Bauer (1939, Sec. 13, ap. p. 48) argue, they are anonymous—you cannot re-identify anything as being the same thing as you observed last time. They are in some sense dependent on our observing them, though not in the naïve way proposed by Berkeley and the modern phenomenalists, nor as according to the phenomenologists.

This is the point of similarity between quantum mechanics and personal knowledge: we cannot give a satisfactory account of what is known without also bringing in the person who does the knowing. Dr. Wigner argues that this is a genuine and significant similarity. Quantum mechanics is unlike relativity theory, where although we often talk about the observer, it is only a *façon de parler,* a vivid way of talking about a particular frame of reference (or its origin). In quantum mechanics, however, although we can shift the boundary between the system under observation and the observer-*cum*-apparatus, *we cannot construe the observer as being just the rest of the universe apart from the system observed.* It must essentially contain a person who is both less than an automatic recording machine—people sometimes forget—and more—people have passions as well as memories. Reality does not exist independently of persons, but comes to be what is through interacting with persons. We are continually, so to speak, asking questions of nature and forcing nature to give us answers. We have a set of questionnaires with multiple-choice answers, but as soon as one question is answered, we cannot say that the next question will be answered by the same person. Or, to use a Biblical analogy, we are wrestling with an unknown stranger and demanding that he tell us not his name but his number, but as soon as he does, he is somebody else. It is extremely difficult to know what to make of such encounters, but at least it is clear that the person is essentially involved, and the knowledge they yield is essentially personal.

PROFESSOR WIGNER:

I think you are entirely right that it is a puzzling and almost eerie situation that we are in.

MR. LUCAS:

May I just press you on a point which I was making earlier, which I took to be the first criticism; namely the point where you were talking about the possible resolution of the gap between psychology and physics, where you were talking of the regularities. I was asking for some sort of explanation which isn't purely a rationally opaque one in terms of regularity—but perhaps I am niggling with the words you use rather than what your central thought is.

PROFESSOR WIGNER:

As Mr. Lucas already implied, there is some misunderstanding of the term "regularity-seeking science" as I used it. It was not my intention to restrict psychology to the description of the simplest phenomena, to a domain which it would find uninteresting. Similarly, we deal not only with the simplest problems in physics. In fact, some of the phenomena that were discovered by physicists would have baffled all people—physicists and nonphysicists alike—only a few years earlier.

I call physics a regularity-seeking science because its questions are of the following nature: given the position of the earth at two instances of time, what will be its position at a third instance? Or, formulated more generally, what are the connections between the positions of the earth at three distinct instances of time? The concerns of some of the sciences, such as astronomy, also include questions such as the number of planets around the sun, their positions at one instance of time, even though the answers to these questions may not exhibit any regularities.

May I say very respectfully that the term "rational explanation" does not have a basis in sensory awareness. In fact, it seems to me that even the word "explanation" has been much misused, and, as I tried to emphasize, what we often call "explanation" is a coordination with a larger group of similar phenomena and the creation of a more encompassing point of view.

I was very much interested in Mr. Lucas's rationalization of Newtonian mechanics and would like to think about it more. I hope he will forgive me if I should not agree with him completely. At present, it is not clear to me why our intervention could not affect the first rather than the second time-derivative of the coordinates. However, this is a technical point which he may be able to clear up.

Let me say, finally, that Mr. Lucas's plastic description of the state of mind into which the epistemology of quantum mechanics puts us, impressed me greatly.

DR. STRAUS:

Is not the physicist in his relation to establishing his findings and laws, is not this whole ensemble *one* topic of psychology? I want to give only one or two examples why I think so. You mention the problem of simultaneity, and we know Einstein's interpretation of simultaneity, but it deals *only* with the observer as a physical body. It leaves out the psychological problem: that one person can unite two separate events, and the condition is that they are separate in one moment of time. This is a psychological problem which is the basis of observations in all ways, because, though I am not so sure about measurement of time in quantum mechanics, in classical physics every measurement is relating two separate events: the event or the observation, and the scale of the clock of some system. The problem is for any measurement of time to establish simultaneities of the beginning, duration, and end of the event, and to relate it to the zero point, to an extension, and to a final point on the clock. All this must be done, and can only be done, by a human observer. In fact, one of the basic problems of physics is that beings like us who live in time can be aware of time and even measure time. And all measurements of time are in some way a reversion of time in so far as the end of a process has to be reverted back to the beginning. The three seconds about which the physicist speaks and which he puts into his equations are something quite different from whatever had happened in the observation of those three seconds. From that point of view, then, I would really think the activities *of* the scientists *transcend* what is given in nature. If you say the velocity of light is 186,000 miles per second, you bring together, let me say, the photons at the beginning and at the end of a second and likewise the whole extension of 186,000 miles which are comprehended in that one numerical term. In all this I think we are not reproducing the picture, but rather we transcend it. But in this way I think it is obvious that one who knows something must reach *beyond* that which is known. The whole possibility of transforming physics into *technique* means that man has a *power* over nature which is given with his whole position and which, as I said before, transcends the natural conditions.

PROFESSOR WIGNER:

I very much agree with most of what you said. Perhaps on the details of physics I could, as a professional, make modifications. However, I do agree with you that the basic difficulty in quantum-theoretical epistemology, which I feel so strongly, is that it considers the physicist or the measurer as an automaton. This would not be the case if it admitted that the observer transcends the observation. The picture used is a caricature of man, and the translation into real understanding must come from very, very much deeper insights into psychology.

PROFESSOR SCOTT:

I wonder if part of the trouble in filling this gap, the difficulty in talking about it, is the difficulty of treating the subject as an object. We like to explain things, whether in regularities or in recognition of a wider rationality, as *objects* which we stand and look at; yet dealing with consciousness is dealing with that which is essentially *subject*. If you treat the world only as one of objects, you have a position which Schrödinger pointed out so nicely: that the self is not in our world at all; it was left out way in the beginning.

PROFESSOR TAYLOR:

I am confused by the way physicists talk; they say it is all a matter of correlating observations. These observations are very precise or mathematical or exact observations, and they *do* get linked by certain mathematics (this I don't have to understand); on the other hand, just in the description of the very simple experiment of the ball in the trough, it is obvious that the equation that comes out of it is embedded in a whole surrounding set of understandings and transitions which are not a question of observation or mathematics. You know this apparatus is going to work, because you have some idea of the thing moving at a certain speed and coming back, and *then* you know, therefore, that the reading is going to have a certain meaning. Now how far does this extend to what we might call the interpretive surrounding around the actual observations which, true, are the ones that are put into the equations? If we tried to reduce them entirely away, we would be left with an inconceivable form of thought; it wouldn't even be a form of thought—it would be without meaning. Well now, surely, this is where the question comes down to the epistemological problem: to what extent can we put this surrounding interpretation on mathematics, and how deeply do we penetrate? In quantum mechanics at the moment we seem to be in some perplexity because the actual, what we might call *physical* interpretations in the ordinary sense of the word, don't seem to be forthcoming. We don't know what this mathematical meaning corresponds to. If we discovered more of the physical interpretation, we might be very surprised, and it might lead to solutions of these problems. For instance, the problem of how to give an epistemological interpretation without introducing the absurd. And this would be the epistemological question which is at stake.

DR. STRAUS:

To the problem which Professor Scott raised, does the world exist objectively, there is a simple answer: it coexists with us or we with it. To put us first outside and then to ask, "Does the world exist?" is, I think, a pseudo argument anyway. But I want to say something about correlation of observations: the plural "observation*s*" presents a problem. Either these observations are really singular (then they cannot be quantitative), or each one of them is already itself a fragment of a larger surrounding whole. Copernicus would never have reached the heliocentric system if he had tried to correlate one of his observations with another. His procedure, I think, was to reach out *completely* from the immediate realm of observable data, and thus he conceived the path of the earth in its totality, far transcending the single positions. The earth's position, at any given time, is only one point of its path; but to understand the path and make astronomical predictions requires us to see the path as a whole. And the means to do that is mathematics. We can do it because the ellipse which we may draw on the blackboard is, in its schematic structure, identical with the ellipse of the dimensions of the earth from the sun. The nonsubstantial character of geometry is, I think, a tool which enables man to transcend his position (which would be a position in any particular observation), and then to *inscribe* the particular observations into a conceptual system which is *not* available in the direct observation.

PROFESSOR WIGNER:

I believe my answer should consist of two parts. First, discovering laws of nature is not the same thing as using them or even verifying them. The discovery of the laws of nature requires first and foremost intuition, conceiving of pictures and a great many subconscious processes. The use and also the confirmation of these laws is another matter. In order to put to work or to verify the laws, it is useful to formulate them sharply and in logical terms. As Professor Polanyi emphasizes, logic comes after intuition. It was not my intention to analyze the process of the discovery of the laws of nature; all I tried was to analyze in general terms how we use them, in which way their statements can be logically formulated. This analysis forced us to the conclusion that the laws of quantum mechanics give correlations between outcomes of measurements or observations (the two are used synonymously in quantum mechanics).

Second, let me reiterate that even though I am convinced that the quantum-mechanical equations cannot be generally interpreted in any other way than the one outlined, as furnishing correlations between results of observations, I do not feel satisfied with this situation. What it presumes is that observation is something simple and primitive, whereas it actually is not. In particular, the carrying out of an observation presupposes a great deal of common knowledge, knowledge of the functioning of our eyes, our apparatuses, sense of time, and probably a million other things.

Hence, even though I can tell you what idealization would render the epistemology of quantum mechanics satisfactory, the idealization that observation is a primitive function, I must also tell you that, in my heart, I do not believe in the validity of this idealization. My statement does not convey a message; it describes a situation.

PROFESSOR POLANYI:

I want to speak for a moment on the question of how far the problem raised by Professor Wigner is a *unique* phenomenon and how far it is a member of a class of similar phenomena, for I do think that perhaps this is characteristic and important in a more general way. What we have heard was that the formal structure of physics is incomplete and has to be supplemented. Now, I think that such incompleteness has been mentioned often in quite different contexts. For example, it is very common among philosophers to say that reflection on ourselves is necessarily incomplete because there is always something which is still reflecting at the last moment which has not been reflected upon. In metamathematics, to talk of another kind of reflection, there is also an incompleteness; metamathematics is intrinsically incomplete in so far as it remains unformalized, because that which reflects *on* the formalisms of mathematics cannot itself be formalized to the same extent as its own subject matter. Another very common and perfectly correct statement, also often made by philosophers, is that all the definitions of classes or external objects must end up with reference to an undefined form of ostensive definition, which is very much like the kind of personal participation which people describe in the matter of the ultimate link of observation. That is, if you have a syllogism, you cannot really conclude anything since all you have before you is a conditional statement; you still have to detach the consequent, and nobody authorizes you to do that except your own common sense. This reminds me, of course, of the Gödelian theorem of the incompleteness of axiomatic systems of a certain richness (as represented perhaps by arithmetic). Moreover, there is an incompleteness of any mathematical theory of experience (I have tried to define that myself), in so far as it is meaningless unless it is supplemented by a process by which it will bear on experience. It always has to be in a kind of tacit relation to something on which it bears. In mathematics we have tried to become more formal than has been usual by completely transposing it into symbols and the operation of symbols. Then it turns out that this only leads to an uninterpreted mathematical or, generally speaking, deductive system which doesn't say anything about anything. And as soon as you interpret a deductive system, you introduce an unformalized procedure. There might be, therefore (I would like to hope that there *could* be), a general theory of incompleteness, a general theory of the incompleteness of formal discourse of any kind. Of course, I have tried myself to say this kind of thing: that knowing certainly goes on in an informal way. Animals do it (animals are really beyond suspicion in that respect; they have no formal system, and also they know something), and so do we, of course, and therefore I think it is very fundamental. To produce from this kind of capacity, which we undeniably have, a formal system (that is, one which consolidates some of our procedure in terms of a formal machinery) is to produce an immensely powerful instrument, but one which, it seems, is always incomplete. And if that is true, then the ideal of a completely formalized thought is logically unobtainable, logically self-contradictory, because it contradicts its own meaning; it contradicts its own bearing on anything at all. I wanted to raise this question because if this direction is promising, I think it should be taken into consideration.

PROFESSOR WIGNER:

I am sure that you are right. The question, however, which is in my mind is this: Is this a manifestation of the fact that science only correlates data, that science correlates everyday experiences? If so, it follows that science cannot be complete. It seems to me that this incompleteness is a manifestation of the fact that the purpose of science is the discovery of new types of correlations of sensory data of everyday experience. Hence the subject of science is something that is by definition *outside* of science, and this is enough to render science incomplete.

PROFESSOR SCOTT:

I wonder if I could add to what you said about essential limitations of formalisms the point that if things were complete, they would be uninteresting to us. Our enterprise of inquiry requires indefiniteness and incompleteness; every time we utter anything, we are doing something unpredictable; but a formal system is essentially a predictable system.

PROFESSOR POLANYI:

The question I would like to raise (not that I think we will necessarily be able to discuss it) is: What kind of theory of knowledge does this indicate? At least may we state what I think is quite obvious: we haven't got a theory of knowledge at all today. Since the demise of logical positivism, there is no theory of knowledge left, and the situation is open to candidates. I think that this is perhaps the most characteristic feature of our situation—we want to produce a theory of knowledge.

[Professor Pantin introduced the problem to be dealt with at length in his own paper—a problem which, like the point raised by Dr. Straus, needs to be followed through to a systematic solution before the paradox set by Professor Wigner's paper can be alleviated.]

PROFESSOR PANTIN:

I would like to suggest that in fact while there are real differences between the biological and other sciences of that sort and the physical ones, nevertheless there are real similarities. I think a great deal of the difficulty comes from the use of the word "descriptive" for such sciences. This is not properly a description of what the sciences, other than the physical sciences, really do. If I can give an example: in my own work, both in taxonomy and in the physiology of the nervous system, what I am doing is not mere description; it is in fact finding the class to which sets of phenomena belong. For instance, in the early work I did with sea anemones and other creatures with very simple nervous systems, I studied the closure reflex. I found that if one takes this simple, straightforward phenomenon, it has all the properties in common with conduction of the nervous impulse in the higher animals and also class characteristics in common with other phenomena of totally different sorts.

A danger in this sort of behavioral analysis—one which I fell into myself—is that it looks so complete that if you are not careful, you may start to imagine that you can explain the whole behavior of a sea anemone by very simple reflexes—like the effect of a coin in a slot machine. But quite by accident, I discovered that apart from reflexes, there was a whole mass of purposive behavior connected with the spontaneous activity of the anemone about which we simply knew nothing. (Actually, this behavior was too slow to be noticed; it was outside our sensory spectrum for the time being.) There is danger here because our way of approach in science is by taking such simple examples (really by an extension of Occam's razor applied to experimental work). That is your only method of attack, but you have to be very, very careful that you are not in fact privately assuming that you have come to the end, that there aren't other aspects of the phenomena, needing other assumptions, that you've missed. That danger is more evident in biology than in physics, but it is true for all science.

Bibliography

London, F., & Bauer, E. (1939), *La Theorie de l'Observation en Mechanique Quantique*. Paris: Hermann.

Von Neumann, J. (1943), *Mathematical Foundations of Quantum Mechanics,* tr. R. T. Beyer. Princeton: Princeton University Press, 1955.

PART II

THE REFORM OF EPISTEMOLOGY

Our problem centers in the sharp dichotomy of matter and mind, with an external "real," "objective" world set against a "merely subjective" inwardness. Caught in this dualism, modern thought has vacillated between a misleading and ultimately self-denying objectivism, and an equally misleading and ultimately despairing philosophy of subjectivity. This impasse arose, in its modern form, out of Descartes's search for a knowledge built up of wholly "clear and distinct" ideas; we can escape its disastrous consequences only by rethinking the principles of our epistemology. Michael Polanyi's theory of tacit knowing provides the framework for such an epistemological reform. His paper, on "The Creative Imagination," is directed to the dynamic of discovery in science. The introduction to the discussion of the paper elaborates more explicitly the central theme of his theory of knowledge, that is, the structure of tacit knowing. Within the philosophy of science, Polanyi's epistemology can put us on the road to resolving Professor Wigner's paradox. But it also offers principles through which we can heal the breach between science and art as vehicles of understanding. In particular, Donald Weismann's paper, "The Collage as Model," exhibits the application of Polanyi's theory to the problem of creation in the visual arts.

3

THE CREATIVE IMAGINATION

MICHAEL POLANYI

The enterprise that I am undertaking here has been severely discouraged by contemporary philosophers. They do not deny that the imagination can produce new ideas which help the pursuit of science or that our personal hunches and intuitions are often to the point. But since our imagination can roam unhindered by argument and our intuitions cannot be accounted for, neither imagination nor intuition are deemed rational ways of making discoveries. They are excluded from the logic of scientific discovery, which can deal then only with the verification or refutation of ideas after they have turned up as possible contributions to science.

However, the distinction between the production and testing of scientific ideas is not really so sharp. No scientific discovery can be strictly verified, or even proved to be probable, yet we bet our lives every day on the correctness of scientific generalizations, for example, those underlying medicine and technology. Admittedly, Sir Karl Popper has pointed out that, though not strictly verifiable, scientific generalizations can be strictly refuted. But the application of this principle cannot be strictly prescribed. It is true that a single piece of contradictory evidence refutes a generalization, but experience can present us only with *apparent contradictions,* and there is no strict rule by which to tell whether any apparent contradiction is an *actual contradiction*. The falsification of a scientific statement can therefore no more be strictly established than can its verifica-

This paper has also appeared in *Chemical and Engineering News,* 44 (No. 17; April 25):85-93.

tion. Verification and falsification are *both formally indeterminate* procedures.

There is in fact no sharp division between science in the making and science in the textbook. The vision which guided the scientist to success lives on in his discovery and is shared by those who recognize it. It is reflected in the confidence they place in the reality of that which has been discovered and in the way in which they sense the depth and fruitfulness of a discovery.

Any student of science will understand—must understand—what I mean by these words. But their teachers in philosophy are likely to raise their eyebrows at such a vague emotional description of scientific discovery. Yet the great controversy over the Copernican system, which first established modern science, turned on just such vague emotional qualities attributed to the system by Copernicus and his followers, which proved in their view that the system was real.

Moreover, after Newton's confirmation of the Copernican system, Copernicus and his followers—Kepler and Galileo—were universally recognized to have been right. For two centuries their steadfastness in defending science against its adversaries was unquestioningly honored. I myself was still brought up on these sentiments. But at that time some eminent writers were already throwing cold water on them. Poincaré wrote that Galileo's insistence that the earth was really circling round the sun was pointless, since all he could legitimately claim was that this view was more convenient. The distinguished physicist, historian, and philosopher, Pierre Duhem, went further and concluded that it was the adversaries of Copernicus and his followers who had recognized the true meaning of science, which the Copernicans had misunderstood. While this extreme form of modern positivism is no longer widely held today, I see no essential alternative to it emerging so far.

Let us look then once more at the facts. Copernicus discovered the solar system by signs which convinced him. But these signs convinced few others. For the Copernican system was far more complicated than that of Ptolemy: it was a veritable jungle of *ad hoc* assumptions. Moreover, the attribution of physical reality to the system met with serious mechanical objections and also involved staggering assumptions about the distance of the fixed stars. Yet Copernicus (*De Revolutionibus,* Preface and Book 1, Chapter

10) claimed that his system had unique harmonies which proved it to be real even though he could describe these harmonies only in a few vague emotional passages. He did not stop to consider how many assumptions he had to make in formulating his system, nor how many difficulties he ignored in doing so. Since his vision showed him an outline of reality, he ignored all its complications and unanswered questions.

Nor did Copernicus remain without followers in his own century. In spite of its vagueness and its extravagances, his vision was shared by great scientists like Kepler and Galileo. Admittedly, their discoveries bore out the reality of the Copernican system, but they could make these discoveries only because they already believed in the reality of that system.

We can see here what is meant by attributing reality to a scientific discovery. It is to believe that it refers to no chance configuration of things, but to a persistent connection of certain features, a connection which, being real, will yet manifest itself in numberless ways, inexhaustibly. It is to believe that it is there, existing independently of us, and that for that reason its consequences can never be fully predicted.

Our knowledge of reality has, then, an essentially indeterminate content: it deserves to be called a *vision*. The vast indeterminacy of the Copernican vision showed itself in the fact that discoveries made later, in the light of this vision, would have horrified its author. Copernicus (Book 1, Chapter 4) would have rejected the elliptic planetary paths of Kepler and, likewise, the extension of terrestrial mechanics to the planets by Galileo and Newton. Kepler (Dingle, 1952, p. 46) noted this by saying that Copernicus had never realized the riches which his theory contained.

This vision, the vision of a hidden reality, which guides a scientist in his quest, is a dynamic force. At the end of the quest the vision is becalmed in the contemplation of the reality revealed by a discovery; but the vision is renewed and becomes dynamic again in other scientists and guides them to new discoveries. I shall now try to show how both the dynamic and the static phases of a scientific vision are due to the strength of the imagination guided by intuition. We shall understand then both the grounds on which established scientific knowledge rests and the powers by which scientific discovery is achieved.

I have pursued this problem for many years by considering science as an extension of ordinary perception. When I look at my hand and move it about, it would keep changing its shape, its size, and its color but for my power of seeing the joint meaning of a host of rapidly changing clues, and seeing that this joint meaning remains unchanged. I recognize a real object before me from my joint awareness of the clues which bear upon it.

Many of these clues cannot be sensed in themselves at all. The contraction of my eye muscles, for example, I cannot experience in itself. Yet I am very much aware of the working of these muscles indirectly, in the way they make me see the object at the right distance and as having the right size. Some clues to this we see from the corner of our eyes. An object looks very different when we see it through a blackened tube, which cuts out these marginal clues.

We can recognize here *two kinds of awareness*. We are obviously aware of the object we are looking at, but are aware also—in a much less positive way—of a hundred different clues which we integrate to the sight of the object. When integrating these clues, we are attending fully to the object while we are aware of the clues themselves without attending to them. We are aware of these clues only *as pointing to the object we are looking at*. I shall say that we have a *subsidiary awareness* of the clues in their bearing on the object to which we are *focally attending*.

While an object on which we are focusing our attention is always identifiable, the clues through which we are attending to the object may often be unspecifiable. We may well be uncertain of clues seen from the corner of our eyes, and we cannot experience in themselves at all such subliminal clues, as for example the effort of contracting our eye muscles.

But it is a mistake to identify subsidiary awareness with unconscious or preconscious awareness, or with the Jamesian fringe of awareness. What makes an awareness subsidiary is *the function it fulfills;* it can have any degree of consciousness so long as it functions as a clue to the object of our focal attention. To perceive something as a clue is sufficient by itself, therefore, to make its identification uncertain.

Let me return now to science. If science is a manner of perceiving things in nature, we might find the prototype of scientific discovery in the way we solve a difficult perceptual problem. Take for example the way we learn to find our way about while wearing inverting spectacles. When you put on spectacles that show things upside down, you feel completely lost and remain helpless for days on end. But if you persist in groping around for a week or more, you find your way again and eventually can even drive a car or climb rocks with the spectacles on. This fact, well-known today, was in essence discovered by Stratton 70 years ago. It is usually said to show that after a time the visual image switches round to the way we normally see it. But some more recent observations have shown that this interpretation is false.

It happened, for example, that a person perfectly trained to get around with upside-down spectacles was shown a row of houses from a distance, and he was then asked whether he saw the houses right side up or upside down. The question puzzled the subject and he replied after a moment that he had not thought about the matter before, but that now that he was asked about it he found that he saw the houses upside down (see Snyder and Pronko, 1952).[1]

Such a reply shows that the visual image of the houses has not turned back to normal; it has remained inverted, but the inverted image no longer means to the subject that the houses themselves are upside down. The inverted image has been reconnected to other sensory clues, to touch and sound and weight. These all hang together with the image once more, and hence, though the image remains inverted, the subject can again find his way by it safely. *A new way of seeing things rightly has been established.* And since the meaning of the upside-down image has changed, the term "upside down" has lost its previous meaning, so that now it is confusing to inquire whether something is seen upside down or right side up. The new kind of right seeing can be talked about only in terms of a new vocabulary.

We see how the wearer of inverting spectacles reorganizes scrambled clues into a new coherence. He again sees *objects,* instead of meaningless impressions. He again sees *real things,* which he can pick up and handle, which have weights pulling in the right direction and make sounds that come from the place at which he sees them. He has made sense out of chaos.

[1] For fuller evidence and its interpretation in the sense given here, see Kottenhoff (1961).

In science, I find the closest parallel to this perceptual achievement in the discovery of relativity. Einstein (Schilpp, 1949, p. 53) has told the story of how from the age of 16 he was obsessed by the following kind of speculations. Experiments with falling bodies were known to give the same results on board a ship in motion as on solid ground. But what would happen to the light which a lamp would emit on board a moving ship? Supposing the ship moved fast enough, would it overtake the beams of its own light, as a bullet overtakes its own sound by crossing the sonic barrier? Einstein thought that this was inconceivable, and, persisting in this assumption, he eventually succeeded in renewing the conceptions of space and time in a way which would make it inconceivable for the ship to overtake, however slightly, its own light rays. After this, questions about a definite span of time or space became meaningless and confusing—exactly as questions of "above" and "below" became meaningless and confusing to a subject who had adapted his vision to inverting spectacles.

It is no accident that it is the most radical innovation in the history of science that appears most similar to the way we acquire the capacity for seeing inverted images rightly. For only a comprehensive problem like relativity can require that we reorganize such basic conceptions as we do in learning to see rightly through inverting spectacles. Relativity alone involves conceptual innovations as strange and paradoxical as those we make in righting an inverted vision.

The experimental verifications of relativity have shown that the coherence discerned by Einstein was real. One of these confirmations has a curious history. Einstein had assumed that a light source would never overtake a beam sent out by it, a fact that had already been established before by Michelson and Morley. In his autobiography Einstein says that he made this assumption intuitively from the start. But this account failed to convince his contemporaries, for intuition was not regarded as a legitimate ground for knowledge. Textbooks of physics therefore described Einstein's theory as his answer to the experiments of Michelson. When I tried to put the record right by accepting Einstein's claim that he had intuitively recognized the facts already demonstrated by Michelson, I was attacked and ridiculed by Professor Grünbaum (1963, pp. 378-

385), who argued that Einstein must have known of Michelson's experiments, since he could not otherwise have based himself on the facts established by these experiments.

However, if science is a generalized form of perception, Einstein's story of his intuition is clear enough. He had started from the principle that it is impossible to observe absolute motion in mechanics, and when he came across the question whether this principle holds also when light is emitted, he felt that it must still hold, but he could not quite tell why he assumed this. However, such unaccountable assumptions are common in the way we perceive things, and this can also affect the way scientists see them. Newton's assumption of absolute rest itself, which Einstein was to refute, owed its convincing power to the way we commonly see things. We see a car traveling along a road and never the road sliding away under the car. We see the road at absolute rest. We generally see things as we do, because this establishes coherence within the context of our experience. So when Einstein extended his vision to the universe and included the case of a light source emitting a beam, he could make sense of what he then faced only by seeing it in such a way that the beam was never overtaken, however slightly, by its source. This is what he meant by saying that he knew intuitively that this was in fact the case.

We understand now also why the grounds on which Copernicus claimed that his system was real could be convincing to him, though not convincing to others. We have seen that the intuitive powers that are at work in perception integrate clues which, being subsidiarily known, are largely unspecifiable; we have seen further that the intuition by which Einstein shaped his novel conceptions of time and space was also based on clues which were largely unspecifiable; we may assume then that this was also true for Copernicus in shaping his vision of reality.

And we may say this generally. Science is based on clues that have a bearing on reality. These clues are not fully specifiable; nor is the process of integration which connects them fully definable; and the future manifestations of the reality indicated by this coherence are inexhaustible. These three indeterminacies defeat any attempt at a strict theory of scientific validity and offer space for the powers of the imagination and intuition.

This gives us a general idea of the way scientific knowledge is established at the end of an inquiry; it tells us how we judge that our result is coherent and real. But it does not show us where to start an inquiry, nor how we know, once we have started, which way to turn for a solution. At the beginning of a quest we can know only quite vaguely what we may hope to discover; we may ask, therefore, how we can ever start and go on with an inquiry without knowing what exactly we are looking for.

This question goes back to antiquity. Plato set it in the *Meno*. He said that if we know the solution of a problem, there is no problem—and if we don't know the solution, we do not know what we are looking for and cannot expect to find anything. He concluded that when we do solve problems, we do it by remembering past incarnations. This strange solution of the dilemma may have prevented it from being taken seriously. Yet the problem is ineluctable and can be answered only by recognizing a kind of intuition more dynamic than the one I have described so far.

I have spoken of our powers to perceive a coherence bearing on reality, with its yet hidden future manifestations. But there exists also a more intensely pointed knowledge of hidden coherence: the kind of foreknowledge we call a problem. And we know that the scientist produces problems, has hunches, and, elated by these anticipations, pursues the quest that should fulfill these anticipations. This quest is guided throughout by feelings of a deepening coherence and these feelings have a fair chance of proving right. We may recognize here the powers of a dynamic intuition.

The mechanism of this power can be illuminated by an analogy. Physics speaks of potential energy that is released when a weight slides down a slope. Our search for deeper coherence is likewise guided by a potentiality. We feel the slope toward deeper insight as we feel the direction in which a heavy weight is pulled along a steep incline. It is this dynamic intuition which guides the pursuit of discovery.

This is how I would resolve the paradox of the *Meno:* we can pursue scientific discovery without knowing what we are looking for, because the gradient of deepening coherence tells us where to start and which way to turn, and eventually brings us to the point where we may stop and claim a discovery.

But we must yet acknowledge further powers of intuition, without which inventors and scientists could neither rationally decide to choose a particular problem nor pursue any chosen problem successfully. Think of Stratton devising his clumsy inverting spectacles and then groping about guided by the inverted vision of a single, narrowly restricted eye for days on end. He must have been fimly convinced that he would learn to find his way about within a reasonable time, and also that the result would be worth all the trouble of his strange enterprise—and he proved right. Or think of Einstein, when as a boy he came across the speculative dilemma of a light source pursuing its own ray. He did not brush the matter aside as a mere oddity, as anybody else would have done. His intuition told him that there must exist a principle which would assure the impossibility of observing absolute motion in any circumstances. Through years of sometimes despairing inquiry, he kept up his conviction that the discovery he was seeking was within his ultimate reach and that it would prove worth the torment of its pursuit; and again, Einstein proved right. Kepler too might reasonably have concluded, after some five years of vain efforts, that he was wasting his time, but he persisted and proved right.

The power by which such long-range assessments are made may be called a *strategic intuition*. It is practiced every day on a high level of responsibility in industrial research laboratories. The director of such a laboratory does not usually make inventions, but is responsible for assessing the value of problems suggested to him, be it from outside or by members of his laboratory. For each such problem the director must jointly estimate the chances of its successful pursuit, the value of its possible solution, and also the cost of achieving it. He must compare this combination with the joint assessment of the same characteristics for rival problems. On these grounds he has to decide whether the pursuit of a problem should be undertaken or not, and if undertaken, what grade of priority should be given to it in the use of available resources.

The scientist is faced with similar decisions. The kind of intuition which points out problems to him cannot tell him which problem to choose. He must be able to estimate the gap separating him from discovery, and he must also be able roughly to assess whether the importance of a possible discovery would warrant the investment of the powers and resources needed for its pursuit. Without this kind of strategic intuition, he would waste his opportunities on wild goose chases and soon be out of a job.

The kind of intuition I have recognized here is clearly quite different from the supreme immediate knowledge called intuition by Leibniz or Spinoza or Husserl. It is a skill for guessing with a reasonable chance of guessing right, a skill guided by an innate sensibility to coherence, improved by schooling. The fact that this faculty often fails does not discredit it; a method for guessing 10% above average chance on roulette would be worth millions.

But to know what to look for does not lend us the power to find it. That power lies in the imagination.

I call all thoughts of things that are not present, or not yet present—or perhaps never to be present—acts of the imagination. When I intend to lift my arm, this intention is an act of my imagination. In this case imagining is not visual but muscular. An athlete keyed up for a high jump is engaged in an intense act of muscular imagination. But even in the effortless lifting of an arm, we can recognize a conscious intention, an act of the imagination, distinct from its muscular execution. For we never decree this muscular performance in itself, since we have no direct control over it. This delicately coordinated feat of muscular contractions can be made to take place only spontaneously, as a sequel to our imaginative act.

This dual structure of deliberate movement was first described by William James 70 years ago. We see now that it corresponds to the two kinds of awareness that we have met in the act of perception. We may say that *we have a focal awareness of lifting our arm, and that this focal act is implemented by the integration of subsidiary muscular particulars*. We may put it exactly as in the case of perception, that we are focally aware of our intended performance and aware of its particulars only subsidiarily, by attending to the performance which they jointly constitute.

A new life, a new intensity, enters into this two-leveled structure the moment our resolve meets with difficulties. The two levels then fall apart, and the imagination sallies forward, seeking to close the gap between them. Take the example of learning to ride a bicycle. The imagination is fixed on this aim, but, our present capabilities being insufficient, its execution falls behind. By straining every nerve to close this gap, we gradually learn to keep our balance on a bicycle.

This effort results in an amazingly sophisticated policy of which we know nothing. Our muscles are set so as to counteract our accidental imbalance at every moment, by turning the bicycle into a curve with a radius proportional to the square of our velocity divided by the angle of our imbalance. Millions of people are cycling all over the world by skillfully applying this formula which they could not remotely understand if they were told about it. This puzzling fact is explained by the two-leveled structure of intentional action. The use of the formula is invented on the subsidiary level in response to the efforts to close the gap between intention and performance; and since the performance has been produced subsidiarily, it can remain focally unknown.

There are many experiments showing how an imaginative intention can evoke covertly, inside our body, the means of its implementation. Spontaneous muscular twitches, imperceptible to the subject, have been singled out by an experimenter and rewarded by a brief pause in an unpleasant noise; and as soon as this was done, the frequency of the twitches—of which the subject knew nothing—multiplied about threefold. Moreover, when the subject's imagination was stimulated by showing him the electrical effect of his twitches on a galvanometer, the frequency of the twitches shot up to about six times their normal rate (Hefferline, 1959, 1962).

This is the mechanism to which I ascribe the evocation of helpful clues by the scientist's imagination in the pursuit of an inquiry. But we have to remember here that scientific problems are not definite tasks. The scientist knows his aim only in broad terms and must rely on his sense of deepening coherence to guide him to discovery. He must keep his imagination fixed on these growing points and force his way to what lies hidden beyond them. We must see how this is done.

Take once more the example of the way we discover how to see rightly through inverting spectacles. We cannot aim specifically at reconnecting sight, touch, and hearing. Any attempt to overcome spatial inversion by telling ourselves that what we see above is really below may actually hinder our progress, since the meaning of the words we would use is inappropriate. We must go on groping our way by sight and touch, and learn to get about in this way. Only by keeping our imagination fixed *on the global result* we are seeking can we induce the requisite sensory reintegration and the accompanying conceptual innovation.

No quest could have been more indeterminate in its aim than Einstein's inquiry which led to the discovery of relativity. Yet he has told how during all the years of his inquiry, "there was a feeling of direction, of going straight towards something definite. Of course," he said, "it is very hard to express that feeling in words; but it was definitely so, and clearly to be distinguished from later thoughts about the rational form of the solution." We meet here the integration of still largely unspecifiable elements into a gradually narrowing context, the coherence of which has not yet become explicit.

The surmises made by Kepler during six years of toil before hitting on the elliptical path of Mars were often explicit. But Arthur Koestler (1959) has shown that Kepler's distinctive guiding idea, to which he owed his success, was the firm conviction that the path of the planet Mars was somehow determined by a kind of mechanical interaction with the sun. This vague vision—foreshadowing Newton's theory—had enough truth in it to make him exclude all epicycles and send his imagination in search of a single formula, covering the whole planetary path both in its speed and in its shape. This is how Kepler hit upon his two laws of elliptical revolution.

We begin to see now how the scientist's vision is formed. The imagination sallies forward, and intuition integrates what the imagination has lit upon. But a fundamental complication comes into sight here. I have acknowledged that the final sanction of discovery lies in the sight of a coherence which our intuition detects and accepts as real; but history suggests that there are no universal standards for assessing such coherence.

Copernicus criticized the Ptolemaic system for its incoherence in assuming other than steady circular planetary paths, and fought for the recognition of the heliocentric system as real because of its superior consistency. But his follower, Kepler, abandoned the postulate of circular paths, as causing meaningless complications in the Copernican system, and boasted that by doing so he had cleansed an Augean stable (Koestler, 1959, p. 334). Kepler based his first two laws on his vision that geometrical coherence is the product of some mechanical interaction (Koestler, 1959, p. 316), but this conception of reality underwent another radical transformation when Galileo, Descartes, and Newton found ultimate reality in the smallest particles of matter obeying the mathematical laws of mechanics.

I have described at some length elsewhere (Polanyi, 1958, pp. 150-160) some of the irreconcilable scientific controversies which have arisen when two sides base their arguments on different conceptions of reality. When this happens neither side can accept the evidence brought up by the other, and the schism leads to a violent mutual rejection of the opponent's whole position. The great controveries about hypnosis, about fermentation, about the bacterial origin of disease, and about spontaneous generation are cases in point (Polanyi, 1958, pp. 150-160).

It becomes necessary to ask, therefore, by what standards we can change the very standards of coherence on which our convictions rest. On what grounds can we change our grounds? We are faced with the existentialist dilemma: how values of our own choosing can have authority over us who decreed them.

We must look once more, then, at the mechanism by which imagination and intuition carry out their joint task. We lift our arm and find that our imagination has issued a command which has evoked its implementation. But the moment feasibility is obstructed, a gap opens up between our faculties and the end at which we are aiming, and our imagination fixes on this gap and evokes attempts to reduce it. Such a quest can go on for years; it will be persistent, deliberate, and transitive; yet its whole purpose is directed on ourselves; it attempts to make us produce ideas. We say then that we are *racking our brain* or *ransacking our brain;* that we are *cudgeling* or *cracking* it, or *beating our brain in trying to get it to work*.

And the action induced in us by this ransacking *is felt as something that is happening to us*. We say that we *tumble* to an idea; or that an idea *crosses* our mind; or that it *comes into* our head; or that it *strikes* us or *dawns* on us, or that it just *presents itself* to us. We are actually surprised and exclaim: Aha! when we suddenly do produce an idea. Ideas may indeed come to us unbidden, hours or even days after we have ceased to rack our brains.

Discovery is made therefore in two moves: one deliberate, the other spontaneous, the spontaneous move being evoked in ourselves by the action of our deliberate effort. The deliberate thrust is a focal act of the imagination, while the spontaneous response to it, which brings discovery, belongs to the same class as the spontaneous coordination of muscles responding to our intention to lift our arm, or the spontaneous coordination of visual clues in response to our looking at something. This spontaneous act of discovery deserves to be recognized as *creative intuition*.

But where does this leave the *creative imagination?* It is there; it is not displaced by intuition but imbued with it. When recognizing a problem and engaging in its pursuit, our imagination is guided both by our dynamic and by our strategic intuition; it ransacks our available faculties, guided by creative intuition. The imaginative effort can evoke its own implementation only because it follows intuitive intimations of its own feasibility. Remember, as an analogy, that a lost memory can be brought back only if we have clues to it; we cannot even start racking our brain for a memory that is wholly forgotten. The imagination must attach itself to clues of feasibility supplied to it by the very intuition that it is stimulating; sallies of the imagination that have no such guidance are idle fancies.

The honors of creativity are due then in one part to the imagination, which imposes on intuition a feasible task, and, in the other part, to intuition, which rises to this task and reveals the discovery that the quest was due to bring forth. *Intuition informs the imagination which, in its turn, releases the powers of intuition.*

But where, then, does the responsibility for changing our criteria of reality rest? To find that place we must probe still deeper. When the quest has ended, imagination and intuition do not vanish from the scene. Our intuition recognizes our final result to be valid, and our imagination points to the inexhaustible future manifestations of it. We return to the quiescent state of mind from which the inquiry started, but return to it with a new vision of coherence and reality. Herein lies the final acceptance of this vision; any new standards of coherence implied in it have become our own standards; we are committed to them.

But can this be true? In his treatise on *The Concept of Law*, Professor H. L. A. Hart (1961) rightly observes that, while it can be reasonable to decide that something will be illegal from tomorrow morning, it is nonsense to decide that something that is immoral today will be morally right from tomorrow. Morality, Hart says, is "immune against deliberate change"; and the same clearly holds also for beauty and truth. Our allegiance to such standards implies that they are not of our making. The existentialist dilemma still faces us unresolved.

But I shall deal with it now. The first step is to remember that scientific discoveries are made in search of reality—of a reality that is there, whether we know it or not. The search is of our own making, but reality is not. We send out our imagination deliberately to ransack promising avenues, but the promise of these paths is already there to guide us; we sense it by our spontaneous intuitive powers. We induce the work of intuition but do not control its operations.

And since our intuition works on a subsidiary level, neither the clues which it uses nor the principles by which it integrates them are fully known. It is difficult to tell what were the clues which convinced Copernicus that his system was real. We have seen that his vision was fraught with implications so far beyond his own ken that, had they been shown to him, he would have rejected them. The discovery of relativity is just as full of unreconciled thoughts. Einstein tells in his autobiography that it was the example of the two great fundamental impossibilities underlying thermodynamics that suggested to him the absolute impossibility of observing absolute motion. But today we can see no connection at all between thermodynamics and relativity. Einstein acknowledged his debt to Mach, and it is generally thought, therefore, that he confirmed Mach's thesis that the Newtonian doctrine of absolute rest is meaningless; but what Einstein actually proved was, on the contrary, that Newton's doctrine, far from being meaningless, was false. Again, Einstein's redefinition of simultaneity originated modern operationalism, but he himself sharply opposed the way Mach would replace the conception of atoms by their directly observable manifestations (Schilpp, 1949, p. 49).

The solution of our problem is approaching here. For the latency of the principles entailed in a discovery indicates how we can change our standards and still uphold their authority over us. It suggests that while we cannot decree our standards *explicitly,* in the abstract, we may change them *covertly* in practice. The deliberate aim of scientific inquiry is to solve a problem, but our intuition may respond to our efforts with a solution entailing new standards of coherence, new values. In affirming the solution we tacitly obey these new values and thus recognize their authority over ourselves, over us who tacitly conceived them.

This is indeed how new values are introduced, whether in science, or in the arts, or in human relations. They enter subsidiarily, embodied in creative action. Only after this can they be spelled out and professed in abstract terms, and this makes them appear to have been deliberately chosen, which is absurd. The actual grounds of a value, and its very meaning, will ever lie hidden in the commitment which originally bore witness to that value.

I must not speculate here about the kind of universe which may justify our reliance on our truth-bearing intuitive powers. I shall speak only of their part in our endorsement of scientific truth. A scientist's originality lies in seeing a problem where others see none and finding a way to its pursuit where others lose their bearings. These acts of his mind are strictly personal, attributable to him and only to him. But they derive their power and receive their guidance from an aim that is impersonal. For the scientist's quest presupposes the existence of an external reality. Research is conducted on these terms from the start and goes on then groping for a hidden truth toward which our clues are pointing; and when discovery terminates the pursuit, its validity is sustained by a vision of reality pointing still further beyond it.

Having relied throughout his inquiry on the presence of something real hidden out there, the scientist will necessarily also rely on that external presence for claiming the validity of the result that satisfies his quest. And as he has accepted throughout the discipline which this external pole of his endeavor imposed upon him, he expects that others, similarly equipped, will likewise recognize the authority that guided him. On the grounds of the self-command which bound him to the quest of reality, he must claim that his results are universally valid; such is the universal intent of a scientific discovery.

I speak not of universality, but of universal intent, for the scientist cannot know whether his claims will be accepted; they may be true and yet fail to carry conviction. He may have reason to expect that this is likely to happen. Nor can he regard a possible acceptance of his claims as a guarantee of their truth. To claim universal validity for a statement indicates merely that it *ought* to be accepted by all. The affirmation of scientific truth has an obligatory character which it shares with other valuations, declared universal by our own respect for them.

Both the anticipation of discovery and discovery itself may be a delusion. But it is futile to seek for explicit impersonal criteria of their validity. The content of any empirical statement is three times indeterminate. It relies on clues which are largely unspecifiable, integrates them by principles which are undefinable, and speaks of a reality which is inexhaustible. Attempts to eliminate these indeterminacies of science merely replace science by a meaningless fiction.

To accept science, in spite of its essential indeterminacies, is an act of our personal judgment. It is to share the kind of commitment on which scientists enter by undertaking an inquiry. You cannot formalize commitment, for you cannot express your commitment noncommittally; to attempt this is to perform the kind of analysis which destroys its subject matter.

We should be glad to recognize that science has come into existence by mental endowments akin to those in which all hopes of excellence are rooted and that science rests ultimately on such intangible powers of our mind. This will help to restore legitimacy to our convictions, which the specious ideals of strict exactitude and detachment have discredited. These false ideals do no harm to physicists, who only pay lip service to them, but they play havoc with other parts of science and with our whole culture, which try to live by them. They will be well lost for truer ideals of science, which will allow us once more to place first things first: the living above the inanimate, man above the animal, and man's duties above man.

Bibliography

Dingle, H. (1952), *The Scientific Adventure*. London: Pitman.

Grünbaum, A. (1963), *Philosophical Problems of Space and Time*. New York: Knopf.

Hart, H. L. A. (1961), *The Concept of Law*. Oxford: Clarendon Press.

Hefferline, R. F. (1962), Learning Theory in Clinical Psychology. In *Experimental Foundations of Clinical Psychology*, ed. A. J. Bachrach. New York: Basic Books.

——— et al. (1959), Escape and Avoidance Conditioning in Human Subjects without Their Observation of the Response. *Science*, 130:1338-1339.

Koestler, A. (1959), *The Sleepwalkers*. London: Hutchinson.
Kottenhoff, H. (1961), Was ist richtiges Sehen mit Umkehrbrillen und in welchem Sinne stellt sich das Sehen um? *Psychologia Universalis,* 5.
Polanyi, M. (1958), *Personal Knowledge*. Chicago: University of Chicago Press.
Schilpp, P. A., ed. (1949), *Albert Einstein, Philosopher-Scientist*. New York: Tudor, 1951.
Snyder, F. W., & Pronko, N. H. (1952), *Vision with Spatial Inversion*. Wichita, Kansas: University of Wichita Press.

DISCUSSION

PROFESSOR POLANYI:

I would like to give an introduction, not so much to my paper as to the thoughts which will guide me, so far as I am concerned, throughout this meeting. I feel that some grammar of the expressions which I want to use should be put to you, although it will be incomplete, as I will mention in passing. Now before I start, I want to make an experiment. Would you all look, please, at that picture? The experiment is over. You don't look at the finger with which I

FIGURE 1

name	thing
features	physiognomy
moves	skill
tool	purpose
clues	perception
	theory

was pointing but at the picture to which I was pointing. Yet you know something about my finger or else you wouldn't know where to look. Now this is the subject which is elaborated on the diagram (see Figure 1), namely that those things which are here on the left of the chart (a name, a feature, a move, a tool, a clue) have a bearing on those which are on the right on the chart: a name denotes a thing; the features belong to and compose a physiognomy; the moves compose a skill; the tool is used for a purpose; the clues guide the perception and also lead to the discovery of a theory. For secret reasons I will call the left-hand terms S and the right, F. At the moment, however, I will only say that this is the illustration of a *from-to* relation between the S's and the F's similar to that which was established between my finger and the picture (which was a *from-to* relation of a kind). Now, these relations which I have listed here often include a number of elements on the left—you see, there are many moves making a skill, a number of features making a physiognomy, many clues used in perception (and also which lead to the establishment of a theory). And if we look at these elements, we find that they vary in the level of consciousness. My finger you saw quite clearly, so that there was no question of your perception of it being unconscious. But the moves of a skill—often you know something about them, but you couldn't tell clearly what those moves are. And in perception we have the whole gambit from the actual things which we see at the center of the visual field, those which are at the edge of the field, those which we see in the corner of our eyes, those which are inside our eyes, and the memories which (heaven knows where they are) are not identifiable—all these are known, of course, to contribute to the way we *see* things, the way we perceive things, and they range over a wide stretch of consciousness from being fully identifiable to being not identifiable in themselves at all, or only with difficulty, or perhaps not capable of being experienced in themselves at all. Now this implies that on the whole the S's are not always identifiable, so that there is a certain measure of unspecifiability in the S's, which is due to the fact that they range over a wide range or gambit of consciousness. And in view of the fact that there are so many of them which we could not identify, there is an element of *tacitness* in the kind of knowledge establishing this kind of relation, this kind of *from-to* relation between the S's and the F's. But there is more to it; there is also a difference in the way in which we are aware of the S's and the F's, whatever the level of their consciousness. You are differently aware of my pointing finger from the way you are aware of the picture at which it points. But the confusion between *degrees* of awareness—that is, conscious and unconscious—and the two *kinds* of awareness is something against which I wanted to warn you.

Now there is another way in which the kind of knowledge which is illustrated here is also tacit. The process by which the S's are made to bear on the F's is an integration, an integration which is difficult to define. It is a problem to what extent one can define it. To the extent to which one cannot define it, it is an *informal* integration. The very fact that it links two different kinds of awareness makes it already clear that it wouldn't be possible fully to formalize such a qualitative change, such a relation between two qualitatively different ways of knowing things. And that is, in fact, what I want to suggest and to go straight on to say that this is characteristic of what is very commonly described as intuitive knowledge, which I will define in a somewhat different way in relation to these illustrations. But this will appear as I go along. Let's for the moment agree that this kind of knowledge, which I have tried to analyze, is an intuitive knowledge of coherence, of the coherence of the subsidiaries with the focals. One could say that the intuition is always a from-to relation, yielding a from-to knowledge.

A curious fact should be mentioned in passing. This whole relationship is somehow involved in the act of attending to F while bearing in mind the S's and being guided by them. In consequence of this structure, therefore, the relation can be destroyed by shifting the focus from F to S. For obviously there is then nothing left of the bearing of these S's on the F, since this was defined as an integrative relation which is determined by the factors we are relying on (the S's) for the purpose of attending to something else, namely, the F's. This is what I call *logical unspecifiability;* that is, there is a logical disjunction between something being known to us as an S or known to us as an F. And if we focus on an S, therefore, it loses its S (subsidiary) character; it no longer bears on what it bore on before, and the coherence has disintegrated.

This description so far has dealt with the *functional* relation of the *from-to* entities, that is, the functional aspect of this tacit process of knowing. There are two or three more aspects which we can note straight away. When such a relation exists, it defines a kind of *meaning*. Those which are on the right, the F's, are the meaning of the S's. The physiognomy is the meaning of the features, and I would therefore call the production of meaning by this from-to relationship the *semantic* aspect of tacit knowing. Naturally the term "meaning" is extended here beyond its common use.

Then there is something more. If you had before you only these S's and you looked at them, and if you could to some extent experience them in themselves and then compare them with the F's—for example, if you looked at the features in themselves and then at the physiognomy which is composed by these features and so on—clearly there is an appearance of coherence each time on the right-hand side of the list. This coherence is established by the tacit pictorial integration of which I have spoken. Thus there is a *phenomenal* aspect of this tacit knowledge. The phenomenal aspect consists of the fact that there is a coherent appearance established by the process of integration.

That makes three aspects which we have identified, and all three will prove of importance. There is a fourth which leads to very difficult problems. It consists in the fact (which I propose to consider to be a fact) that these relationships, when justifiably established, define a reality—they are a knowledge of reality. We could call this the *ontological* aspect of the tacit relation which we established between the S's and the F's. They have a bearing on reality, a bearing which we will sometimes be able to identify in terms of a comprehensive entity. We will hear later about a person being analyzed as a comprehensive entity of this kind. But you see, it is in a large company—the person—of quite different and much less distinguished things than it perhaps appeared to be in philosophic discussion in the past.

All this is to introduce the grammar, at any rate parts of the grammar, of tacit knowledge which I want to use from time to time and have used in the paper which I have presented to you. There is an important chapter of the analysis of the ontological aspect which I will completely omit here.

It should be added, however, that all this kind of knowledge is, in a very clear sense, *personal*. It is *we* who are achieving these integrations, *we* who are using the moves to perform a skill, or the tool for a particular purpose, or pursuing the clues either in achieving a clear perception, or in making a discovery, of a theory. This is, therefore, also a theory of personal knowledge, an attenuated general outline of such a theory.

PROFESSOR MURRAY:

Could I start with the person? As I understand it, you are putting the person, the one who has personal knowledge, at the center of the scheme; he is the perceiver—the man who is moving toward a theory. He is also the one who has purpose, for instance to see certain phenomena accurately and then to arrive at theory to explain them. And then on both sides of the chart, the moves and the skill, they are also the person; he has some kind of ability, maybe with a tool, which he can rely on to achieve his purpose. But the physiognomy: is that *this* person's physiognomy?

PROFESSOR POLANYI:

No, the left-hand side is, what shall we call it, the first person. This may be another person, on the right, who is subject to the observation of his features by a mechanism of this kind. But I must say a little more. Clearly the whole range of these phenomena, as analyzed by me, can be thought to be another person's skills, physiognomy, discoveries, and so on. And I am analyzing them by a process of the same kind. But this is the kind of thing that leads on to the ontology of the coherent entities which one sees in this way. In other words, the relationship is duplicated in the observer, who integrates from the outside, and in the observed.

PROFESSOR MURRAY:

I can see that almost everything on the chart might be aspects of another person. The man you are observing is working toward a theory, say; he is the reporting perceiver of clues, but these are *outside* himself. He uses a tool with a purpose, and he has a skill as you can see. And he has features and a physiognomy. But now if you put all this inside the first person, the person with personal knowledge, how do you get the *thing,* the physiognomy and the clues inside *him?*

PROFESSOR POLANYI:

I see your point. This reflection is not taken into account here.

PROFESSOR TAYLOR:

But surely it isn't necessary for the things on the left to be one thing or person and the things on the right to be another thing or person. A skill is one's own skill, can be one's own skill.

PROFESSOR SILBER:

Or in self-portraits by an artist . . . I don't see any reason to divide the first person and the third person vertically except to recognize the *possibility* of doing so. But you wouldn't want to commit yourself to the necessity of that split?

PROFESSOR POLANYI:

No, this is a description, which is quite naïve (and solitary) for the moment, of what is going on in one person—this is, of course, my own experience which I am describing, but you could have a more complex situation. Let's say you want to study the process of thought of a chess master. Well, you have that complex entity, his projects, which you analyze in terms of the clues which you have toward understanding; this naturally includes that range of inquiries and that range of knowledge—in fact, that is one of the most important parts. I can't develop it quite because there is one important fact I haven't mentioned until now: our knowledge of our own body is almost invariably an S knowledge.

DR. STRAUS:

About skills: one has to read one's own body objectively. The first step is really to be aware of your body as a kind of object: you have to take a position, e.g., hold a racket. The process of learning a skill with this never-ending requirement of practice is, if I see it correctly, just to turn from the focused motion to a kind of performance where the motion is no longer focused; it would be among the S's.

PROFESSOR POLANYI:

I am glad you mentioned that. You see, this is the thing of which I said much can be stated. The motion of our attention from right to left and left to right again is the dialectic of *detailing* and *integrating,* and I am sure that is what you are referring to. There are many ways in which one can amplify this scheme, and that is one of them.

PROFESSOR POTEAT:

From the point of view of this distinction—between detailing and integrating—may I ask what bearing this distinction has on your use of "personal"? For example, if I am performing a skill and the vectorial thrust is therefore from the details of the skill to the skillful performance as integrated, and if I then attempt further to practice and improve the skill, is *detail* less personal when the hitherto integrated entity is the skill that I am myself performing?

PROFESSOR POLANYI:

Well, I think that "personal" is the effort of this integration and the sustaining of this integration; they are all-important. It is conceptually misleading, I think, to believe that such an integration can exist without somebody being there to sustain it, because only in ourselves can two levels of awareness exist. They can't exist outside somebody, and therefore there is the ineluctable presence of the person in knowledge, so far as it is knowledge with that structure (and of course all knowledge has that structure); this ineluctable presence is logically necessary in view of the two levels of awareness which can be present only in a person.

PROFESSOR MURRAY:

Would you agree that there may be a continuous organization of differentiated processes or functions in learning, for example, a somewhat complicated skill (such as doing a figure eight on skates)? A person starts by acquiring a small microskill which, for him, is a minor achievement, and he says, "Ah, I got that today." He rehearses it, and then the next time he tries to get a little more. Soon he acquires a larger integration, a larger system of subsidiary processes, etc. In short, there would be an organization of minor skills leading up to one major achievement, the realization of a purpose. Would you agree to that?

PROFESSOR POLANYI:

Yes indeed. I am glad you called our attention to it. This is really an expanding system. It is a universe of culture which is indicated. Take language, for example; it produces meanings which produce emotions and the understanding of phenomena far beyond anything which, without this earlier achievement, would have been conceivable. And the whole universe of art, which of course is indefinitely expansive—I think that Cassirer has in this respect said something fundamental: this whole universe of the mind in which we live is an expansion of a symbol-making, that is, of a semantic function of an elemental kind.

DR. STRAUS:

In order to distinguish between two types of skills I would say "transitive" and "intransitive" skills. By transitive I mean something meant to effect something. By intransitive I mean something like jumping (or maybe the ice-skating just mentioned). But the attitudes in these two cases must be different at some point.

PROFESSOR POLANYI:

I would go further, with your permission, in your direction, actually. Because what is left out here and what I have never worked out, but I think is absolutely essential to work out, perhaps on these lines, is the self-integration on which the psychiatrists, of course, insist more and more. It is not quite easy to see how this diagram applies to a person with a disintegrated personality which he tries to recover and bring into balance and control by wisdom and prudence and joy. All this is, I think, not clearly included, but must be included by an extension to the purely existential purposes which can be achieved by integration. The term "integration" promises to carry through because it is one which psychiatrists particularly have used for characterizing improvements in personality.

PROFESSOR CROSSON:

I have several questions. One concerns the relation between the subsidiary and focal. Returning to Dr. Straus's first comment, he remarked that in learning a skill we first have a schematic or focal awareness of the parts that are finally integrated into the skill. I want to raise the question whether this is always the case, whether one can acquire skills *without* that schematic or specific awareness of the parts; in relation to this I also want to ask whether the logical relation between subsidiary and focal awarenesses is also chronological. One of your five instances up there seems to me to stand out from the others—the relation between features and physiognomy. I myself suppose that, in this case, the focal awareness never *follows* chronologically the observation of features. A young child, for instance, is aware of a friendly face before he is aware of smiling lips and green eyes. Now this does not necessarily apply to the other instances. There you can find examples where the subsidiary awareness itself is schematic and separate before it is integrated into a whole.

PROFESSOR POLANYI:

I don't think Dr. Straus intended quite exclusively to say that we always know first the parts of a skill. I think he was satisfied with my modifying, somewhat, what he said in my reply that this is a dialectical process. I think we usually see somebody doing the thing as a whole, for otherwise our imagination—our muscular imagination—would not be invoked. On the other hand, if we break a world record in jumping, then of course we haven't got anything to go by except the task which we define in a very abstract way. I don't know how far we have also a feeling about, a conception or awareness of, the means of doing it. I think that one could actually go on about cases where the whole thing is inverted, too. Supposing you take the name and the thing. Sometimes you know a thing—say you have discovered a new species, then you want to name it; or you have to give a name to what those things are on the left and what those things are on the right and you have to make up your mind to give them names which are in some sense opposite. I am still struggling after many years to decide whether all the subsidiaries are the kind of thing I called them. This is a case when one has to make a thing and not a name; on the other hand, if the child listens to some grownups talking around him, he may hear names (or what he presumes to be names) but not know to what they are referring—this same game may be played with theory: a clue to a theory is *also* an illustration of a theory; you look upon the world with a subsidiary awareness of the theory and see it in a different light in consequence. This is not to be taken as guiding, in that detail, the understanding of what's going on—it is the *type* of process.

MR. LUCAS:

I wonder if I could indicate where Professor Polanyi's position is often open to attack and suggest one or two defenses. I think the normal attack comes on two points: first of all, personal knowledge is personal, and it is also knowledge. How do we share it with others; what is the technique of argument by which the universal intent can be supported? And second (a different aspect of the same point), what about the case where people *have* some creative vision which is wrong (this can happen)? These two points become linked: in order to be right, it is not enough simply to have inspiration; it is necessary first of all for this to be intersubjective (at least under some conditions). Now the attraction of the very negative position, for instance, of Mill, is that he *does* give rules for knocking out wrong ideas, and he does express these rules universally. So when we read Mill, he gives some clear idea of the procedure which we can go through, and it is one which occasionally (though it is not predictable) *will* show that this particular hypothesis is a bad one. Now the whole sense of Professor Polanyi's position is that things aren't as simple as that. That you just can't simply run through a set of necessary and sufficient conditions in the S column and then produce a clear answer with a yes or no decision. On the contrary, he points out that the relation is inexhaustible, and this in three ways: we don't know all the S things that are relevant; we don't know all the ways in which they are relevant, what the logic of the argument is; and third, there are a great many further pictures which we don't know yet but which we expect *will* turn up in the F category which will turn out to be relevant again. That is, on the third one, we can expect that if we were right on the F perception or the F theory, it will be indicated in all sorts of ways which we have not yet understood. What, then, is going to be the correct way to supplement the ideal that Mill and Popper have of necessary rules for determining, if not the truth, at least the falsity, of hypotheses: rules objective enough for computers to formulate? I think the answer is given in the idea of an argument where you say what you can and then leave yourself open to attack. This was pointed out as a possibility by Hart, whom Dr. Polanyi has referred to elsewhere. Hart points out that in the law we don't have a strict logic of necessary and sufficient conditions, but of, roughly, presumption and counterpresumption. And I think it is here that Polanyi should be able to develop much more—not so much the logic of personal knowledge, but the logic of the controversy, which must go with this when we are (a) trying to show other people that our ideas are right, and (b) on occasion trying to show other people that their ideas are wrong. It's going to be a logic which isn't nearly so tightly formulated. So for a physiognomy, for instance, we don't give *all* the proofs that are relevant; but if we are trying to show someone that this *is* a portrait, or this is a portrait of a friendly man, we have to be able to show *some* of the points about it. We have to show that the mouth is curved in a way that is like a smile, rather than a sardonic grin. That is, although we can't say *all* there is about the S features, the S column, we *do* need to be able upon occasion to point out certain things. When a man is trying to imitate skating and is getting it completely wrong, the skilled instructor will point out some of the things which he is doing wrong, although he can't tell him all the things he is doing wrong.

Now on the second point, the way that the argument goes, even when I have pointed out what factors I think are relevant, I have still got to lay myself open to a man failing to see the relevance or to his objecting that the relevance is inadequate. When I argue that this portrait is that of a friendly face, I have got to leave room for the person to come back and say: ah, but if you look at the whites of his knuckles, that shows he is not as friendly as the face shows him. It is, as it were, necessary that one's argument shall have gaps in it for other people to enter their objections.

PROFESSOR POLANYI:

I am afraid I would disagree with the hint which John Lucas has given—I don't think I would use the idea that of course one *has* to have universal acceptance, an intersubjectivity. I am against intersubjectivity, in theory at any rate. If philosophers are sure that there is always a doubt (we all feel that there is something in that), and particularly if one has personal knowledge (there is always a kind of personal factor involved in what we are concluding), then I don't see what advantage it is to have the views about it of other people who are subject to the same disability. We are responsible ultimately for making up our own minds, and I don't think there is any way in which we can shift that responsibility to other people. And this is, I think, the most serious part of my answer: that I do suggest that we should draw the conclusion that this is all that we are under obligation to do, that this is what we can do, and no more. We can know what we decided to believe, having allowed for such delay as is reasonable, such examination as is available. This point we come to with the declaration that we have got in touch with reality, that we have got in touch with *something* which lends a claim of universality to our conclusion. Whether that claim will be accepted or not is, of course, of great importance to us, but it does not *define* the success of our enterprise. I cannot accept the thesis that it does so. I think that if we accepted that, we should get into an absurd situation, because we would be laboring to persuade other people instead of persuading ourselves. And this clearly would be an infinite and futile regress.

That's how I see the difficulty, but then we have been in a difficulty for a long time. We have been through three hundred years of effort, since the Copernican revolution, to do something which was a noble and immensely fruitful aspiration but which is not practicable—it can't be done. Therefore we must expect to be in a difficult position and to have something difficult to do to get out of it or, at any rate, to get on terms with the difficulty. And this is what I suggest—that we *must* have the state of mind which I have outlined. You cannot say I am indifferent to the possibility of convincing people, for otherwise I wouldn't have tried to get this meeting together. This may be a trivial answer, but it is nevertheless, I think, a substantial one. I am doing everything I can, but I don't think I can, with all due respect to this gathering, make my conclusions and my convictions dependent on what the gathering will decide about them.

MR. LUCAS:

Could I answer Professor Polanyi's use of the word "intersubjective"? I don't want to suggest it is a *criterion* of the truth of one's own ideas that other people think they are true. If this were so, then clearly one could never start to propagate new ideas, because by admission other people don't hold them to begin with. And in *that* sense I don't regard intersubjectivity as essential. It is not that other people hold these ideas, but rather that we *want* them to hold these ideas. One doesn't present one's theories to other people and then say that one doesn't worry about any of them agreeing. What I want to resist—and I want to reaffirm this resistance in view of what Professor Polanyi has said—is this: I want to resist the implicit solipsism in his confession of faith. I want to do this on two levels. First of all, by a declaration of independence; when I feel sufficiently sure of my ideas, I want other people to share them, and I want to know their comments, their criticisms, for I want to check up on my own. And I think that in fact Professor Polanyi could be consistent and still keep the first person of personal knowledge if he used the first person plural rather than the first person singular. But even if he would not do this, I would attack him on the other point, which I think is absolutely central, and that is the question of fallibility. It is clear and necessarily true that if one can hope to achieve anything in one's personal investigations, the necessary condition is that one *could* be wrong, and leaving aside all other people, one *must* be self-critical, for only if one is prepared to be self-critical can one hope to avoid the errors which are a possibility, which are the necessary concomitant of the possibility of success. Leaving aside all other people, one must have some logic of a *critical* kind to make sure that when one has got some idea, some vision, it is not mad, not trivial, not in some other way faulty.

DR. KLEIN:

I think Professor Polanyi has discussed this with a distinction that I hoped would have come up by now, between the *personal* and the *subjective*.

PROFESSOR POLANYI:

About fallibility: I don't see that I am here in disagreement with John Lucas. On the contrary, I am rather proud of having *introduced* fallibility, because intuition once was used as unfailing, but the intuition I am talking about is one which can, and probably very often does, go wrong, because it is only the *structure* which characterizes my kind of "intuition" and not its *result* as something which is beyond criticism. It is only that I believe that the chances of this intuition are sufficient to justify our reliance on it. Now I have said this in my paper, and it is very important; if we are going to use the term "intuition," anybody who wants to follow me in *this* usage must realize that this is the decisive point, that this is a *fallible* intuition—it is just as fallible as any other form of inference and it is, of course, informal—that is its characteristic.

As to what Klein says—I am glad he reminds me of it—I have, of course, tried my best to distinguish between the subjective, the passive, states of consciousness, and those which I call personal knowledge. And again and again I have pointed out the claim, inherent in from-to knowledge, which we must have in ourselves: that we are establishing a bearing on reality. That is the point which gives not intersubjectivity but universal *intent*. Because it is something which is outside, postulated through our commitment, it gives us, necessarily and logically, the claim of contributions to be shared by others, because they face the same kind of reality we do. And as

I have also said in my paper, this gives us a claim to know what people *ought* to believe, what they ought to do. Just as we have decided what we ought to do, on the same grounds, we know what they ought to do. And there is, therefore, in this view, a primacy of the *normative* over the *descriptive*. The normative is the more general and the more responsible way of expressing our conclusion. The descriptive form varies precisely to the extent to which it is not just another way of putting the normative conclusion, the conclusion that this is, as far as we can see, that which *ought* to be concluded. There is nothing here to suggest that the opinions of others should not be taken into account or that one should have an uncritical acceptance of one's own conclusions. Nor do I think that Lucas meant that I said that, but I just want to say that there is not the slightest hint of that: the struggle for coming to the right conclusion is just one of the things which I have tried to dramatize.

PROFESSOR SCOTT:

Going back to the intersubjective business, puzzling over what you mean, isn't it so that one takes personal responsibility for deciding whether to seek the assistance of someone else on the subject one is concerned about? That is to say, if you listen to others, it is because you have confidence that the reality you seek has been perceived by them. That is where you can do it—you decide whether to rely on your direct observation or on those of others—mostly you learn from others, of course.

PROFESSOR POLANYI:

Well, yes, of course. I hope I can learn, and I certainly would encourage people to do so. I think I have expressed myself paradoxically in abjuring intersubjectivity. We are 99% made up of what we learn and get from others. So I only was arguing perhaps a little crudely about the ultimate sanction of our convictions, which I think has often been described as if it were identical with the mere fact of intersubjectivity. Science has been described as that which is intersubjective. Now I think that is misleading—that is, science is something which ought to be intersubjective if you believe in it, but I don't think it should be universal *assent* which is the criterion. Besides, it isn't even true. There are lots of parts of science which few people believe in. The most important ideas of science, as John Lucas has hinted, are those which are not shared by anybody else, but they are in the minds of those who will continue in pursuit of a discovery. Yet textbooks are just full of these statements: that *this is the nature of science,* that *it is intersubjective.* That is wrong, but only to this extent: that it is logically mistaken and ought to be replaced by a more careful formulation. Of course, that which satisfies ourselves as a discovery has also the power of enriching and guiding other people. Of course, the great triumph of the human mind, which I celebrate as far as I can every time I have an occasion for it, is that we have these powers; this is a cosmic fact, a fact which ought to be able to inspire us, but doesn't do so now because we constantly try to run it down. We give it some trivial explanation which, fortunately, is false. Take the example of the people who invented chess, and then I don't know for how many years (certainly a matter of thousands of years at least), people have gone on playing chess without improving on it; if I ever find new combinations in it, then this achievement will be profoundly impressive and should not for a moment be reduced; it should be exalted by whatever I have to say about it.

PROFESSOR HAAS:

I am still not satisfied with your answer to Mr. Lucas on the question of intersubjectivity. There is, perhaps, after all, this aspect of our desire to be intersubjective—namely, that there is some kind of *argument* relevant to our opinions and conclusions. True, it cannot be such as would normally be claimed to be a formal argument. It cannot be deductive; it cannot be inductive. I think there was no conflict at all between what Lucas said and your saying that the argument was informal and of the kind, for instance, that a jury would apply in asking whether the accused is guilty or innocent. John Wisdom has examined such arguments (e.g., in his paper entitled "Gods"). These arguments are not simply about the truth or falsity of judgments used in analysis. We are not proceeding here from F to S, asking whether *all* the features that make up a particular physiognomy, or *all* the clues for the perception are present. We cannot enumerate *all* the conditions that are relevant to the theory. No such argument would be used in a court of law. One *would* ask for an analytic judgment if one asked, "Has this been a case of *killing?*" One would want to know whether the victim is dead or not, etc. But if one asks whether this is a case of *murder,* then the question is different. One never has sufficient conditions for saying that this was a case of murder. One could think of cases, say, of a patient dying under the knife of a surgeon and someone who had never heard of surgical operations saying that this was a case of murder. He might then be informed that the surgeon had been acting in a professional capacity, so there was no murder. But then someone might object that the surgeon was acting unskillfully and with neglect. So, again, perhaps, "culpable homicide." Now this is a very difficult question to decide: did he act with neglect or not? There are no sufficient conditions of neglect. And yet, I think there *is* a kind of relevant argument. And if we want intersubjectivity, then we must acknowledge that there is a kind of argument that we allow to take place here. I think this was one of the questions Mr. Lucas asked: what is this kind of argument that is neither inductive nor deductive? To say it is just informal, is only a negative characterization. We ask: what sort of argument is relevant here which, though it does not give us logical necessity, is nevertheless a convincing argument?

PROFESSOR POLANYI:

I think that first of all there are rules for that in a court of law—rules of evidence—which tell you what you can take into account and how, but of course, they are not exhaustive and are subject to interpretation. But I would like to mention the name of Professor Perelman, a Belgian philosopher who has come to a similar conclusion about the difficulties of conclusive demonstration in such cases—difficulties which of course are no secret; everybody knows about them. But he has decided to try to develop a logic of persuasion, rather than of entailment, by using the procedure of courts and so on. He has written about that in a very illuminating way. He has tried to revive the study of rhetoric and has developed it starting from this point of view—from this position of the uncertainty of the conclusion. So it is a possibility to pursue the philosophic sense of this situation more systematically.

PROFESSOR PANTIN:

May I raise a point? In your final conclusion you were speaking of the way in which discovery could be treated in two stages, the deliberate stage and the spontaneous stage. If I may take a few minutes, I would like to give an illustration of failure of intuition. I may be wrong, but let me just give you a picture of the district near Ben Nevis and Lochaber in Scotland.

This concerns a great mistake Charles Darwin made when he was quite a young man, soon after he came back from the voyage of the *Beagle*. He had been working on papers for the Geological Society and was doing very well, but he wanted a week off. He went to the northwest of Scotland, where there is a tremendous, deep fault running through Loch Ness down to the sea; there are also various valleys deepened, as we now know, by ice. There are some very odd geological features there, commonly known as "the parallel roads of Glen Roy." They consist of three absolutely level terraces, and they can be seen very clearly. These "roads" had interested people from a very early time—in the 18th century they were said to be hunting roads; later they were said to be the remains of the shores of a lake which was blocked by a great dam here.

Darwin went to have a look at the "roads." His initial purpose was simply to take a holiday to clear his mind of all the studying he had been doing. His interpretation of the phenomena was based quite clearly on what he had just seen in Tierra del Fuego in South America. To his eyes Glen Roy became the Beagle Channel; the "parallel roads" appeared as raised marine beaches. He wrote a long paper concerning them, but the paper is open to difficulties: Darwin couldn't find certain things that he had expected. Had he come to these conclusions in the south of Wales instead of the west of Scotland, his intuitive solution (that the "roads" were due to a rise in the sea level as was the case in Tierra del Fuego) would have been quite correct, and all he would have had to do was to prove his point logically and scientifically.

The following year, Agassiz visited these "roads" after visiting the glaciers in Switzerland where he had seen things of this same sort—valleys, for instance in Chamonix, where there had once been two glaciers, with water impounded in between them, blocking up a valley. He stated that similarly there had been an immense glacier at Ben Nevis which came down from what is now known as Loch Treig. It blocked the valley at two points and formed a barrier which impounded a lake in Glen Roy. The ice barriers made lakes at high levels. The lakes of these various "parallel roads" escaped through fissures; they overflowed at the various cols. However, Agassiz went too far with his theory. He said, seeing it all with what I call "Chamonix eyes," that all the parallel roads ought to be along the main Glen Spean into which Glen Roy opens. There is one such road in Glen Spean, but it is only the very lowest one. What had happened was that the ice sheet was ever so much larger than Agassiz had expected—it filled Glen Spean. This is actually the proof of the matter, but Agassiz "saw" all three roads.

Now compare the two cases. Darwin knew there was something interesting at Glen Roy, but he wasn't going there deliberately to investigate the "roads" at all. He simply looked at things and "saw" exactly what he had seen at Tierra del Fuego. He, then, assumed that they had the same explanation. Agassiz "saw" exactly what he had seen in Chamonix. He was very nearly right. But notice he wasn't quite right—he also made a mistake in intuition. The point is that both men made spontaneous guesses: neither first set out to give a deliberate explanation. These were worked out afterward.

PROFESSOR POLANYI:

I have no objection to your account. Perhaps you would explain what the relation of your observation is to what I said about discovery.

PROFESSOR PANTIN:

Well, you *start* with a deliberate attack.

PROFESSOR POLANYI:

Oh yes, I see. I do think that if you pursue a problem, this is how you do it. If you haven't got to pursue it, because you have a solution without pursuing it, of course the problem doesn't arise.

PROFESSOR PANTIN:

Oh, yes, you *can* do it your way, as it were, but what I am trying to say is that it is by no means the only way. The problem can arise intuitively to start with. In fact, even in the case where you deliberately set out to discover how something works, this may happen.

PROFESSOR POLANYI:

Let me make that clear. I said that the act of discovery is in two moves, but there is no need for them to be consecutive; that is precisely why I brought in the elementary case of lifting my arm. Surely I need no imaginative effort to do that. It takes a little time, but after that my arm goes up. The structure which I suggested is analogous to the more dramatic case when somebody racks his brain for weeks and years on end, as Einstein did about relativity, and then something comes out. That case is a change in the parameters of the structure, but I would still think that the structure can be applied. In your example, too, both men looked at the situation and thought about it, and imagination played a part in their discoveries.

PROFESSOR CROSSON:

Couldn't you also say that it is just a matter of where the deliberation began? In one case it was off the coast of Tierra del Fuego and in the second case it was in Switzerland, but the deliberation had begun long before.

PROFESSOR PANTIN:

Yes, as long as one makes "deliberation" cover all sorts of things which were not directly connected with what happens afterward.

PROFESSOR POLANYI:

Yes. But my problem was to try to give a structure which would tell us what people are doing when they *are* trying to discover something and how they possibly can do it because they don't know what they are doing. If they knew what they were doing, there would be nothing to discover. In other words, the initial sallying forth of imagination of which I spoke is focal, indeed, but of something incomplete, which calls forth the effort of completing it. In fact, I think your case of Darwin and Agassiz fits my account very well.

DR. STRAUS:

I would like to bring up one other question: whether the real task in the situation you are describing is not rather the discovery of the *problem*. If you have the problem, then you can proceed in certain ways. And so I would wonder whether the tacit knowledge in the column S is not at the same time a tacit ignorance of psychology.

PROFESSOR POLANYI:

I am very glad you bring up our understanding of the problem, which is one of my main problems, and what I am trying to say about it is: this is something similar to knowing a comprehensive entity, but to know it in an incomplete but promising situation. In other words, it is, as it were, a knowledge of the gradient of coherence—the slope of coherence, the tendency of it to be present and capable of being discovered. I have said something about that in my paper. It is, I think, a rather daring hypothesis, but I think it is quite unavoidable: we have not only the capacity of identifying significant, real coherence but also the capacity of identifying the presence of potential coherence, the presence of the *promise* of coherence. I have tried to give the phenomenology of that, to use that term, and show the importance of it, but I have recently come across the work of some Russian psychologists which has impressed me very much. They have introduced a term which can be experimentally identified: the orientation reflex which an animal shows (or a human being may show) if something puzzling is presented to it. Well, we ought to have noticed that long ago, because, of course, animals *do* turn their heads in a certain direction if something puzzles them. But we didn't recognize this, because it wasn't the kind of thing we liked. Now these psychologists have not only recognized it; they have developed a series of symbols of what they call OR—orientation reflex—and studied how often the orientation reflex recurs if they repeat the same kind of surprising thing. Different species of animals are very different from one another in that respect. After three orientation reflexes, a dog will no longer be interested and no longer surprised and no longer puzzled and will not try to come to terms with the thing, whereas a cat will be surprised 173 times. But I think that this is now well on its way to being recognized at least by nonbehaviorist psychology—that is, simply the fact that the dog has a problem. I shall go on about this because I think it is immensely promising. For example, the Russians' work about intestinal stimuli, which can be conditioned, shows how pervasive this orientation reflex is; it goes through the whole of the autonomic system. And this is why: it is an aspect of something which is a part of the definition of a problem, namely, that *it bothers us*. Something that doesn't bother us is not a problem. Not only can a problem worry us, it can worry our alimentary canal —it really has an unsettling emotional content. And that shows again, I think, that the emotional component of an inquiry is important: unless you want to find out and are passionately interested, you will never find out anything. And so, of course, that is one of the reasons one has to allow for personal knowledge, because it is simply ridiculous to say that there are methods of making discoveries impersonally.

PROFESSOR TAYLOR:

One of the things that I don't understand is why, in your analysis, the concept of the society figures not at all. Why do you insist only on the personal; why is the individual never placed within his community for you? Is there some reason for that?

PROFESSOR POLANYI:

No, just the lack of space, you see.

4

THE COLLAGE AS MODEL

DONALD L. WEISMANN

In recent years, especially since the end of World War II, the artist has more and more been asked into the conference room and the lecture hall. Unlike a generation ago, the artist is now often asked to speak before religious groups, in churches, to scientific, educational, and even political groups. His advice is solicited and, wonderfully, it is often valued to the extent of its becoming part of new emphases and revised patterns of operation in situations which traditionally have had no visible relation to the arts.

As an artist primarily concerned with the kind of reality arrived at via the formulation of personal experience, I am not at all averse to speaking of myself and my work. In fact, I feel this is the best way for me to make my point concerning this expanding role—and responsibility—of the artist.

I estimate that I have been an artist since the age of 15; it is easy for me to contrast the role of the artist in the very early 1930's with his role since about 1946. As an artist I went to school with scholars, and after that I was still an artist but with such academic appurtenances as made it easy to go on being an artist—as teacher—inside these wonderful and autonomy-developing powerhouses we call universities. I started out teaching drawing and painting, and did that for something like 10 years. The longer I taught in these areas, and the longer I worked at my own painting, the more interesting and insistent became the conceptual notions bred by them. After a while these notions took on the character of problems which in turn led me into the history, philosophy, and criticism of art. Not being able to solve enough of these problems fast enough by myself, I went back to being a G. I. Bill type of graduate student in the history and criticism of art. And after that I went back to teaching—but not in the studio. I moved into the lecture hall with all the oversize, souped-up projection equipment now at our disposal. My shift from teaching drawing and painting to teaching the history and criticism of art did not mean that I had lost interest in the studio. In fact, my own painting continued and, if anything, increased in amount and quality. This may have been because, removed from the teaching studio, the temptation to traffic in my untested insights before I myself had had the opportunity to grapple with them was also removed.

Now, because of the special gifts of wisdom or ignorance in which we all share, I have a habit of allowing my closest convictions to have pretty much their own way. I have difficulty, and it makes me sick in a very subtle and pervasive way, when I persist in trying to read these convictions—and hence, so much of myself—out of the act. And, as I said earlier, I think of myself as an artist who went to school with scholars. So, in crucial ways I remained an artist while teaching courses in "Nineteenth and Twentieth Century Art," "The Art of Flanders and Holland," and directed theses ranging from "The George Washington of Horatio Greenough" to "Title Pages from the Sixteenth and Seventeenth Centuries in the Latin American Collection of The University of Texas." At times, and mainly for the benefits of perspective by incongruity, I have played at impersonating the nonartist in my teaching of art history. Certain benefits have accrued, I feel, to both students and me with impersonations of such specialists as Chandler Post, Gisela Richter, Erwin Panofsky, and Wylie Sypher. But ever since the last time I taught painting in the studios of Wayne University in 1950, I have been an artist teaching the history and criticism of art. I feel it is what I have learned from the creative processes in art, especially in painting and collage, that lends to my present teaching whatever real value it may have.[1] I feel that the same relationship is true for my performance as director of a university fine arts gallery, as head of two university art departments, as director of graduate studies in art, as director of a university-wide program in the arts, and as University Professor in the Arts at The University of Texas. And

[1] Long ago I touched on this relationship of the creative process to the history and criticism of art (see Weismann, 1949).

this is, rather artificially, limiting my considerations only to those of an academic and academic-administrative kind.

I feel that what has been found valuable—or *real and true*—in the creative processes of art is what others want to know about. Certainly they are not so eagerly lusting after the knowledge of what makes the color green, or how old Titian was when he died. They, whoever they are—businessmen, politicians, ministers, heads of educational programs and institutions, medical groups, and still others—sense, in the operations of the artist, clues to solutions of their own problems, in no matter what context. And I think they are right. With this in mind I have taken the Organization Committee's suggestion—that one way to get our individual views before the group might be by reporting on some special aspect of our current work—and have chosen to speak of my recent and continuing work with collage and, to a lesser degree, assemblage.

By collage, nowadays, we mean a kind of paste-up—a configuration composed of various materials pasted in their respective positions on some kind of support. Generally speaking, a collage has the surface characteristics of a painting: it is flat. An assemblage, in the accepted connotation of metropolitan America of the 1950's and 1960's, is a three-dimensional additive sort of sculpture—either relief or sculpture in-the-round. It is accomplished by gluing, nailing, welding, tying, wiring, or keying together parts, often of *other* things, to form a new ensemble.

If one started out consciously and by design to create collages or assemblages, as I did not, I suppose one would begin by getting a lot of stuff and things and parts of things with which to work. In my case it seems I looked up one day about two years ago to find that, indeed, I had *en passant* amassed a great variety of stuff and things and parts and splinters. But truer, perhaps, would be that I had been "unsystematically" but continually amassing a great variety of particular things over a long period of time, slowly, as if for some purpose. I think I can be fair to the past and to the person I may have been then and still say that the particular things I had corralled were all things which, in themselves, for whatever reason or nonreason, had had some other than ordinary effect on me. This effect, I should like to make clear, seems to me not to have been in any essential way "aesthetic" at the outset. At the first stage when these particular things were come upon or salvaged and then retained, it seems to me that this took place simply because some more than average intensity of interest was engendered. This interest might just as well have been of the qualities of dislike and uneasiness as of high admiration and satisfaction—and my memory, even of particulars, would have me attest to this. It is, I feel, the level of *intensity* of effect, no matter the *quality* or *kind* of that effect, which determines whether or not I pick up, purchase, or salvage a particular thing.

In my case particular things either purposely amassed or dumbly rescued along the way have been coming together in boxes, drawers, bundles, piles, and on tabletops for the last 40 years. Among them are fiddles and phonograph parts, newspapers and toilet seats, Italian circus tickets and prize-fight programs, bus tokens and gramophone records; photographs, signs, and sheet music; posters, letters, and streetcar transfers; tongue blades, belt buckles, and shoe tongues; ribbons, cloth, and fishline; slivers of wood, laminated wood beams, and pieces of stone; books impossible to read, hopelessly foxed engravings, and sea shells; celluloid, wallpaper, glass negatives, and radio parts; labels, stamps, coins, and x-ray photographs; gloves, false teeth, chair seats, valentines, diplomas, paintings, prints, drawings, calling cards, and handwriting.

In a way this sort of uncatalogued collection of things is what each of us has, even after wars and floods. My collection may be larger than some; maybe its range is greater, too. This may be only because I, unlike a Stephen Hero (Joyce, 1944, pp. 210 ff.) who for a while collected *verbal* "epiphanies," fell early to saving concrete things—but with something similar to Stephen Hero's faith in the power and promise of words to precipitate radiant manifestations.[2]

So, beside the easy will to discover and value objects and bits of things because of some more than ordinary pull on us, there is the stronger will to hold on to them, to give them safety in one's keeping—to save them out of one time and into others. This amassing and careful saving of so much creates obvious physical problems. This is why, often regretfully and with feelings of personal loss, we

[2] It is perhaps of crucial significance here that when Joyce goes on to expose and develop his Augustinian theory of epiphanies he cites *objects,* not words, as the key agents: i.e., "the clock in the Ballast Office" (p. 211).

"clean house" and throw away. Partly in an effort to avoid this, I have in recent years constructed a building of good size separate from the house. It, too, is filling up nicely. Ideally, there ought to be enough space so that these things could remain spread out, so that one thing need not overlap and hide another—so that they could show and be seen. For one of the "reasons" this or that thing was discovered and saved was that it had not at all finished being what I was somehow encouraged to suspect it was or is. One of the virtues of each of these things, from the beginning, was its beguiling incompleteness and its power to generate in me something like a faith in its ultimate potential for pointing to its own completeness if allowed the chance.

Now, in order to allow for the possibility of any of these objects to complete itself, my perception of them must be completed or greatly enriched. Consequently, at some stage, I find myself looking at one object or at a group of particular objects which hold my attention in such ways as tend to heighten a mood of anticipation in me. I turn these objects in my hands; I place them alone and in various ways together in a variety of fields of associational contexts, colors, depths, and textures. I move them, adjust, overlap, remove, modify, substitute; and I move myself around them. As I become more and more aware of the qualities of these things they gain or lose interest for me. Those of more or continuing interest remain; those of less are usually put aside, at least for the time being. In any event, however, it is my habit to work with a considerable number of objects and bits of objects—anywhere from 10 to 50 with the ever present possibility of extending this last number to tens of thousands. And it is part of my habit to work for considerable lengths of time—three to 10 or 12 hours at a stretch. I have found that it is essential to stay with things long enough to fatigue the obvious in both the objects and in me.

This dwelling in prolonged acts of perception is most often accomplished in my studio, alone, but not necessarily so. The experience always feels purposeful to me—at least as purposeful as acts of trial and error feel in working toward the solution of a specific problem or the mastery of a skill. And trial-and-error procedures are certainly a great part of this experience, for I am continuously trying a great variety of objects for their size, shape, color, position —for all their visual qualities—in a constantly changing configuration. But for what do I keep trying them? What is the model or the dream? And how do I know when I have succeeded or failed?

It all goes something like this. Beginning with an object of particular visual and associational qualities, *and* with its power to affect me at that very time with considerably more than ordinary intensity, I begin to seek its context. Or, I could say that I begin to seek for the ideal context, a gestalt, in which this incomplete thing will appear completed. As I have said, I move the object as I move in relation to it; I see it in a variety of visual environments, a continually running trial-and-error kind of seeking. After a while, in just enough cases, the object begins to ask for certain kinds of support—for the color violet, for the metallic gray qualities of the daguerreotype, for lines that lose to a *sfumato*. I try other objects, bits, and pieces in the vicinity of the first. I paint and draw around some parts, modulate others with the cloudiness of overlaid x-ray photographs. I enhance and obliterate until something like a neighborhood of compatibles begins to assert itself. This assertion shifts, but at a stage it begins to limit these shifts through a much narrower range. Then a direction is sensed and followed with a finer care. I find myself "tasting" the colors as they come together, savoring them and rejecting, or savoring and saving, all within a more limited range than any time up to this. I have a sense of "hefting" the sizes and shapes, the "pictorial weights"; I physically feel the textures through my hands and my eyes, all the while any photographic or printed, drawn or painted images are adjusted for maximum effect. Then, ultimately, like the last split second before the forgotten name of someone moves from the tip of one's tongue to full recovery and clear articulation, I feel the impact of completion—the discovery or realization of a *coherency* existing among the formerly disparate and incomplete things. Each time it is arrived at, this coherency comes as a surprise even though it is that, precisely, toward which I must have been working. This end which is sought, this new coherency, unity, or radiance which does not actually exist for me until it comes into evidence at the end of the creative process, is yet present in some way throughout that whole process. From beginning to end, it haunts the voyage of discovery as an ambivalent allure, and it is that from which the searcher does his dead reckoning—or so I sense I do mine.

For a long time I have enjoyed the pleasures and quiet terrors of the utterly human quest for coherence through formulations of personal experience. I have come out successful just about often enough. This means that to a significant degree I dwell, so to speak, in that neighborhood of compatibles of which I have spoken. Through the years I have developed a strong sympathy for that neighborhood, for its architecture, its weather, and its residents. When I set out to make a collage, I set out for that now old neighborhood as if it were my very own. In a quite natural and even casual way, it is upon this neighborhood that I focus as I take up the first bit of a potential collage, be it a picture postcard mailed from Tonnerre in 1903 or a hand generator bought in the Toluca market last summer. I sense that it is this very focus which is crucial in determining how certain objects affect my interests at the time. As a result it is difficult to know the clues which signal the thousands of steps that are taken in all directions to the completion of such a work, since these clues have, for me, no importance in themselves. Still, it is the stuff of all the clues in every visual quality, in every image, that leads to the achievement of a new coherency in the completed collage.

If I were asked how I chose between this bit of wallpaper and that bit of Greek theatre-ticket stub, I might say that the one "looked better" in relation to the rest of the growing configuration. If pressed, I might add that I did not have much difficulty choosing the bit of wallpaper because it felt like a clue to success, while the Greek theatre stub seemed to adumbrate failure. Now, were I asked against what I had measured these two things, I more than likely would have to say that I had measured them *against the still unformed coherence of the still only potential collage,* because in a very real way that is exactly what I did: I physically placed first one and then the other of these material bits in the forming pattern of the collage and, after looking, rejected one and saved the other.

This is, indeed, a fascinating situation: I find myself saying that in working toward a coherency or "rightness" I use as a standard—an exemplar of correctness—something which for me does not yet actually exist, and which will not exist until the collage has been completed. About this, some might say—come, let's not be so mysterious; after all, you do have "art principles" and when you "try" things in the context of the developing collage you are doing no more than checking the appearance of a provisional arrangement against those "art principles." Well, it may be true that there are such principles, but I must confess I am not the man able to isolate them, nor am I the man to use them—should they so exist—in this accessory-after-the-fact manner.

Some people, even some who remain identified with the visual arts in one way or another, speak for instance of proportion as if *certain specific* relationships of size, amount, and degree are, in fact and in themselves, better than others. Not curiously, these stated proportions are most often traceable to preferences exercised in 5th-century Greece. Hence, we still have today the fetish function of the "golden section"—an amulet worn against "bad proportion." But what if our insight and outlook are less Romanly historicized, more phenomenological? Then we hold, I say, that proportion is an expressive means, and that proportion is "correct" when the specific size, amount, and degree relationships are either engaging in themselves, or when the proportion has been developed for purposes of a specific expression and, vis-à-vis, succeeds.

So, in any work of such caliber as makes overtures in the direction of philosophy or art, we are not concerned with exercises given over to illustrating in visual form this or that language version of "art principles." The artist, it seems to me, does not start from any such principles, although his finished work may give rise to ideas—in him or in others—which then might be set forth in words and even construed by some, in some circumstances, as principles of art.

In my own case I begin making a collage by beginning to make it. I do not always end up with a collage; so it may be more accurate to say that I begin making a collage or *failing to make one* by beginning to make one. There seems no other way. The materials, objects, images which I either create or select as part of the search for a collage are not arrived at randomly. In those prolonged acts of visual perception of which I have spoken, I become aware of chains of events running inside me. These events feel like special impressions made upon the steadily running continuous wave of visual perception. It is as if the means of visual perception, so long as we are awake, run more or less steadily like an electric current. This is a kind of strong constant. Now, when these prolonged or more intense acts of visual perception are experienced, no matter how subtly or delicately, it is as if the special form or pattern of these acts becomes the modulating force for the entire and powerful current of perception. The whole continuous flow of visual perception seems to take on the qualities of these special perceptions, and in the process these qualities are immensely amplified. With these specific qualities now modulating the general current of visual perception, the whole body feels as if it also has taken on their character. One begins to act in accordance with the prevailing mood set up by the particular chain of perceptual events. And one "plays along," much as the players do in the best of musical jam sessions *after* they have "gotten with it."

To remain in the mood and to act in accordance with this mood as it shifts with the linkages in the chain of perceptual events—that is the trick. In the case of creating collages it is accomplished, it seems to me, by continuing to perceive in richer and broader ways as the materials of the potential coherence are shifted into this and that provisional relationship. And how these trial configurations appear to me I take as compendiums of what is going on inside of me. When things are going well I have the feeling of stretching toward that neighborhood of compatibles I have mentioned. And if things go so well that the neighborhood is actually approached and entered, then I seek to remain there as long as possible. To remain any length of time, I have found, requires successive acts of finer perception and fuller attainments of unity and radiance in the work at hand. In a real way the completed collage declares what went on inside of me. It is both the proof and the meaning of consciousness and engagement. And then, for a while, its ambience of truth and reality lingers—just long enough and strong enough to portend something of the quality and tone of the next undertaking.

I realize that the foregoing is hardly a full report of my collage-making activities. For one thing, I have all but omitted consideration of the fact that many of my recent collages make extensive use of photographs and photographic negatives on glass, as well as large plastic x-ray negatives—along with almost everything else. These collages are often built with images of people and things, and several of them have the superficial appearance of expressionist or surrealist art as categorically typified in 20th-century art history and criticism. Still, as I have gone along in the previous pages, my comments have been largely limited to the "formal" qualities of the visual arts—to the visual elements[3] and their configuration. Of course, these visual elements have the power, of themselves and in concert, to stand for generalized feelings or moods. We say, for instance, that these visual elements, when presented without attempting specific reference to actual, physical objects or particular situations in the surrounding visual world, have this power to express and communicate generalized qualities of sentience.

Now, when the visual elements are so configured that representations of the surrounding visual world are made, then the generalized feelings or moods set up by the visual elements are specified into the context of the things represented. Hence a generalized quality of sharp, cold presence set up through a configuration of bluish color in large clear-edged masses which crowd the format can be specified into a particular context if those same visual elements are given the shape qualities of ruined buildings and human beings. This is the kind of specification or particularization that takes place with my most recent collages. It allows not only for the large abstract reference—the kind we respond to in the work of Mondrian, Soulages, and de Kooning—but for the kind of focused, particular, concrete reference managed in the work of such men as Breughel, Rembrandt, Goya, and Rouault. This kind of concrete particularization is related to my concern for the human module as the crucial scale in our affairs. Most of my collages achieve their coherence not only in the structural terms of the visual elements, but also by virtue of the associational potential of the descriptive subject matter. As a result they satisfy me in having gotten a purchase on something as general as a principle as well as on a particular instance of which I feel myself an integral part. The collages I make relate to my wish to know things I can see and feel, things that give up their natures through the action of myself as a thinking, feeling, and prehensive person.

I suppose there is nothing new or especially gripping about someone's reporting on his work, especially if that work has the avocational, hobbylike character that the making of collages may seem to have. If there is anything of more than routine consequence in this quite incomplete summary, it may be what I have intended to

[3] In recent years I have settled for eight of these: position, movement, size, color, shape, line, texture, and density.

imply throughout: that the "operations" I experience in making these collages have proved to be the models for what I do and for much of what I have done with just about all the bits and pieces and stuff and things and events and occasions of the entire life I live.

Bibliography

Joyce, J. (1944), *Stephen Hero*. New York: New Directions.

Weismann, D. (1949), On the Function of the Creative Process in Art Criticism. *College Art Journal*, 9(1).

DISCUSSION

PROFESSOR POLANYI:

I'm still not quite clear about one point which was raised—that you are describing a personal experience. From what you said, I did not find any reason to assume that. I thought that you described potential coherence and perception and didn't say anything to imply that nobody else would share your knowledge, when once achieved, of these coherences and perceptions. Reading your paper, I was continuously impressed by the universal intent that seemed to be implied in your description of your achievement.

PROFESSOR WEISMANN:

I'm cagey about this, about zeroing right in on it and saying, "That's how it is," but it is true, I do feel that way about it; it is a universal thing. But when I say it, then it's too easy to get rid of. If I say, I had a universal experience, that does something to what I'm talking about, even though it may be true.

PROFESSOR POLANYI:

No, I don't think so. You actually brought out an old analysis, which obviously was an analysis of technology, and inventions, and science; you are entirely on the lines of the process of discovery—except that yours is in another direction and is, in some ways, more enterprising, because if you do make a technical invention, usually you know what you are after; you haven't got to discover yourself. Like a scientist, you have to discover your problem, but in the end the scientist has a certain amount of external zest for possessing his success, his achievement, that you don't have to the same extent. I'm saying all this only to contradict you when you say that if you declare your universal intent, you claim something for yourself that you would prefer not to claim because you are then submitting yourself to a discipline which is something you recognize as not simply a part of your own nature.

PROFESSOR SILBER:

I want to argue with you with regard to your statements about coherency. You say that the visual elements have the power to stand for generalized feelings or moods, and you talk about this movement toward coherency in them. And yet it seemed to me that only once did you get close to a richer, more accurate, conception of coherency—when you said the collages achieved their coherency not only in the structural terms of the visual elements but also in virtue of the associational potentials of the descriptive subject matter. I should like to hear you expand on that, because I gathered that the titles were an integral and supporting part of the collages. For example, I think it would have been an interesting experiment to see what would have happened if we had all the people in this room try to give a title to something like the "Pelvic Memories of a 1914 Dodge" (Plate 1). I think that much of that title would have been brought out just from looking at it. It is interesting to see a pelvic area used as a kind of stylized death's head before which you find the fully textured face of the woman, for whom this is both the remains and also a structural element, and in the central position you find the automobile which has become a symbol of the mass age and the site of the fertility rites of American civilization. All of the sardonic commentary, however funny and however sad it may be, I'm sure is intentional. It seems to me that in most of these you've clearly got the eye of the satirist and social commentator, and not just an eye interested in visual qualities. I think that also supports a kind of objectivity. Consider the island picture (Plate 2). Unless I'm mistaken, you've got Adam and Eve expelled from the garden. Somehow you got a black and white out of that, and put it into this thing coming out of the backbone of what would seem to be an abdominal region. All of this—the womb as an island, human existence as an island—has a very high cognitive content. These collages have almost as high a cognitive content as some paintings like Raphael's "School of Athens." And I'd like to hear you enlarge more on the actual rational coherence, the conceptual coherence, that goes through your work, quite apart from its visual coherence.

PROFESSOR WEISMANN:

When I got the cut-out 1914 Dodge near that pelvis, it was a ridiculous combination, and yet on the cognitive side I was thinking, I suppose, of all the things we remember about the feelings in the pit of the stomach, the region of the solar plexus, memories that lie in the guts like thorny eggs, indigestible and irremovable. You have this feeling for even a physical object being a point of tangency or purchase where in the remembrance of this object you held so much together. My father had long ago a 1914 Chevrolet, which we didn't have very long, because he was an unusual man. He bought it in the morning, with his friend Heimie Otzleburger, and it ran out of gas near the ski slide on the Milwaukee River's Jordan Park; they, having had their good time with it, just pushed it down the slope. But they did have it for a good part of the day. And of all the 1914 Chevrolets that came into being and went out of existence, I know them all for that 1914 Dodge I will forever have, and with it I shall always have Heimie Otzleburger and my father forever yelling down the hall, "*unbedingt,* Heimie!"

Then the girl comes in, and she is a sort of 19th-century pre-Raphaelite person. Besides this formalistic thing of textures and shapes, it certainly has a cognitive, or literary, or whatever, quality also. Is that all right?

PROFESSOR SILBER:

Do you think you would ever have put it together that way visually?

PROFESSOR WEISMANN:

It's hard to say, but I think we could guess that the likelihood of its happening would have been lessened. I think it's related to that.

PROFESSOR POTEAT:

How could you possibly have put it together visually in some sense that was distinct visually *cum* all the rest you're talking about? The very fact that you've got a human pelvis here to start with already has you well on the way to doing something other than just a design (which after all, a human pelvis has, and a rather fine one).

PROFESSOR WEISMANN:

As you say that, all these things come back. My father worked with Heimie a long time. Heimie was killed; he fell off a building. And my father fell off a building, but later. They used to do their work on high buildings, and they must have thought they were angels—or feathers. Among other things my father broke was his pelvis, in five places. We were all very proud of it, because no one we knew had a father with a pelvis broken in five places.

PROFESSOR POLS:

My question is in a way related to John Silber's. He put very clearly one I was groping for, but I want to try to push it on a bit in the direction of the problem of coherence, either private or public. I think in the first place you did perhaps stress the perceptual coherence too much; now that we have been at you a bit, we see that the emotional coherence is very much bound up with it. One of the things you seem to be saying is that you're going to create a coherence that is not there, but that you think *ought* to be there. And because it ought to be there, in some other sense it's perhaps already there; that's part of the normative claim you make on us. You demand that we should see the same kind of coherence that you do. To what degree is this public and universal, to what degree is it a purely private coherence? We have to hear about Heimie, and even then, some of it does not have the kind of coherence . . .

PROFESSOR WEISMANN:

There's a difficult step here that's hard for me to make; I don't quite know how to do it. I have this feeling that the deeper I go into myself, the closer I get to the other guy. Yes, I do expect . . .

PROFESSOR POLS:

You make that demand upon us?

PROFESSOR WEISMANN:

I don't expect that it will happen at any specific time, nor do I expect that it will happen in any really specific way, but I hope that that new object becomes the means for making it, for making this connection.

PROFESSOR POLS:

Yes, so you're again arguing about reality in two senses, aren't you? One is the reality that you find, the other the reality that you leave behind because you say it's a reality that somehow was there as an undiscovered order all the time. May I push this just a little further? You are, I understand, although I have not seen your paintings, a figurative painter of great distinction. When you are engaged in that kind of activity, would you regard the collage as an effective model for what you are doing?

PROFESSOR WEISMANN:

It's a very interesting difference. I can and have and still do paint figurative paintings. It's a different process, because when I paint, the requirements and the restrictions are different. When I paint, I make all the shapes myself. Oil paints ask for this to be done, and you determine the shapes, like your handwriting; but now when you go to the pile of junk, you have to accept a world you never made, and that's the kind of world I was born into, a world I didn't make. Out of what was given at birth I couldn't in the craft of painting, make my life that way. Do you see what I mean?

PROFESSOR GRENE:

In other words, a figurative painting is more subjective?

PROFESSOR POLS:

But it doesn't deal with a world you made in any absolute sense.

DR. KOCH:

May I ask whether or not one of the primary differences between what you are doing when you make these collages and when you paint (your collages, everybody agrees, do have high cognitive content) is somewhat as follows. When you make the collages, you obviously use the elements of a given language; you use the given elements that you yourself have not set but which have become available. You are creating both a formal and cognitive effect by certain types of juxtaposition, which presumably are realized in both cases as valuable relationships. And in fact, you have a kind of interplay actually between the purely visual formal relationships and the cognitive relationships: these can cohere, significantly clash, or interact in other ways. But when you paint, you are in a sense creating your own language at the same time that you are denoting with it.

PROFESSOR WEISMANN:

That's right.

PROFESSOR STALLKNECHT:

I wonder whether Coleridge's distinction between "fancy" and "imagination" is in any way pertinent here. You have pointed out that the objects as they are chosen from the scrap heap reveal a certain strangeness. It becomes obvious that on their own they are in a world the artist never made. This gives them a certain dignity that one easily overlooks. Perhaps the chosen objects are like words that pre-exist their own position in a poem. In isolation—the scrap heap is a sort of chaotic vocabulary—these words may take on a strange and unfamiliar character, especially if repeated aloud in a monotone. Again, these words may acquire a new meaning as they are drawn into new contexts. This may also apply to the objects in the scrap heap.

Once we resist seeing these objects as commonplace instruments ready for practical use, their "strangeness" challenges our imagination and we may come upon new possibilities of significance or of significant combinations. This is Coleridge's imagination as opposed to fancy—or to a mere arrangement of objects, tasteful perhaps, but without the power of transformation.

PROFESSOR POLS:

Yes, as Coleridge puts it, the poet, acting as the model for the creator in general, takes the world as it is and does with it what he will. He puts it into a new shape, as you have in a sense done with these real objects. But Coleridge's point always is that through what is thus made you see something: you see a higher reality than was there before. Now would you make any such claim for what you're doing? It seems to me that, if you claim that you discover a nonprivate coherence, you tend toward the Platonic approach to the imagination that one finds in Coleridge—and that would indeed be different from fancy.

PROFESSOR WEISMANN:

To some degree I think again this is true, that this new reality displaces the old requirement, because now knowing that, you become responsible to what you now have, and you can never do that one again.

MISS SEWELL:

I want to ask further about the objects that you collect. In ways they belong to the same field: you feel they are incomplete, because at that point already they are clues, they are signs, but you have no idea as to signs to what. How do you know it's a clue before you know that? I know this is tacit knowing, but how on earth do we *know?* We don't know. Are we just guessing? Are we just all junk collectors?

PROFESSOR WEISMANN:

Yes, but there's also something more. We know that there are clues sent up that we don't even know about.

PROFESSOR POLS:

The whole physical world, though, offers clues of this sort; it's true of anything you want to fasten upon. Why fasten upon just these? They are private clues to he knows not what, but he doesn't want to say something private with them. It may be that he only manages to say something private with them, but he doesn't want to do only that.

PROFESSOR CROSSON:

On this question again of psychological genesis and universal intent: it seems to be clear that in so far as a work is successful it must have universal meaning, but what strikes me here is that you are far more capable of expounding the psychological meanings than you are at giving any hint of what, as it were, the collage in itself might mean.

PROFESSOR WEISMANN:

The only thing I hope to do is use language to point at the thing I've made in visual form. Rather than trying to describe it, I try to analogize it and hope that the analogies will work.

PART III

SCIENCE AND THE LIVING SUBJECT

The paradox put by Professor Wigner at the outset—the gap between physics and psychology—can be resolved only by the mediation of the sciences of life. And epistemological problems also, the problem of how we, as living beings, forge our way forward to make sense of the world around us, will depend for their resolution on rethinking the concept of organic reality. The topic of the relation of the sciences and their subject matters to one another, therefore, and in particular the question of the conceptual structure of biology loom large on the Study Group's horizon. Part III, on "Science and the Living Subject," includes three papers which deal with aspects of this theme. Professor C.F.A. Pantin's paper develops the difference between what he calls the "restricted" and the "unrestricted" sciences. Professor Helmuth Plessner recalls the concept of "positionality" which he has used as a central theme for a theory of the organic. Dr. Chance emphasizes, from the point of view of ethology, the importance of seeing man within the horizon of biological research.

All three of these papers, as well as Professor Wigner's paper, and, by implication, Professor Polanyi's, suggest the theme which Professor Pols's essay had made explicit; even though that paper cannot be included within the compass of this volume, it is indispensable to the aims of the Study Group to indicate, at least briefly, the type of metaphysical problem which arises in connection with all these papers and our discussion of them. The problem I refer to, which comes up so urgently whenever the relation between physics and biology is in question, is the problem of levels of reality. This problem was raised by Professor Polanyi at the conclusion of the discussion of Professor Plessner's paper and I include a brief statement of it at the close of this section.

5

ORGANISM AND ENVIRONMENT

C. F. A. PANTIN

Charles Darwin entitled his work: *On the Origin of the Species by Means of Natural Selection, or the Preservation of Favoured Races in the Struggle for Life*. In discussing natural selection he says (1859, p. 80): "Let it be borne in mind how infinitely close-fitting are the mutual relations of all organic beings to each other and to their physical conditions of life." Those "close-fitting" relations were the result of natural selection. Long after, in 1913, L. J. Henderson, in that remarkable book *The Fitness of the Environment*, noted that while biologists had given much thought to the adaptations of the living organism to the environment, they had given little to the nature of the environment itself:

> But although Darwin's fitness involves that which fits and that which is fitted, or more correctly a reciprocal relationship, it has been the habit of biologists since Darwin to consider only the adaptations of the living organism to the environment. For them, in fact, the environment, in its past, present, and future, has been an independent variable, and it has not entered into any of the modern speculations to consider if by chance the material universe also may be subjected to laws which are in the largest sense important in organic evolution. Yet fitness there must be, in environment as well as in the organism. How, for example, could man adapt his civilization to water power if no water power existed within his reach? [Henderson, 1913, pp. 5-6].

Surprisingly, this absence of attention still continues. In pre-Darwinian days it was not so, and the peculiar fitness of the en-

This paper has also appeared in *The Relations between the Sciences*. New York: Cambridge University Press, 1968.

vironment for living things was as well recognized as was the apparent element of design in organisms themselves. But consideration of Henderson's statement shows us that there are two very different aspects of the environment which have not been properly separated. There is (1) the world of physical objects, including other creatures, by which an organism is surrounded, and (2) the set of conditions, peculiar to this universe, governing organism and external world alike. Irrespective of the fact that living organisms may display additional special features of their own, in *both* organism and environment the same kinds of matter and energy appear to follow the same "laws" and changes in time. Indeed, one of the most remarkable conclusions of astronomy is still that even in the most strange and distant galaxies we find the same elements and the same kinds of energy following the same familiar configurations.

Moreover, as I have said, there are only certain possible configurations with certain properties. The conditions of existence are such that there are only a limited number of real solutions to the engineering problems confronting the construction of a machine, or to the viable construction of a living organism. There are only certain ways in which an eye or camera can be made, and there are only certain ways in which a computing machine designed to predict the future can be made. In living organisms such limitations determine the possible solutions to the engineering problems of an animal for it to be a successful predictor behavior machine. It is convenient to speak of these as the conditions of existence to which both living and nonliving matter are subject, and to distinguish this from the environment of external objects which surrounds an organism or a nonliving entity.

There is a boundary, though not a precise one, between organism and environment. Even in the physical world the boundary of objects is not wholly precise. Michael Faraday noted long ago (1844), in his attack on Dalton's atomic theory, that we knew an object only by the forces it exerted and that these might extend, with attenuation, throughout the universe.

In the prosecution of the physical sciences this external environment is commonly made as simple as possible by the observer, so that the number of necessary controls is few. For the biologist generally, the environment of his organisms is exceedingly complex —and he must put up with it. This may be overlooked in some analytical biological work. Thus in genetics the environment is at times treated as a simple constant thing providing an asymptote for natural selection. In fact, it is exceedingly complex in both time and space; the same species may be found in environments which vary discontinuously. A successful species of bacterium may be found developing in very different food sources. The action of natural selection in the field is far more complex than the selective preservation of mutant *Drosophila* in an experiment.

In all this description, it will be noticed that we have tacitly assented to an external world of real objects. The attitude to this external world varies greatly in the different sciences, a fact of particular importance today, when science itself and its nature are popularly identified with the technically successful parts of physical science. As I said in a recent essay:

> When we look at the different sciences a very important distinction becomes evident. Natural phenomena are extremely complex. The physical sciences as they now dominate us have achieved their rapid success in a great measure by deliberately restricting their attack to simple systems, thereby excluding many classes of natural phenomena from their study. Until in the end the nuclear physicist has to take into account the fact that the observer is a biological system, there is no need for him to burden his hypotheses with other sciences. Because of this I speak of physics as one of the "restricted sciences." Biology and geology on the other hand are among the "unrestricted sciences." The solution of their problems may at any moment force biologists to study physics, chemistry, mathematics or any branch of human learning, just as Louis Pasteur had to become bacteriologist, entomologist, chemist, biochemist and physicist to achieve his goal. Almost every biological problem is a piece of operational research using other sciences for its solution [Pantin, 1963, p. 12].

It should of course be borne in mind that certain sciences such as meteorology, commonly classed in the physical sciences, are in fact unrestricted, involving, as they do, biology, geology, and so on. But their very complexity places them outside the pure physical sciences. Likewise the development of certain special fields of biology may lead to their becoming to some degree restricted, as was at one period the case with taxonomy, and as at present is the case with molecular biology.

There are many differences between the restricted and unrestricted sciences. For one, their interpretation of the scientific method is not the same. But here I want to discuss their different attitudes toward an external world of "real" objects. That such a difference exists can be seen very simply in the percentage of practical marks against theory in a recent university examination in various natural sciences: Geology 40, most biological subjects 33, Chemistry 30, Physics 20, Theoretical Physics 0.

The difference appears in two ways. The unrestricted sciences deal with a richer variety of phenomena than the restricted: and in particular the goals of their study may be phenomena at many different levels of size and complexity, as in the large-scale problems of the geologist, the taxonomic relationships of starfish, the machinery of the central nervous system, the conduction of the nervous impulse, the molecular-biological problems of the replication of nucleic acids, and so on. Scientific attack is based partly upon analysis of factors which bear upon a phenomenon. This can rather easily lead to what I might call the "analytical fallacy": that understanding of a phenomenon is only to be gained by study of rules governing its component parts. Particularly in the restricted sciences we seem to see a progressive analysis starting with gross physical objects, the understanding of which depends upon molecular analysis by the chemist, which in turn depends upon our knowledge of isotopes, which in turn depends on the ever-increasing number of "ultimate" particles dispensed to us by the nuclear physicist. From here it is easy to pass to the fallacy that once we have found the correct assumptions necessary for the description of ultimate particles we have only to work out the consequences of these, together with the theory of probability, to describe the properties of all material configurations of higher and higher orders. As Price (1932, p. 1) says in his work *Perception:* "Thus the not uncommon view that the world we perceive is an illusion and only the 'scientific' world of protons and electrons is real, is based upon a gross fallacy, and would destroy the very premises upon which science itself depends." That is a view based upon the analytical fallacy. Price's statement will do well so long as we remember that it describes a common error arising from the present state of the sciences, and not the view of the informed man of science.

Now as we pass to higher orders of configurations we find new, so-called "emergent" properties, such as the special properties of living systems which distinguish them from the nonliving, or the predictor properties of brains and computing machines. Do the assumptions for ultimate particles suffice for these emergent properties? At the outset, empirically, they do not. That is, even if the physicist one day gets to some really ultimate particles, it would be long before we could extrapolate upward in the manner required —and in practice, novel features of complex configurations would still require new assumptions. But in fact the present position of nuclear physics suggests that the quest for ultimate particles may never reach finality. In the 1930's Eddington could indeed suggest that the universe consisted of 10^{79} protons and 10^{79} electrons, a number bound up with the dimensions of the universe itself. Later, as Heisenberg said (1958), neutrons were added to these two components. But hope was deferred. Soon after this temporary breathing space other particles were discovered, and their number already exceeds that of the 92-odd fixed elements of an earlier day. The biologist may be forgiven a doubt whether in fact there is an end to this particular analysis. And if that is so, where is the foundation upon which we can build a superstructure for the description of higher systems?

But that is not the main difficulty with the analytical fallacy. It is this: higher-order configurations may have properties to be studied in their own right. We can make observations to enable us to understand how a gasoline engine works without calling upon the molecular hypothesis. Chemical analysis may help us to make more enduring cylinders; but that is a problem with a different goal. In the same way, electron microscope sections of the components of a computing machine will not help us to understand how it works or the origin of the highly significant parallels between the principles of its action and some of those which seem to govern central nervous action.

It is simple systems that occupy the particular attention of the restricted sciences. The unrestricted sciences deal with innumerable complex systems with seemingly emergent properties. Understanding of these is not to be obtained by extrapolation of their simpler components. What has to be done here is essentially a taxonomic operation—the determination of the class to which a phenomenon belongs. That was the key to our understanding of nervous action. Equally, I consider that the vitally important and most intractable problems of ecology and population studies can only be advanced by seeking comparisons of class with models from physical chemistry. We need a new Willard Gibbs with a biological slant.

But for our present purposes, the unrestricted scientist is always deeply aware of the multitude and variety of higher-order systems, with their emergent properties. Unlike the restricted scientist, we cannot shelve the study of phenomena which seem too complex—thereby introducing a systematic bias into the treatment of phenomena in general. The multitude and reality of these higher-order systems give the biologist an immense respect for the reality of natural phenomena, as opposed to hypotheses about them.

The nuclear physicist today presents us with a world of elementary particles which seem to have nothing in common with the everyday objects of our experience. Indeed for him these particles are not observable as things. He seems concerned only to establish relations between them which observation can show to be constantly obeyed and which thus permit successful predictions. As Michael Faraday said in 1844: "What thought remains on which to hang the imagination of an *a* independent of the acknowledged forces?" (p. 141).

Heisenberg (1958) refers to such particles as "the building stones" of matter. The term will do so long as we do not suppose that description of their relationships will necessarily suffice to describe the special properties of material configurations of a higher order; that they are the sole "building stones." But with respect to the reality of the external world, the nuclear physicist leaves us only with the conclusion that the demonstrable relationships between these particles are not mere products of our own minds, but must arise from something external to us.

The basis of acceptance of the real world in the unrestricted sciences is very different. Such a scientist at work accepts absolutely the existence of a world of real objects. He does so more completely than does a physicist or a philosopher in his everyday life, or indeed than does the everyday man. The reason for this is the complete congruence between this acceptance, and this alone, with the experience and predictions in everyday life; and that in the enormous number and variety of phenomena which through his job he critically witnesses, all seem consistent with a real world of objects.

Craik (1952), in his admirable essay on the nature of explanation, points out that one can never prove the existence of an external thing, or its obedience to a particular law, by trying to wring the truth out of a particular example. He says: "You must vary the conditions, repeat the experiments, make a hypothesis and a remote inference from that hypothesis and test it out" (p. 3). That is indeed a way of approaching the matter inductively. But I do not think this conscious logical procedure is the source of our conviction of the existence of external things.

Some years ago (Pantin, 1954), while engaged upon the taxonomic identification of the species of certain worms, I was greatly struck by the entirely different procedure I used when in the field I concluded beyond doubt, "there is a specimen of *Rhyncodemus bilineatus,*" and the procedure I used in the laboratory. In the latter I slowly followed a conscious logical process of identification based upon certain well-defined "yes or no" characters of the worm's internal anatomy. In the field I instantly recognized the species of the worm. The two methods are quite different, and are subject to quite different kinds of error. Field recognition, which I have called "aesthetic recognition," depends enormously upon past experience, much of which is not even conscious. When I see a shore crab today, and at once say, "There is a *Carcinus maenas,*" the whole machinery of my perception of it is different from what it was when I was a child. In an important sense my recognition of a specimen of *Carcinus maenas* today is only the end of a long series of all sorts of experience, unconscious as well as conscious. And the end of all this is not arrival at a logical conclusion that shore crabs must exist, but the tacit absolute conviction that they do, through all sorts of past experience. The appearance of colors of a shore crab or of a tomato are not basic units from which, with similar units, we can build evidence for or against the existence of a world of real objects. A "tomato" that appeared bright red in the dark or under a sodium lamp should be a highly suspicious object to any chef. The acceptance of the external reality of such objects depends upon the whole of past experience.

That conviction of reality is enormously enhanced by the variety and indirectness of the evidence with which it is congruent. This is most strikingly shown by a study of the behavior of insects. The simplest cellular animals, sea anemones, jellyfish, and the like, can show remarkably complex motor reactions to natural stimuli. But it is to stimuli that they react, not to the presence of objects, as in our own behavior. Among insects, on the other hand, the matter stands very differently. The hunting wasp, *Ammophila pubescens,* digs burrows for its young (Thorpe, 1950). It hunts over a considerable distance for spiders and caterpillars, which it paralyzes and puts in its burrows. Later the eggs hatch and the young feed upon the paralyzed prey. If the prey is too large to be carried by flight, the wasp will drag its prey around obstacles along the ground toward the burrow. If wasp and prey are transferred in a closed box to a new place some distance away the prey will nevertheless be dragged toward the burrow. The wasp behaves in fact as though it had an internal model of the district round its burrow, just as Craik suggests that we ourselves have an internal model of the external world which we use to control and predict action. The wasp is behaving not to stimuli but to a world of objects, and to a world of objects identical with that accepted by our own everyday naïve realism. This is carrying congruence of phenomena with the world we naturally accept very far.

But the matter does not end here. Physiological study of men and animals shows that much of their behavior can be usefully described by considering them as predictor behavior machines. The primary need is to foretell the future. Such prophecy is possible with high probability on the assumptions that:

1. information collected about past events can be a guide to the course of events in the future;
2. however different an organism is from ourselves, and however different the sources of information which it appears to utilize, on analysis its behavior is completely consistent with the occurrence of the external objects and events presented to us by the naïve realism implicit in our own everyday behavior.

Physical studies can tell us the kinds of physical and chemical information which organisms or predictor machines can receive. When we examine animals we often find that very different kinds of sensory instruments from our own are used to receive that information. Bees have color vision, but they behave as though their colors are quite different from those we ourselves recognize (von Frisch, 1954). Cabbage white butterflies, on the other hand, seem to have color appreciation very close to our own (Ilse, 1937). Sound in insects is generally detected only at low frequencies (below the C above middle C). But crickets have an ingenious mechanical rectification device by which they can receive the high-pitched chirrup of their stridulation (Pumphrey, 1940). And yet, for all these great differences in the kind of information received, the resulting behavior remains completely consistent with a real world of the objects familiar to us. Thus the congruence between the impressions we receive and the existence of an external world of real objects is not just something inferred from our own direct observation of particular phenomena. We can seek our phenomena through far-distant and wholly unexpected channels—and the congruence of the phenomena with a real world of external objects never fails; the experience in support of this is far greater for a trained naturalist than it is even for the ordinary man.

And there is yet one more thing of interest. Charles Darwin (1871) once said:

> It is certain that there may be extraordinary mental activity with an extremely small absolute mass of nervous matter: thus the wonderfully diversified instincts, mental powers and affections of ants are notorious, yet their cerebral ganglia are not so large as the quarter of a small pin's head. Under this point of view the brain of an ant is one of the most marvelous atoms of matter in the world, perhaps more so than the brain of a man [p. 145].

Even the astonishing behavior of which von Frisch (1954) has shown the honey bee to be capable is operated through a brain of about 0.62 cu. mm., and that of a larger ant by one about one tenth of this size, against the 1,600 cu. cm. of our own. Certainly, the apparent appreciation of a real world of real objects seems to require only an utterly trivial number of nerve cells compared with our own. When we consider the problems of the mind-brain relationship, perhaps a biologist of the behavior of the lower animals may be forgiven a doubt about whether we have as yet even begun to see the questions that must be asked about our own brain and mind (see Pantin, 1965).

I think the question we must ask is not, "Can we find any premises from which the existence of an external world can be proved with certainty?"; it should be, "Why do we accept with conviction an external world of real objects?" It is important to realize that by this we do not simply refer to tomatoes and bent sticks and so on, but to something much more complicated and unique. We recognize enduring objects, like tables and mountains, liable to denudation. We also recognize objects which are open steady states, such as rivers and the ocean. These various objects exist at many levels, from that of nuclear particles up to ecological systems and to the universe itself. All behave with respect to time according to elaborate rules, from which, for example, the physical chemist can distill such statements as the second law of thermodynamics, or the biologist that of natural selection, which, like the second law, tells us something about the probable future of material configurations. Of course, the physical chemist will tell us that the second law is truly applicable only to ideal systems of a certain sort. But it must not be forgotten that it holds well enough in everyday life for it originally to have been based upon experimental observations. It must not be supposed that such well-defined rules are consciously present in our minds when we deal with everyday life: but our uninformed and indeed unconscious expectation of what will happen in the world follows these rules closely.

All this elaborate system of material objects changing with time follows a pattern consistent with past and present experience: stones follow the same rules for mice and men. One feature of these patterns is of particular importance. Phenomena fall into classes. That is both a character of the "real world," and it is the basis of the fact that models can be made showing identical essential features, so that the behavior of the phenomena can be predicted from that of the model. A system in relaxation oscillation can be built either electronically or hydraulically. Either can be used as a model to predict the behavior of the other.

Behavior patterns tacitly accepting the reality of material objects and their changes in time are to be seen in ourselves, other men, and, as I have said, in quite lowly animals. Our recognition of shore crabs and tomatoes is based upon the consistency of that recognition with the whole of past experience. On occasion we may make errors, or suffer hallucinations: but it is only a question of time before these come into collision with the expectations of experience. Often such errors are due to incomplete present information leading to wrong classification. When the conjuror saws the lady in two, all experience leads us to suppose that behind the scenes we should "see how it was done."

I think that it is this whole consistent pattern of things and their changes in time which engenders the tacit acceptance of reality of the external world. Particularly for the biologist, who observes that even lowly creatures behave as though they tacitly accepted the same external world as we do, the question arises whether our own acceptance is a conscious process at all. If there is a square-topped table in the room, I react appropriately to it whether or not I am consciously aware of it. If questioned I may consciously note features of it, color, shape, and so on. But it does not follow that such features as I can consciously perceive about it are the essential basis of my conviction of its reality. That conviction arises from the whole of my past experience, conscious and unconscious, and the consistency of the phenomena which it presents; my everyday acceptance of the reality of the external world depends particularly upon the unconscious assumption that the present kind of consistency will not suddenly fail. The past would then be no guide to the future, and the basis of any such unconscious assumption would collapse. It is impossible to prove that that failure might not occur, for all our prediction of the future depends upon past experience. It is only on the assumptions implicit in that that we can form an inductive proof of the reality of the external world. There can be no deductive proof.

As a biologist, it seems to me that the problem of our acceptance of external reality has often been complicated by concentration upon conscious perception. Thus, Price in his book on *Perception* (1932) begins:

> Every man entertains a great number of beliefs concerning material things, e.g., that there is a square-topped table in this room, that the earth is a spheroid, that water is composed of hydrogen and oxygen. It is plain that all these beliefs are based on sight and touch (from which organic sensation cannot be separated): based upon them in the sense that if we had not had certain particular experiences of seeing and touching, it would be neither *possible* nor *reasonable* to entertain these beliefs [p. 1].

He then goes on:

> . . . to examine those experiences in the way of seeing and touching upon which our beliefs concerning material things are based, and to inquire in what way and to what extent they justify these beliefs. Other

> modes of sense experience, e.g. hearing and smelling, will be dealt with only incidentally. For it is plain that they are only auxiliary. If we possessed them, but did not possess either sight or touch, we should have no beliefs about the material world at all, and should lack even the very conception of it [p. 2].

In the first place, as I have said, it does not seem to me proven that my assent to the existence of such things as a square-topped table is purely the result of conscious perception. It seems possible to consider that what are commonly referred to as sense data are not the elements from which our assent to the existence of an object is derived, but rather that they are to be considered as labels of which we can become consciously aware, and which are attached to certain kinds of information we receive about an object.

Second, the statement about sight and touch does not seem to me to be true. A man blind from birth can have all the beliefs to which Price refers. Touch is an exceedingly complex and ill-defined sense. It is worth bearing in mind the physiologist's view. Winton and Bayliss (1948), reviewing the effects of cortical lesions, say:

> In man, the destruction of the sensory area does not abolish sensations of pin prick, touch, heat or cold. It does diminish the power of localising a stimulus sharply and appreciating accurately fine differences. Stereognosis, the power of recognising the shape of an object when it is held in the hand, is always severely impaired in these lesions. The recognition of an object by touch, which seems childishly simple to a normal subject, requires sensations of touch, pressure, joint and muscle sense, the fusion of the separate sensory data, and the recollection of previous similar experiences [p. 436].

Though it is dangerous to isolate and commend the relative importance of any of the senses, the importance of hearing and smelling should not be belittled—particularly when extended to the lower animals.

The really important question is: are there unconscious sources of information which contribute to our behavioral assent to a real world of external objects? A comparative physiologist who studies the behavior—and the powers of intercommunication—of bees and of ants is at least forced to be aware of this question. And in ourselves, when we drive an automobile correctly through a maze of traffic lights it is hard to suppose that we consciously perceived each

—even though some of them could subsequently be recalled to consciousness. Vision itself may be unconscious as well as conscious, and since in both cases behavior is affected, the word perception itself needs qualification.

But most interesting of all are those classes of sensory information which undoubtedly contribute to knowledge of the world around us unaccompanied by sense data. Such senses are particularly the sense of orientation associated with the inner ear and above all that of proprioception. That 60-year-old term of Sherrington's (1906), proprioception, has crept into the supplement of the 12-volume Oxford English Dictionary, though older and imprecise terms such as "kinesthetic sense" are well established in even the smaller brethren of that great work. Since proprioception is one of the fundamental necessities of animal life, its importance should be appreciated. By orientation and proprioception an organism is aware of its position in space and the relationship of its parts. We cannot assign sense data to proprioception in the way we can conceive of patches of redness in vision. Position and orientation seem simply inherent in our parts. Yet notwithstanding Price's statement, a good case could be made for supposing proprioception to be even more important than vision to our primary assented notions about space and its physical objects. All the visual difficulties of telling whether a stick partly immersed in water is straight or bent are overcome by running your hand down it, even in the dark and when your fingers are numb with cold.

Conscious perception therefore at best provides only part of the information contributing to our notions of the external world. It is noteworthy that we owe it to the physiologist that this has been brought to our notice. At times, the attempt is made to exclude the physiologist from discussing matters of this sort on the grounds that his experiments presuppose the very things at issue. But this is scarcely right since he has in fact repeatedly drawn attention to possibilities which have been overlooked: and too often the attempt to evade him succeeds only in an unconscious return to the physiological premises of an earlier day. The five senses that hold sway in so much discussion are merely the supposed physiological sources of information of 200 or more years ago.

This still leaves us with the interesting question of why it is that only certain sources of information about the external world are accompanied by sense-data labels. I have no answer to this except to note that our orientation and position are not good taxonomic features of the objects in the world; whereas consciously seen red patches, musical notes, odors, taste, and touch are exactly the kind of taxonomic features which, fed into a digital computing machine, could deliver to us far-reaching, reasoned, logical conclusions.

Bibliography

Craik, K. J. W. (1952), *The Nature of Explanation.* Cambridge: Cambridge University Press.

Darwin, C. (1859), *On the Origin of the Species,* Vol. 1. London: Murray.

——— (1871), *The Descent of Man.* London: Murray.

Eddington, A. (1952), *The Expanding Universe.* Cambridge: Cambridge University Press.

Faraday, M. (1844), A Speculation Touching Electric Conduction and the Nature of matter. *Phil. Mag.* (3rd s.), 24:136-144.

Frisch, K. von. (1954), *The Dancing Bees.* London: Methuen.

Heisenberg, W. (1958), *The Physicist's Conception of Nature.* London: Hutchinson.

Henderson, L. J. (1913), *The Fitness of the Environment.* New York: Macmillan.

Ilse, D. (1937), New Observations on Response to Colours in Egg-Laying Butterflies. *Nature,* 140:544.

Pantin, C. F. A. (1954), The Recognition of Species. *Sci. Progr.,* 42:587-598.

——— (1963), The Ballard Mathews Lectures. *Science and Education.* Cardiff: University of Wales Press, pp. 1-53.

——— (1965), Learning, World-Models, and Pre-adaptation. *Animal Behav.,* Suppl. 1:1-8.

Price, H. H. (1932), *Perception.* London: Methuen.

Pumphrey, R. J. (1940), Hearing in Insects. *Biol. Rev.,* 15:107-132.

Sherrington, C. S. (1906), *The Integrative Action of the Nervous System.* New Haven: Yale University Press.

Thorpe, W. H. (1950), A Note on Detour Experiments with *Ammophila pubescens* Curt (Hymenoptera; Specidae). *Behaviour,* 2:257-263.

Winton, F. R., & Bayliss, L. E. (1948), *Human Physiology.* London: Churchill.

DISCUSSION

PROFESSOR POTEAT:

I would like to ask Professor Pantin what he means by sense data in the context in which he was using that expression. This is a highly technical term that is used by philosophers to talk nonsense, and I didn't think what he was saying was at all nonsense. But I was not quite sure what kind of nonnonsense it was! Perhaps you were using "sense data" as a means of distinguishing simply the sorts of things that we can say we see (as when we see a color) together with the surface on which it appears (we might want to say it's reddish, or roundish, or what not). Or things we might hear—someone with the perfect pitch might say "I seem to be hearing middle C, and it seems to be propagated by a French horn." This would be opposed to the sort of case where, as in proprioception, it is not possible to make a reference to an object in the same sort of way.

PROFESSOR PANTIN:

I was trying to use it in what I thought was Price's expression of it in his book on perception. It did involve actually the fact that you could be aware of the red patch on a tomato. You could be conscious of it; what's more, you could record it.

PROFESSOR POTEAT:

But do you hold that one is aware of a red patch on a tomato or aware of a tomato by means of sight?

PROFESSOR PANTIN:

Well, logically look at it the other way around. I recognize a tomato just as I recognize the worm, *Rhyncodemus*. Under correct illumination it will seem red, and I can attach a red label to it.

Now that's fine, because the moment I've attached a red label, I can sort the red and not-red, ripe and not-ripe tomatoes, and I can get logical machinery to work on the thing.

PROFESSOR POTEAT:

Then what is good taxonomy or a good taxonomic device, as you use this expression, in the light of what you just said?

PROFESSOR PANTIN:

A good taxonomic device, good in the sense of most museum taxonomists (this is not what I would say is a really good device), is one where you can actually extract yes-or-no features from an object. You see and are conscious of them, and then you can argue logically about them. This is the kind of thing you see in all biological keys, and it's very, very different from the aesthetic conviction of the identity of an object when in the field. For one thing, the error to which it's subject is very different.

PROFESSOR POTEAT:

To go back to your tomato illustration: you would ask of a tomato which you recognize to be such, is it red and therefore ripe, or green and therefore unripe. And this would provide some sort of taxonomic distinction. And then you might say it has a certain mass, and you can feel it as having three dimensions when you hold it in your hand (and a tomato that didn't feel that way in your hand would be a very suspect tomato). This, then, is a sense of taxonomic devices that are more or less clear that you want to use, as opposed to the kind of thing that Price talks about in his book on perception?

PROFESSOR PANTIN:

Yes, I think that is right.

PROFESSOR POTEAT:

That is, you're not going around classifying patches of color, and that sort of thing? You are going around classifying *tomatoes* that are either red or green, that have three dimensions or are perhaps pictures of tomatoes?

PROFESSOR PANTIN:

That's right, yes.

PROFESSOR POLANYI:

May I try to sell some of my own wares on this occasion by saying that the difference between what you described as the museum method, going key by key with yes-no distinctions, and the other picture called an aesthetic one, is that in one case you use a series of *focal* observations, whereas in the other you integrate a large number of *subsidiary* elements which you called unconscious. This brings up something which, if true, seems to me of very great importance, namely, that focally we can integrate only a very few elements. The only way of integrating a large number of elements and joint meaning is by doing so subsidiarily, by relying on them to attend to their joint meaning. That is why one has to go so clumsily from key to key, because the focal awareness is so much limited in its operations. Attention can only be given to one or two or three, or according to some authors, as many as 11 elements, focally at the same time, but on the subsidiary level, you can have hundreds of elements of which you are aware at the same time. And I think what you said about the proprioceptive element being so important in giving us a sense of the external world was very much to the point. It occurs to me that this is probably due to the fact that proprioceptive observation is one that cannot be made focally at all. And it has therefore a privileged position (though it's not the only one that has this privileged position) of being integrated into a complex awareness of the external world. I think this has something to do with what I was trying to show about the process of discovery: that the intentional sallying forth of the imagination is a very clumsy thing and can never really integrate that which we are after and which we are proposing to discover. That has to be done spontaneously on a subsidiary level. This is the kind of story which I think is a continuation of what you have told us today.

PROFESSOR PANTIN:

May I make just one point about what Polanyi has said. The only thing that I'm not quite sure about is whether in the use of "subsidiary" features like that, one isn't really trying to split up something which is in fact a continuum. Whether, in fact, the means by which you recognize things may not really have a digital element in it at all, just as a purely analogue computing machine doesn't have one. I may very well have misunderstood you, but taking the case, for instance, of taxonomic characters—you have clear-cut taxonomic factors. That's fine, and you mark off on your scale, as it were, three whiskers, two whiskers, one whisker, or whatever it is. But there are other cases where things get a little bit difficult (I mean small whiskers or something like that coming in between, and so on.) One gets over that difficulty very often by trying to have subsidiary divisions. It's got four big whiskers anyway, but there's so many smaller whiskers. It's rather like trying to cover a whole panorama by dealing with more and more individual points in it. What I'm really suggesting is that I haven't excluded from my own mind the possibility that dealing with things of this sort is really a continuum and doesn't really split things up at all. Because of the logical machinery of our own minds, we tend to split things up, and if we get half a chance, we do bring things into a digital form for the sake of expression. The subsidiary element may have a hidden weakness there. But perhaps I haven't quite understood.

PROFESSOR POLS:

Could one say perhaps that subsidiary awareness is never of precise data? Subsidiary awareness *is* continuous . . .

PROFESSOR PANTIN:

Yes, that's all right; as long as it's a continuum, that's all right.

MR. LUCAS:

I want to pull these two together. I'm very much in agreement with both what Professor Pantin has said and what Professor Polanyi has said. The two points can be brought together to make it clear what is at stake. That is, if we take Professor Pantin's taxonomy and generalize that taxonomical complex—the point is that we *start* by recognizing, for instance, a particular kind of worm, then we sometimes have doubts about it or other people misrecognize it; we then have two biologists disagreeing about whether this is or is not a *Rhyncodemus bilineatus,* and at *that* stage you begin introducing the taxonomic details. We start to specify Professor Polanyi's features, the things which hitherto have been unspecified, in order to resolve the dispute. We *then* start shifting our focus from the initial, quick, instinctive glance of recognition to details which might be able to decide this thing. And therefore, we start setting up an arrangement of classification. Professor Pantin's question, then, is answered; the answer *isn't* given once and for all on two levels—one of subsidiary clues, the other of focal awareness—but rather this varies with the dispute, and at one stage it's a question of counting the number of stamens or the number of whiskers, at another stage a chemist, perhaps, begins to discriminate very fine distinctions of color (a man who's been engaged for a long time in judging litmus can see the difference betwen pH's with a degree of fineness which other people can't see at all). We don't have two levels with a great gap between them which we then have to integrate, but rather we have a whole lot of different problems. Then when things are running through easily, we can concentrate on our main problem. We just simply read off at once: yes, this is an alkali, yes, this is pH_8, or, in Professor Pantin's case, yes, this is that sort of worm. When we are in doubt, either it's because someone is disagreeing with us or because we are professional skeptics and are trying to make a foolproof classification. We then go through step by step, going over what we already know (as Professor Pantin told us, he already knew that it was *Rhyncodemus bilineatus*), very carefully going over its features so that if anyone at any later stage *were* to ask us, we could point to all these things. The digital character is given by the logic which we are imposing. We are specifying some, but of course, not all, of the subsidiary features. We *couldn't* specify them all, because there are an unlimited number. But since the dispute isn't unlimited, but finite, a limited number is enough for the purpose. Hence the digital number character. So we pick out just those qualities which make *good* arguing points if we come to disagree. Colors and shapes are easy to specify. On the other hand, take the case of features which Professor Polanyi mentioned much earlier: we recognize if a person is friendly or not, but it's difficult to argue about. The other tack is to go to the shape of the mouth or the color on the knuckles, or something which I can point to, about which there is less discrepancy. The great mistake of the phenomenalist and sense-data people was to set themselves in an atmosphere of universal skepticism; whereas in fact given a particular dispute, we can work further and further back into more and more minimal descriptions until we've got one sufficiently minimal for our purpose. What we *can't* do is to start in this position and then try to go the other way. That is, we've got to embed our language of sense data in a language of real objects, then it's all right. We can use it upon occasion, but though we can use it sometimes, we can't use it at all times.

One further point I think ties in to this. You raised the question of our propriosenses. Now this, of course, is going to be different from the ordinary case of perception. We're going to be (a) relying on these senses much more, but (b) going to be able to argue about them much less, just because they are proprio—that is, not shared. I know instinctively the way in which I'm looking, whether I'm falling or not, but this is something I can't argue about. It's one of the traditional points of the skeptical philosophers. And indeed you can't argue about propriosenses for this very reason. There isn't a language of the basis of normal sense experience; it's something you've got to allow before you specify anything. The propriosenses may be wrong, but if they are, we can't do anything about it, because they are necessarily our own; they're not shared, and therefore are essentially unarguable. Therefore, propriosenses are very, very important but are something about which we have no easily articulable knowledge and which we therefore tend to overlook.

PROFESSOR CROSSON:

I want at this point to say one small thing: it seemed important to me that Professor Pantin, in speaking of his worm, told us that in one case the worm was observed in the laboratory and in the other case it was observed in the field. Now I am wondering about the function of, for instance, peripheral clues definitely related to the worm when you come upon him in *his* world. And again having or not having (I don't know which) to resort to other means when you come upon the worm in *your* world. I think you are saying that meeting the worm in the field is very important because you are meeting more than the worm, you're meeting him on his home ground, so to speak. This makes it easier, doesn't it?

PROFESSOR PANTIN:

Yes, and this, of course, is very important. I not only recognize the worm, but I also put up a net of "this is the sort of place this worm ought to be." Occasionally you find the worm where it "didn't ought to be," as it were, and that gives you an awful shock and you try to explain it away; but it can lead to some very interesting situations. As a matter of fact, there's another worm rather like this which comes from Western Australia. Again in that case I not only know the worm, but presumably I can say, oh, this is just the place where you'll get *Geonemertes dendyi*. Yet when I found the worm in Australia, it didn't look to me like the sort of place in which I would expect to find the worm.

DR. STRAUS:

To come back to your basic question about the senses and the external world, I wonder what is meant by "external world"? Where is the *other* position in relation to the other world, let me say the "internal world," from which you figure out the external world? What's the relationship of your own body, in this case, to the external world? Is not this whole term, "external world," which has a long history, just as bad as its history? Is the external world of the worm and your external world the same, and how are they related?

PROFESSOR PANTIN:

This is a point I did want to make. One of the odd things about the biologist's world, for instance in the case of the hunting wasp, is the naïve assumption that it's living in exactly the same world as he does. There are color relations and the same sorts of deceptions and everything else; it's exactly the same as his. And that is to say that that assumption about the wasp's behavior in relation to the external world is something the biologist needn't even think about, because that is just, in fact, exactly what the animal will do! It won't walk through stones, for instance, it will walk around them.

PROFESSOR CROSSON:

I'd still like to pursue this external-world theme, but I think there's a more important point to come back to: the one about the continuum. There seem to me to be two sharply different questions: one is whether or not when we identify something we can be said to be performing a rapid or habitual explicit integration of many items. And I would want to say here: we are not. At least one can give instances where the answer seems to be no. For example, I can distinguish at a glance the type face of *The New York Times* and the *Chicago Tribune;* all I need is a small paragraph. I haven't the vaguest idea how I do it; I couldn't enumerate the criteria by which I do it even if I wanted to. Clearly here there isn't any kind of integration in the sense of running through a digital operation. The other question is whether, even if that were the case, it would still be possible to simulate that kind of achievement by a digital process, or whether (and this raises the question to which Mr. Lucas referred) whenever we have recourse to a digital process we do not always presuppose another subsidiary context with other unspecifiable clues.

PROFESSOR PANTIN:

To my mind the two methods are very, very different indeed. In the case of the digital method, for instance with the keys, if you make a mistake the effect is absolutely disastrous, and it takes an awfully long time to see that the disaster is there. You see this in teaching students how to identify animals; they get them all wrong. They will say, look, I know this is a tomato, but I've got it down for a potato, and I can't get it to be anything else. In the other kind, the errors are very different: "I'm so sorry, I thought you were your brother." You can always explain this, and that has one very important consequence for the aesthetic versus the discontinuous method. It brings in integrity, moral questions, and all sorts of things as well. There are various other differences also.

PROFESSOR POLANYI:

Just one word. I do think it is a fact that the "museum method" can be operated only by experts who have clues which cannot be communicated in a way which beginning students could at once grasp.

PROFESSOR PANTIN:

Could I give just one answer to that? I absolutely agree, because I think one of the most important things that the logical procedure of a key is doing is, not merely that it's helping you to arrive at a logical conclusion, but that you are enriching the aesthetic impression which you've got, on which you make the other sort of judgment.

6

"A NEWTON OF A BLADE OF GRASS"?

HELMUTH PLESSNER

I

In the *Critique of Judgment* (1799, pp. 337 f.), Kant says:

It is quite certain that we cannot even arrive at an adequate acquaintance with organized beings and their inner possibilities according to merely mechanical principles, let alone explain them [by such principles]. Indeed, this is so certain, that one can say flatly, it is absurd for human beings even to conceive of such a project, or to hope that some day a Newton might arise, who would make intelligible so little as the production of a blade of grass according to laws of nature unordered by purpose. On the contrary, such an insight must be absolutely denied to me. But it would be likewise too audacious of us to judge that, if we *could* penetrate to the principle of nature in the specification of her known general laws, a sufficient ground of the possibility of organized beings *could* not lie hidden there, without the presupposition of a purpose for their production (that is, in their mere mechanism). For from what source could we know this? Probabilities are wholly excluded here, where it is entirely a question of judgments of pure reason.

To whom is the warning directed? A contemporary biology could not really feel itself affected. As is clear from Kant's *Archaeology of Nature,* comparative anatomy and paleontology were in their early stages (indeed they were rather inclined to speculative hypotheses, and in their later stages with good reason), but they could make no contribution to the problem of the autonomy of living matter. The dawning knowledge of evolution and metamorphosis, which is suggested, for example, by the note on page 370 of the *Critique of Judgment* (Kant, 1799), naturally brings into view the old question of the origin of life, the alternatives of preformation and epigenesis. But there could be no talk of possibilities of deciding this question on the basis of empirical data. Kant's praise for Blumenbach's decision in favor of epigenesis, together with the clear rejection of a "formative force" (*Bildungskraft*) of "raw matter" (an *Urzeugung*), and his approval of a "formative drive" (*Bildungstrieb*) subject to "the higher guidance and direction, as it were" of the principle of organization (Kant, 1799, p. 379) are directed to restraint in a matter on which, empirically, there was at the time nothing to be said.

It is *theology* to which Kant's remarks are really addressed:

> Thus natural beings, which we find possible only as purposes, provide the finest demonstration for the contingency of the cosmos, and are the only . . . valid evidence for the demonstration of its dependence and its origin at the hand of a being existing outside the world and, because of that purposive form, an intelligent being; so that teleology finds no completion of the opening for its researches into nature except in theology [p. 335].

In this connection one must bear in mind that purposiveness is, according to Kant, lawfulness of the accidental (p. 344), which represents a compromise between reason's longing for lawfulness and unity and the discursiveness of our understanding. Impotent to derive particular phenomena from the general laws of nature and to proceed, like an intuitive understanding, from the whole to the parts, the concept of the purposiveness of nature in its products becomes a subjective principle for the judgment, regulative, but just as necessary "as if it were an objective principle" (p. 344). Necessarily, but without demonstrative force, teleological thought asserts itself as a heuristic device in the fields of both biology and theology. Only under the guidance of a concept of functional reciprocity do we penetrate into the systematic structure of the organism.

> On the other hand, a physical (really physico-teleological) theology can at least serve as a propadeutic to theology proper: since . . . through the contemplation of natural purposes it gives occasion to the idea of a final purpose, and so can indeed make the need for a theology perceptible, although it cannot produce it or found it adequately on its own lines of demonstration [p. 482].
>
> But of man as a moral being . . . we cannot go on to ask: for what . . . he exists. His being has its highest purpose in itself [p. 398].

Through the limitation of the theoretical validity of the idea of purpose, faith and knowledge are both to win back their specific uniqueness and mutual independence, as against the fatal practice of enlightenment theology, which places knowledge in the service of faith and wishes by this means to take the wind out of the sails of an increasingly prominent unbelief. In this undertaking, the preservation of the purity of knowledge plays a decisive role. Its restriction to exact procedures, which excludes the invocation of purposive factors, guiding forces, or entelechies, forms an essential link in the chain of the Kantian demonstration. But taken in itself, on the other hand, as a pure methodological problem of biology and without any polemical edge against theological claims, it meant little as yet to that age. The fashionable Newtonianism which took delight in judging life, man, and society by mechanical principles did not get beyond analogies. There were at that time simply no compelling facts which brought a "mechanical" explanation of organic phenomena perceptibly within reach.

The scene changed only in the 19th century with the rise of organic chemistry and experimental physiology. Wöhler's synthesis of urea, Helmholtz's measurement of the impulse velocity of the peripheral nerves, were not only important as discoveries, but were also significant as symptoms, because they established new directions of research. The organic world became subject to the same methods which had established themselves in the inorganic in the course of the two preceding centuries. The problem of the possibility of uniting mechanical and teleological regularities, which Kant had transferred to the sphere of the "in-itself," became accessible to experimental treatment and thus acquired an essential change of accent: purposiveness became the epiphenomenon of the "mechanical" play of forces. The most famous example: Darwin's theory of natural selection. It was the first to popularize the idea of the unity of inorganic and organic nature and of the relativity of the realms of nature, and assisted in the breakthrough of the neutralization of purposive phenomena. A presupposition for this process, assisted by social change, was the rapidly increasing indifference of the century to theology, even to the liberal Protestantism with which Kant had sympathized. The system of adjusting knowledge to pure faith, the limitation of theoretical argumentation in order to make room for faith, lost its religious meaning in neo-Kantianism and became a justification of the autonomy of cultural spheres: faith and science were to have nothing more to do with one another.

II

The neutralization of purposive phenomena came to full fruition, however, only with the triumph of experimental method in the biological sciences at the beginning of this century. Developmental physiology—which was even called, at the start, developmental mechanics—genetics, and ethology have set themselves the task of analyzing protoplasm and intracellular structures as well as the reactions of the organism as a whole to its environment. If we add ecological research, the study of population forms and biological equilibria, we see purposive events in nature, both on a large and a small scale, grasped by exact methods, objectivized as phenomena, and thus brought to that symptomatic value for a world view which they already had for Kant.

Characteristic for the beginnings of this change to the exact treatment of finalistic phenomena is the vitalism of Driesch. Misled by too rigid and simple a conception of "mechanical" systems, he believed it necessary to explain the phenomena of regeneration and regulation in the early stages of ontogeny through the introduction of guiding factors. He thought of these "entelechies" not in Aristotelian fashion—a type of thinking which cannot by its nature be adapted to factor analysis—but as corresponding to other physicochemically definable forces or energies and acting as their completion. Yet, on the other hand, these entelechies cannot be forms of energy, since, unlike those, they have no spatiotemporal specifiability. They act not "in" space but "into" it. But such a property contradicts the methodological rules according to which "factors" are handled in an analytical procedure.

Driesch never admitted the validity of this objection; on the contrary, he took it as a confirmation of his thesis of the autonomy of living substance, which forces us to abandon the methodological framework of physicochemical analysis, yet without giving it up as a guide to research. Later experiments brought to light the fragmentariness of his results, and since Spemann's discovery of organizers the situation looks quite different. Today we know that the fluid equilibria of protoplasm contain possibilities for future analysis which have no longer anything to do with the rigid models of Driesch.

Another example for the early stages of the exact treatment of final systems is Uexküll's doctrine of the environment, from which modern ethology took its start. From the beginning, Uexküll took issue both with the kind of animal psychology that uses anthropomorphic analogies and with a prematurely mechanistic behaviorism in the style of Loeb and Watson. On the middle path that he followed, it was always an organism in confrontation with an environment—a confrontation peculiar to organisms, that is, to subjects—which guided the investigation. A piece of sulfur confronts nothing and has no environment, in the sense of a limited whole prescribed by sensory and motor organs, of a "world." The medium in which the piece of sulfur happens to be influences it and is influenced by it. Needless to say, that is true also of the organism; but the latter suffers and acts, because it is at the same time divided from its medium. Modern ethology does not deny this but nevertheless does not allow the fact to distract it from causal analysis. Ethology brings into view the guiding mechanisms in behavior and does not concern itself with their "meaning," that is, with the perspective effect which they have for the structuring of the world of the organism in question. It considers this superfluous, because, for the method of exact analysis, the "behavior" of an organism is necessarily to be studied only on the level of observed and measurable "movements." Uexküll, on the other hand, believes he can make visible the way a fly sees my room, for example, by photographing the picture that a facet eye produces. He knows, too, that it is we who thus see through the fly's eye, and not the fly. How it experiences the room we do not know. We do not even know this about our fellow men. But that the fly "sees" when it receives light must demand, according to Uexküll, an interpretation of behavior in response to a "world" and not only a factor analysis according to the stimulus-response schema.

Driesch's vitalism and Uexküll's environment theory, for all their difference in starting point and theme, and without prejudice to their suggestive power, have had the same fate: research takes no heed of their theories. Not because their experiments are no longer correct, but because the way in which they evaluate them does not correspond to the method of exact factor analysis. A magnitude such as Driesch introduces evades measurable control, not, to be sure, in the sense of an uncertainty constant, which itself can again be expressed in measurable values, but in the sense of rejecting measurement as such. Considerations like those of Uexküll with respect to the organism as a whole, in the perspective of its closed environment, seem to the exact ethologist not indeed to be necessarily false, but to be an interpretive addendum, which can perhaps be suggested but not convincingly established through the methods of research. But what made both men, in spite of everything, into classical exponents of experimental biology in the eyes of their successors, who were less weighed down by philosophical cares, was their courage and their ability to subject phenomena of purposive order to a causal inquiry.

They were not the first and certainly not the only ones, but for the period of Darwin's reception, especially in Germany, their break with the then dominant fashion of constructing evolutionary genealogies had special significance. For the chances of romanticizing such constructions were especially favorable in Germany. There was a tradition of the philosophy of nature reaching back to the time of Goethe; there was the political motive for softening dialectical materialism through evolutionary considerations, and making it, in the double meaning of that term, presentable (Engels, Kautsky); and there was the increased resonance for ideas of competition, adaptation, and selection of a young industrial nation like the Reich founded in 1871. The reaction to this hurrah-evolutionism began as early as the end of the century and not only after the European debacle. For analytical-experimental biology it was a blessing.

III

In 1957 a memorable congress took place in Moscow. A symposium with the theme "The Origin of Life on Earth" was organized at the suggestion of the International Union of Biochemistry. The host was the Academy of Sciences of the U.S.S.R. In his opening address, A. I. Oparin (1959) stated that even 20 or 30 years ago the idea of such a symposium would have been impracticable and that for nearly the first half of our century there had been only occasional and isolated attempts in the direction of the proposed question. Scientists were dominated by the idea "that living things (though only the most primitive ones) could arise directly from inorganic material." Allegedly successful attempts at such a "spontaneous generation" constantly proved false. Thus the conviction was established that the problem was insoluble, unworthy of serious effort. According to the present view the trouble lay in the mistaken way in which the question was attacked: "The problem of the origin of life cannot be solved in isolation from the study of the whole course of the development of matter which preceded this origin. Life is not separated from the inorganic world by an impassable gulf—it arose as a new quality during the process of the development of that world." The matter must be treated historically, in terms of evolution, in cooperation with astrophysics, geophysics, and geochemistry. Thus Oparin assumes a sequence of three stages: (1) The simplest organic compounds, carbohydrates and their immediate derivatives; (2) increase in complexity of the appropriate compounds in the lithosphere, atmosphere, and hydrosphere. Results of the process: extremely complex substances with high molecular weight, especially compounds like the proteins, nucleic acids, and others characteristic of present-day protoplasm. On this basis "one may postulate the emergence of some sorts of primary systems," which changed under the influence of the external medium and were capable of selection. With the development of such systems stage (3) would be achieved, the stage which concludes with the formation of the simplest primary organisms.

It can of course be asked whether the history of matter has in fact proceeded according to the established pedagogical principle, "from simple to complex"; but in any case the scheme can serve as a guide for analysis. It used to be assumed that even the simplest organic compounds, the carbohydrates, could be produced only in a living medium. Today we know that there are other ways. It used to be held that the asymmetry of the compounds characteristic of protoplasm was a monopoly of living matter. Today we know that asymmetric compounds can be synthesized under the influence of circularly polarized ultraviolet light, or in catalytic reactions on the surface of quartz crystals, or spontaneously in slow crystallization out of solutions, etc. And we have the same experimental support today for the possibility of abiogenetic formation of amino acids, porphyrins, proteinlike polynucleotides, and other macromolecular compounds, whose role, for example, as the building material of the genes is known.

Finally, through the investigation of genes and viruses, the question has gained currency: at what stage should we let "life" begin? Oparin says: "Can life be attributed to individual molecules even if they are very complex, or only to the multimolecular systems which served as basis for the emergence of life?" The answer depends on the question, what criteria are considered indispensable for life, and on this the authorities are not agreed. Schramm (Oparin et al., 1959, p. 311), for example, says: "It appears by no means permissible to see a virus as a forerunner of organisms, for the presupposition for the multiplication of viruses is the existence of living cells—the significance of virus research for the problem of the origin of life seems to me to lie rather in this, that it offers us an insight into the biochemical bases of reproduction." Wendell M. Stanley takes a different view: "The essence of life is the ability to reproduce. This is accomplished by the utilization of energy to create order out of disorder, to bring together into a specific predetermined pattern from semi-order or even from chaos all of the component parts of that pattern with the perpetuation of that pattern with time. This is life" (Oparin et al., 1959, p. 315). The capacity for mutation, for change, or response to stimulus, he does not consider to be an indispensable criterion, even though decisive for evolution. Nevertheless, nature provides for "a built-in error, so that the replication process is not perfect," and this change we recognize as mutation. Accumulated and stabilized as differences, we call them genes. Thus viruses not only do not constitute a *pre*-stage of life, they *live*. The usual objection, such as Schramm raises, Stanley meets by pointing to parasites: many tapeworms can reproduce only in the organism of the host. He points out also that many viruses exhibit morphological differences "which can hardly be called molecular in nature and [are] rather more organismal or cell-like" (Oparin et al., 1959, p. 316).

Only the biochemist can judge the weight of these arguments, so far as their confirmability is concerned, and here everything is in flux. But the nature of the argument is instructive also in a fundamental sense. For in all these controversies it is a question of formulating the necessary and sufficient conditions for the occurrence of the quality "living" in chemically definable compounds or systems of such compounds. Their formal characterization, for example, in the sense of J. B. S. Haldane as a "self-perpetuating pattern of chemical reaction," or the formulation of Bertalanffy in terms of hierarchical ordering of an open system which maintains itself in the exchange of its components thanks to its systematic conditions, constantly recurs as a guide for models (P. Jordan, Schrödinger, Linus Pauling, Calvin, and so on). This persistence of a structure, however, cannot be understood without a unique relation to the environment, no matter what degree of complication the system in question possesses in its stability. In order to maintain itself against the surrounding medium in its exchange with it, the system must fulfill specific presuppositions. Haldane specifies them as follows: "The critical event which may best be called the origin of life was the enclosure of several different self-reproducing polymers within a semi-permeable membrane." Impermeable isolation is not sufficient. On the contrary, the materials of the membrane must have been synthesized or accumulated from the environment "and must be organized in a stable arrangement between the environment and the inner aqueous medium of the organism" (P. Mitchell, in Oparin et al., 1959, p. 440). Certain observations of Stanley's in the case of a number of virus forms confirm this statement.

Special significance is to be attached, therefore, to the formation of natural membranes. With it organic materials achieve the character of organisms, becoming living beings in the strict sense of the word. We may leave aside the question whether we have thus arrived at an adequate definition of life. The ambivalent nature of viruses (and genes?) warns us to take care. But what is certain is that, with the formation of a membrane, that stabilization of the boundary is achieved which we call the form of an organism. It may be that the cohesive forces of large molecules and their interlocking in systems are sufficient to achieve the status of a membraneless living being. Again we may think of viruses and genes. But the formation of a membrane is in any case a step beyond this in the direction of a "higher" level of boundary formation. It marks the living "being" as an individual, and acts in two senses: enclosing-and-protecting against the environment, and disclosing-and-mediating in relation to it.

Membranes are not mere surfaces, which every body has in accordance with its state as an aggregate against the neighboring media of another aggregate and its state. They are *mediating* surfaces. In them the body is not simply at an end, but is set in relation to its medium. The molecular complex constituting it (or perhaps even the molecule) maintains its pattern, not only in the state of multiplication, but in its constant contact with the sphere of influence by which it is bounded. Its own sphere, protected against the neighboring sphere and opened to it, stands in contact with it at a distance. It is in such circumstances that metabolism takes place, a process which always consists in a selection under conditions of exchangeability. But clearly this filter function of semipermeable membranes is decisive also for the property of reactivity of living substances to stimuli, a property which presupposes a relatively stable inner sphere set off from an environment. When a body stands in contact at a distance with its medium through the stop-and-go achievement of its mediating external layer, then the chance of preserving its own inner sphere is increased. There is no question here of sensation, let alone consciousness—although both these are to be understood as developed forms of contact at a distance, but under special organic conditions. If we are to relate discussion of the origin of consciousness to a precise conception, this is where we start. But the term "consciousness" is significant only within a limited range. To tie consciousness to organic material as such, as Teilhard de Chardin, for example, still suggests (and he is the last of a long line), is to rob the word of its meaning—even though it is not, as is sometimes said, a procedure wholly without foundation.

Membrane or not, "life could originate only as a result of the evolution of a multimolecular organic system, separated from it by a distinct boundary, but constantly interacting with this environment in the manner of 'open' systems. Since . . . present-day protoplasm possesses a coarcevate structure, the mentioned systems . . . could have been coarcevate drops" (Oparin et al., 1959, p. 428). The effect of such structure-conditioned cohesive forces on the surface is the decisive point. For it makes out of the edge a *boundary,* in which two spheres acting on one another are brought to a reciprocal mediation, without disturbing in its structure the inner sphere of the body so bounded. This fact gives the body *positionality,* that is, it sets it off against the area outside it. Thus it acquires in its medium a surrounding area of the sort that becomes, in later stages of development, an *environment*. With positionality the so-called character of wholeness is given, which develops as form, though not necessarily as a constant form. Membranes naturally favor the stabilization of form. But it is to be assumed that the effect of the limiting form on the enclosed system, through the braking and at the same time canalizing function which it inevitably possesses (whether through a membrane or not), in turn produces new qualities, to which the original pattern does not entirely conform. An evolutionary perspective can take account of such discrepancies. Indeed it must do so, if it wishes to rely on the idea of an open system with a certain constancy.

A whole has parts or components, over against which it must maintain a certain independence, otherwise it is not a whole, but only an aggregate. Its configuration makes possible a certain area of flexibility (*Spielraum*) within which components can either disappear or be replaced. For the clarification of the cohesive forces governing such an area of flexibility, special significance attaches to quantum biology. Properties of living systems such as the capacity for regeneration and change of function (the substitution of one part of not yet differentiated protoplasm for another in the early stages of embryonic development, or of determinate parts of a network for one another, e.g., Monakow's vicarious function in the central nervous system) can no longer be adduced as evidence for a Drieschian vitalism. The occurrence of a whole which uses its components as means to its self-maintenance no longer justifies our resorting to a factor like the entelechy, which contradicts the basic rules of analytic method in empirical science. Without damage to the independence and uniqueness of living systems, their autonomy is sacrificed to the extent that a special agent is not needed to explain them. Physical and chemical ways of thinking no longer need any additional external factor when they are confronted with the phenomenon of a whole, that is, of a purposive configuration.

IV

Should we then conclude that the autonomy of living systems, because it can be reduced to laws of a physical and chemical kind, is in the last analysis only illusion, only epiphenomenon? In 1928 I sent Driesch my book *Die Stufen des Organischen und der Mensch*, in which I had tried to develop logically the specific characters of organic levels, starting from the concept of the boundary. He called me a hylozoist. Such concepts drawn from textbooks of the history of philosophy are always untrustworthy, because they are seldom coined by the holders of the view in question, but are polemic or expository in origin. There are supposed to have been hylozoists even in ancient times, in an age that knew nothing of scientific analysis in the sense of the past 300 years. Yet there is a kernel of truth in the term. Driesch might also have called me a materialist, better yet a dialectical materialist, since the analysis of the phenomenon of the boundary exhibits a strict sequence of contradictions, the solution of which is connected at each step with the achievement of a new level of organization. He avoided this expression. For we associate with "dialectical materialism" the problems of Marxism, history, and class struggle, and not a dialectic of nature, as sketched by Engels. But why didn't he at least call me a materialist? Obviously because he saw that I not only took seriously the autonomy of living things in their appearance, but wanted to provide a foundation for this autonomy under the guidance of one of their specific properties. Such a person was in Driesch's eyes (and in the eyes of his generation) no materialist or mechanist, who really denies to life its full dimensionality. The popular materialism of the 18th and 19th centuries had indeed proceeded in this way. Thoughts were secretions of cerebral ganglion cells and acts of will were chains of reflexes. It was on this model that the behaviorists worked in their heyday and that Pavlov produced his school. It would not have done to count the "hylozoist" among this group of *terribles simplificateurs*. He was no vitalist, but also no mechanist. The cryptological procedure of vitalism, rescuing the specific capacities of living bodies by taking refuge in entelechies, which can indeed be brought in, but not carried through, as natural factors—such a procedure seemed to him nonsensical. But neither was he satisfied with the opposite position, which denied reality to the specific powers of living matter and equated its methodological reduction to physicochemical processes with its denial.

But was not the future to belong to this so-called hylozoism? As the plumb line of an undeviating analysis of organic phenomena by scientific methods it can show successes of which, in 1928, no one yet dared to dream. Perhaps it was really a happy stroke of mine to make the phenomenon of the boundary the starting point of an argument intended to resolve the paradox of the immaterial dimension achieved by living matter. What carriers and instruments of such an immaterial dimension are available in terms of the system to be defined by biochemistry can be discovered, or at least inquired into, by scientific research. But this dimensionality itself, which research has in view in its proceedings, for example, reactivity to stimuli on the basis of the positional character of a living thing—this dimensionality itself escapes the method of science. Thanks to the saving effect of the boundary surfaces—whether enclosed by a membrane or "naked"—an organism lives in an environment which needs to present itself to it or even simply to become noticeable, and not in a mere medium. This fact, which I cite here as an example of a specific dimensionality of life, is not an empty verbal formula, even though it cannot be stated in biochemical language. Biochemistry will not want to deny, but neither will it want to demonstrate, that living things, thanks to their positionality, are centers about which an environment can develop in a fashion capable of increasing complexity, an environment to which they disclose themselves and against which they delimit themselves as centers not only of metabolism, but, beyond that, of a perspective assisted by organs of sensory discrimination. But biochemistry always has to do only with the means of dimensionality and not with dimensionality itself. Today existential ontology and behaviorism, which have otherwise nothing in common, are agreed on one point: that there is no psychophysical problem—the first evades it by using the concept of existence, the second by the concept of behavior. This procedure, with its talk of pseudo-problems and of out-of-date questions, does indeed commend itself, but the problem nevertheless remains with all its weight. It will not be solved by neurochemistry, unless the analysis of positionality is combined with that discipline, that is, unless the problem of the achievement of dimensions of existence for a cerebralized organism is taken seriously.

The old materialism with its slogan: "sensations, ideas, thoughts, feelings are in reality nothing but physiological processes," has thrown out the baby with the bath water. What can be reduced in this situation (as also with the nonconscious properties of life) is not the dimensional character of the psychical or the vital, but the means of its genesis in (or for) a biochemically definable system. It is there that the limitations lie for a Newton of a blade of grass and not, as Kant thought, in the phenomenon of purposiveness. The latter *does* lie within the sphere of biochemical analysis. A Wendell M. Stanley (Oparin et al., 1959, p. 320) knows about the difficulties and nevertheless says: "Eventually chemists should be able to synthesize a small polynucleotide specifically arranged, hence one may now dare to think of synthesizing in the laboratory a structure possessing genetic continuity and of all the tremendous implications of such an accomplishment."

We know Kant's motive for considering such a step impossible: a theological motive. But Kant's argument is grounded on the impossibility, for an intellect like ours, of penetrating "to the principle of nature in the specification of its known general laws." To deny to nature a sufficient ground of the possibility of organized beings in mere mechanism, that is without presupposing a purpose for their origin, is said to exceed our powers. It would be possible that there should be such a ground, but hidden from us in that zone of the in-itself in which it can exist together with teleological order. Only: "Whence should we know this?"

We do know it now; that is, we are beginning to know it. The problem, no longer held up at the barrier of specification, has become an empirical question of biochemistry and of a series of other sciences, which are competent to illuminate the history of matter on our planet. No one can say at what speed they will achieve this, nor is that a decisive question. But such questions as, by the nature of their subject matter, do not belong in the sphere of natural science—such questions as those suggested above concerning the immaterial dimensionality of a living body—these remain outside scientific inquiry and set limits to a "Newtonian" treatment. Precisely because the chemical understanding of protoplasm "as possessing a pattern which so regulates the course of the changes that go on within it that a specific form or activity tends to result" can no longer be excluded, the biological consideration of the immaterial dimensionality that is indubitably posited along with such understanding must become conscious of its logical limits. Does Sinnott go too far when he continues: "This pattern is the 'purpose' which leads to the achievement of the 'goal'—the form or activity produced"? Is the spontaneity of living substance to be understood through the introduction of a control function which the "pattern" can exercise? He sees that it is here already a question of a relation between material and immaterial aspects of life,

> . . . but the impasse in biological philosophy which . . . still resists solution requires some bold attempts to break it down. To this end it may be worthwhile to push our present thesis still further. If mind—conscious mind—is simply an exalted extension, inwardly experienced, of protoplasmic self-regulation . . . then we have access not only to its lower levels such as instincts, but even to the problem of bodily development itself [Sinnott, 1962, p. 56].

Sinnott—one example for many—does not want to provide any new edition of materialist theories, even though he also declares himself against the vitalism of Driesch and Reinke and the holism of Smuts. He stresses the difficulty of bringing the immaterial aspects of life into relation with its material aspects. But how are we to arrive at the immaterial aspects, which nevertheless achieve reality and are eventually to unfold themselves into consciousness and self-consciousness? This is no objection to Sinnott's way of putting the problem. Both in the statement of the problem and in general perspective we are agreed. But his thesis cannot be carried through as he states it, because it does not go beyond drawing analogies between the "small" organism and the "large" one, man. Forced solutions will not do here, if, for the sake of the immaterial aspect of the matter, we fail to preserve the connection with the basic question of the scientist. It is: What conditions must be fulfilled in order that we can speak of a chemically definable structure as living? A concept of what it means to be living is here guiding the biochemist also. He needs some guiding image in order to determine the degree of approximation to it in the progress of his analysis. If, for example, he considers reproduction to be a specific criterion of living matter, he will orient himself to this phenomenon. If this is not enough for him and if he considers the state peculiar to life to be fulfilled only with inheritance or irritability or metabolism, then he will perhaps orient his work differently, or at least judge with more circumspection the elucidation of the reproductive mechanism. A certain understanding of what is meant by these phenomena constantly guides the investigation. What the phenomena are, as defined with a view to carrying through their investigation, will be determined in view of the means available for biochemical research; but the definition does not fall from heaven, nor is it a product of sheer caprice. A certain imaginative understanding for life precedes it, even though such understanding is no longer wholly naïve. Its naïve criteria are broader in scope, if you like, conceptually less clear, but more flexible: growth, development, aging, death of the individual organism.

Must all these criteria be fulfilled before we can speak of a chemically definable body as living? If that were so, biochemical research would be faced with an insoluble riddle. It is therefore forced, on grounds of method, to seek for minimal conditions, the elucidation of which permits an approach to the problem. The investigation must proceed through preliminary stages, and a promising stage of this preliminary kind seems to come to hand in the analysis of the cohesive forces of an open system. Here phenomena which also belong to the perceptible criteria of living things, phenomena of individuation, development of form and constancy of form as well as of reproduction, can be understood as they occur in specific materials.

Is it, with such phenomena, a question of more than external similarities? In the last analysis, what are produced in test tubes are no homunculi nor even blades of grass; what is observed are macromolecular compounds, which are indeed necessary but not yet sufficient conditions for the living state. When are the conditions sufficient? At what point has chemical analysis run through the series of preliminary stages? If the chemists knew this, they would already be at their goal. Because they do not know it, they can only hold to their guiding image, which sets certain minimal demands, and it looks as if biochemistry sees these in the "open" limiting of a bounded system. A body that finds itself in such a reciprocal exchange with its medium is related to it as to an environment. It is not only a gestalt, not only a whole, but, however primitively its "parts" may be articulated, *a center of relations*. These characters of positionality result necessarily from the fact of having a boundary, and constitute its immaterial aspect, its achievement of immaterial dimensions. By what chemically definable means this is achieved, maintained, and developed (semipermeable surfaces, membrane formation) is the material aspect of the matter. Whether bodies with such properties may be called living is an open question.

But that they form a preliminary stage to life is certain, since life includes immaterial aspects. What constitutes the living state is the independence of a whole in relation to its parts and to its medium, to both of which it is always, and at one and the same time, directed. For this reason it would be false to give a preferential status to the material aspect and to declare the immaterial aspect its mere epiphenomenon. Both have equal weight. If we succeed in penetrating further into the interplay of the specific binding forces of protoplasm, on which the power of regulation, that is, the supremacy of the whole over its parts, depends, then there comes in sight a road, not to the triumph of mechanism over teleology—its heuristic value is still assured in any case—but to the transcendence of both views. Once a system has been formed, it has acquired properties which change its position. This change consists, without damage to its physical and chemical nature, in an increase in positionality, that is, in an immaterial dimension, which we have in view when we attribute life to a body.

SUPPLEMENT[1]

A conception of the human mode of existence as a natural process and a product of its history is to be achieved only by contrasting it with the other modes of existence known to us in living nature. To do this we need a guiding central concept. I chose for this purpose the concept of *positionality,* a fundamental criterion, I believe, through which living natural systems are distinguished from nonliving. The character of positionality, for all its perceptibility, is broad enough to allow us to present the modes of existence of plants, animals, and men as its variations, without falling back on psychological categories. But on the other hand the concept of positionality is no mere construct; it is obtained from the visible structure of . . . perceptible objects. Thus if the investigation begins with the question, what conditions must be fulfilled in the perceived character of a given structure in order that we should be able to call it living, it is also well aware of the limitation of its scope. Not everything that gives the impression of being alive must "really" be so according to the criteria of common sense, let alone

1 From the Preface to the Second Edition of *Die Stufen des Organischen und der Mensch,* 1965.

of biology. In the sphere of the perceptible criteria of the organic there are possibilities of error. But that does not absolve us of the duty—or should I rather say, that does not make it a worthless enterprise—to concern oneself seriously with them. The nature lover and the biologist can usually avoid occupying themselves with the criteria of life, but such concern is not to be avoided when, as for example in biochemistry, a problem is sharpened to the point where one has to put the alternative: does the behavior of a compound of known structure correspond to the criteria of life, to what extent does it correspond to them, or does it fall completely outside their range? In other words, we must know what we are talking about when we use the terms "life," "living," "alive." Granted that they are used metaphorically and derive from a conceptual history which includes religious and metaphysical meanings; granted also that their meaning as limited to organisms need by no means take priority over their other meanings. All this in no way alters the urgency of the need to clarify the situation to which they refer. Nor is this need affected by the history of science, that is, by the fact that the number, independence, and importance of the criteria characterizing life have changed and will change under the influence of further research.

In dealing with this problem, the investigation remains strictly within the confines of external perception, on which the operations of the biologist and the ethologist are founded. Wherever reference to theoretical statements of natural, or, in the last chapter, social science seems indicated, this is done only as exemplification. Such statements are never taken as supports of the argument. "We demand," it is stated on p. 107, "a development of the essential criteria of the organic, and in the place of the usual purely inductive enumeration, at least the attempt at a strict demonstration. Our task is an a priori theory of the essential criteria of the organic," or, to use Helmholtz's term, of organic *modals*. Such a theory can be a priori only in the sense that it investigates the conditions which must be fulfilled in order that a certain definite fact of our experience can exist. Thus the theory is a priori, not in virtue of its starting point, as if it were meant to develop a deductive system out of pure concepts on the basis of axioms, but only in virtue of its regressive method, of seeking to find the inner enabling conditions of a given state of affairs.

What *given* forms the starting point for the theory of organic modals? The immediate answer can only be: the fact of the delimitation of a physical body acknowledged to be alive and of the independence achieved through such delimitation. This criterion, which is to be found in all organisms, of whatever level of organization, has then to be shown to be the minimal condition which, so far as it is fulfilled, constitutes the state of being alive. Thus the thesis of the minimal condition underlies, as a hypothesis, the whole argument of the book. In this connection it must be kept in mind that the term "delimitation" or bounding (*Begrenzung*) of a physical body is to be taken, not in any derived sense, but in its visual and tactile perceptibility. The concept of forming a perimeter or a contour *points* to the fact, but is not identical with it. Perimeter, contour can be drawn; the fact of the delimitation can only be understood, not drawn. The factors on which the delimitation depends, and which are physically and chemically determined as cohesive or combining forces and so on, must remain outside the scope of the logical analysis of the basic state of affairs.

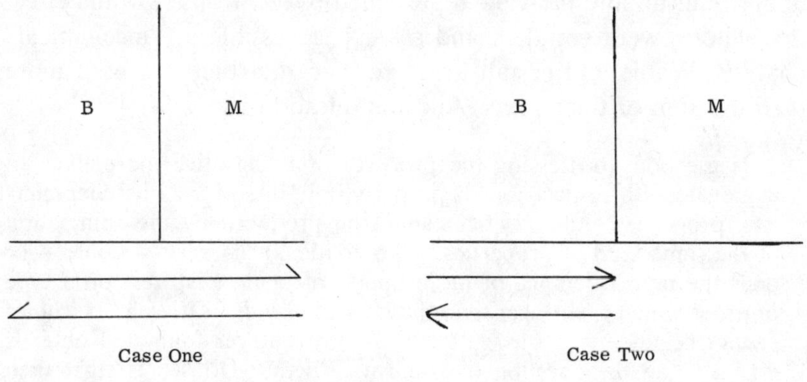

FIGURE 1

The emphasis falls on the relation of the bounded body to its boundary. Here there are two possible cases. Either (Case One) the boundary forms only the virtual in-between of the body and its adjacent medium. Then, however sharp the contour formation, the body does not have a boundary, or has one only in the external sense that it stops here or there and is at an end. Or, in contrast, in Case Two the boundary belongs in a real sense to the body, it is set off against the adjacent medium and in relation to it, no matter how sharp the contour formation, whether through membranes or other superficial structures. The boundary is no longer a virtual in-between, but a property of the body itself, through which it achieves its own existence (p. 103). "If we can develop, out of the situation given in Case Two, those basic functions, the presence of which in living bodies is accepted as validly characteristic for their special status," then the real significance of the difference between the two cases cannot be called in question, even though it cannot be confirmed directly, but only in its consequences for the structure of certain phenomena. If we succeed in developing the characteristic criteria of life from this starting point, "the situation represented in Case Two turns out to be the foundation and principle of the constitutive criteria of organic nature. Case Two would then signify the ground (not the cause) of living phenomena" (p. 106).

The occasion that gave rise to these reflections was the controversy about vitalism between the conception represented by Driesch, according to which the organism possessed a wholeness inaccessible to mechanism, and the view represented by W. Köhler, to the effect that wholes were gestalten and as such accessible to "mechanical" analysis. Whole and gestalt are agreed in that they are both more than the sum of their parts. And the question is:

> Is the body possessing the property of being alive more than an aggregate with respect to this property only in so far as its characteristic properties and activities cannot be produced by the summation of the same kind of properties and activities of its parts—Köhler—or does the preponderance of the property of being alive rest on a type of order which is stronger than the laws of *gestalt*—Driesch? If wholes cannot be understood as *gestalten,* then, whatever follows, Köhler is mistaken on the question of vitalism. Whether Driesch is right then remains to be considered [p. 99].

In fact he is not right, for the disjunction is not exhaustive. But the controversy is not decided simply in favor of mechanism, to which the autonomy of all life must be sacrificed; it is resolved in a different manner. From the point of view of method, there are no impassable barriers for the physicochemical analysis of organic phenomena. Through his too narrow version of the concept of a machine, Driesch found himself forced to put the rules of exact analysis out of action and to take refuge in nonenergic factors. With the introduction of the entelechy as a natural factor which is supposed to be exempted on principle from every kind of measurement, we have an untenable solution of the difficulty and a self-contradiction. Nor was the progress of research disturbed by his "solution." Spemann's discovery of organizers in ontogenesis was a decisive step forward from Driesch, to say nothing of the discoveries made with the help of biochemistry in the analysis of genes and in virus research. For exact analysis, the reduction of the essential criteria of life to laws of inorganic matter is only a question of time.

But this reduction means the dissolution of these criteria only in the operational sense. As phenomena they are not touched by this reduction. They present appearances whose quality can indeed be put into univocal correlation with a quantitatively determinable constellation of chemical and physical characters, but which, in their qualitative appearance, retain their irreducibility. We know of such relations also in the inorganic sphere. A certain color is defined through a certain wave length, but as quality it corresponds to this wave length only when it appears for a seeing subject, by means of a normally functioning retina and a nervous apparatus, as precisely this color. The modals of life are such qualities, the genesis of which can be analytically understood (and thus made available for experimentation), in so far as this is possible for qualities. A theory of organic modals, which is concerned not with the elucidation of their genesis, but with the elucidation of their logical location and logical contribution to the phenomenon of life, can be carried through only in an axiomatics of the organic (not to be confused with an axiomatic of biology, from which, however, it has something to learn).

Life is a quality of the appearance of certain bodily entities, of their type of construction, of their behavior in a medium, a milieu, even, indeed, their behavior in relation to a "world." Many of the "essential" criteria of life can be observed in them, and they can also present the illusion of life. In order that life should in fact be present, a certain collection of such essential criteria is necessary, and about these there is general agreement, in common sense as in science. Yet there are cases about which the authorities disagree, such as viruses. Is it a question here of intermediate forms or of parasitic molecules, of pseudo forms, primitive forms, or genuine forms of life? One thing is certain: the more explicit, the clearer the individuation and independence of a phenomenon through a relatively constant form, the more do we incline to hold such a bodily entity to be alive. Form as the manifestation of the boundary is an essential index of life. For this reason, external appearance is of significance for the organism in the scale from primitive to higher organization. In the higher case the observed entity not only appears to be alive, but its appearance becomes an organ, a means of its existence. External appearance as lure, protection (mimicry), means of frightening or of appearing impressive, is built into the cycle of life. But as appearance and display, the gestalt of the organism becomes, as A. Portmann says, "an authentic phenomenon." "Display must be understood as a basic character of living things, on a plane with self-maintenance and the preservation of the species" (1957, p. 40). And taking up my theory of the boundary, he says:

> The boundary surface becomes opaque, it represents a higher level of the "possibilities of the boundary" which play a significant role in the higher organism. Through the patterning of the surface, display in the broadest field of simpler organisation is "unaddressed," not directed to other living forms, but, in the simplest way, manifestation in lighted space. But it already carries within itself all the powers which at a higher level of organization give rise to directed, "addressed" display—an expression of life to which so much more attention is paid than to the primary expression of undirected being-in-light.

Bibliography

Kant, I. (1799), *Critique of Judgment.* Hamburg: Felix Meiner, 1924.

Oparin, A. I., et al. (1959), *International Union of Biochemistry Symposium Series,* Vol. 1. London: Pergamon Press.

Portmann, A. (1957), *Wesen und Wirklichkeit des Menschen.* Göttingen.

Sinnott, E. W. (1962), *The Biology of Human Nature.* New York: Athenaeum Press.

DISCUSSION

DR. CHANCE:

I can only say how this particular concept strikes me as a biologist who has had experience in quite a variety of fields of biology and who is an active pursuer of ethological methods. It is a delight and a surprise to see this mentioned in such a broad context, for I feel your desire to exclude the psychological frame of reference is compensated for by your inclusion of ethological method, suggesting at any rate that ethology and the rest of biology are congruent. I think I can deal with the subject in two modes—at the cellular level and in behavior. It seems, from what I know of the boundary conditions of cells or of viruses or of similar relatively microscopic forms, that the boundary is essentially, in its living state at any rate, a vehicle for the transport of water. It is possible that in this sense we can still see ourselves as a flow of water. And this is an essential part of the nature of the boundary defined in this context. But in a more philosophical context, that is to say observed as, seen as, a position, as a shape in a position, the concept can be treated at the molecular level. I would like to refer you to the work of Lancelot Whyte, who has suggested the possible relationship of form to life and nonlife. He has suggested that in symmetry and in asymmetry there is a distinction between the nonliving and the living, and he has drawn attention to the possibilities of two forms of the asymmetrical, the squew and the screw. These are both forms which have a unique axis, and I think that it is in the relationship of positionality to axial forms that we may find a common feature of most living systems. This is even extendable into the vectorial relations that go *between* living entities. Here I wish to go straight into the behavioral field where I know in detail what is to be found. In my own contribution I distinguish two forms in which the term social behavior is used. I'm going to use here the one which refers to the pattern of social interactions that can be seen in a group. Until the faith of the ethologists came along, groups were considered to be too complex for simple observation, but it's quite possible for anyone to sit down in front of a group of monkeys and within a few weeks to know the structure of their society. You start with no preconceptions whatever: you do not divide them into sexes; you do not divide them into young and old (the obvious ways to do it). You say to yourself: let me see what are the emergent subgroups, and then you find that the dominant males do form a major subgroup in all primate societies. How do you do that? You find that they are found, persistently and over long periods of time, in each other's company, and in such a form they move over a large area of territory. You can then begin to confine your attention to these subgroups, and when you do, you will find that very much of the behavior can be understood in terms of vectorial relations between the individuals of the subgroup. Specifically stated, there is a rank order between these males, and the order of rank can be changed only by one animal's operating spatially in relation to the other animals of that rank order: one male upgrades himself by getting between an animal of higher status and the one above that, propitiating the one at the top and threatening the one below. He does this only by getting himself in a direct line between the dominant one and the one toward which he is operating to upgrade himself. This is true of many other animal societies. You have a direct vectorial operation which is dependent on the positionality of each of the individuals. I could illustrate this in a variety of ways, but I will merely say that I feel the concept has, at any rate, heuristic value of quite considerable power.

PROFESSOR MURRAY:

It seems to me that Professor Plessner is operating with a metaphor or metaphysics of space, substance, and structural relationships rather than of time and process. The boundary of the organism or the cell can be observed when the cell is dead or can be thought of as an instantaneous abstraction from the reality of an ongoing process. If I were going to consider the boundary (and I do think the boundary is essential to life), I would think of it in terms of functions, of properties, what it does, why it is essential. I would say there are many reasons why it is essential, but I would prefer to represent the organic system in terms of process, in this case in terms of metabolism. From this point of view, the boundary must be semipermeable with selective properties, the capacity to keep out noxious, harmful particles and to admit the substances that are needed to keep the metabolic process going. For instance, if this were an aerobic organism, oxygen would have to come in, as well as water, food particles, salt, and a few other things, and then it would have to be permeable to the waste products (carbon dioxide, urea, etc.) of the catabolic process. When life stops, the boundary is still there as a structure, but gas exchange has stopped and water exchange has stopped, etc., etc.

PROFESSOR PLESSNER:

I believe that this relation between process and the structure of positionality is very essential. Indeed, although I can't repeat the whole argument here, one can demonstrate the logical necessity for a structure of this peculiar kind to *develop,* that is, one can demonstrate that it must shape itself and that it must have a determinate end. And within the framework which you have indicated, I believe that metabolism is an absolutely essential expression of this structure, and in fact, we do have genuine metabolism only in organic beings. Naturally we also have in the inorganic an exchange with the media, with the surroundings, but we never have a genuine metabolism, an exchange which is capable of self-regulation. That surely is the criterion that is decisive here.

PROFESSOR POLS:

To put it in that dynamic way is to suggest a sense in which the animal is a causal agent of some sort. The animal establishes its boundary. Yet I take it you wanted to stay away from a causal way of regarding the entity in favor of regarding it in terms of a logical ground.

PROFESSOR GRENE:

I think there is a misunderstanding there. Professor Plessner wants to take the criterion of positionality, which is a perceptible criterion, yet not identical just with the semipermeable membrane as such (that's the part I find difficult to grasp), but you can take this as a logical ground from which other criteria of life will follow:

that there is development, that there is death, that there is organization, and so on. That is not to say that the organism itself, this example of *Rhyncodemus* or this rat in your laboratory, *is* itself a logical ground. But the concept is the logical ground in Professor Plessner's argument. I don't think he would object to saying that the organism itself as a living entity has causal power.

PROFESSOR POLS:

Perhaps the misunderstanding stems from the analogy between secondary qualities (like color) and life. At least in that section of his paper Professor Plessner seems to be saying that life is a phenomenon in somewhat the same sense in which color is a phenomenon.

PROFESSOR PLESSNER:

All I meant with this comparison was the relation of the modal to a causally analyzable state of matter. That and no more is the *tertium comparationis*. I am taking finitude as a phenomenal structure. My intention is phenomenological.

PROFESSOR GRENE:

I think that in the parallel which Professor Plessner drew he does not mean us to take it as closely as that; it's simply that in the case of color and its physical explanation, and in the case of life and its biochemical explanation, there is this parallel: in both cases you have a phenomenon which can be described phenomenologically and which is given a physical explanation, but is not thereby reduced to nothingness. But no closer parallel was intended.

PROFESSOR TAYLOR:

I don't think I understand yet what you mean by positionality and how the other features which you accept as being features of life follow from it. You said that they follow logically from this concept, but I don't quite grasp it.

DR. STRAUS:

I think the best model to illustrate Professor Plessner's position is "an animal living in *what*?" To maintain its identity, it needs the boundary which separates it from the immediately touching environment and keeps it as an individual animal. This boundary is one (I'm not thinking now of genesis of life or such a thing) grown with and growing with the individual animal. The boundary is mutual exchange. To permit this mutual exchange, the organism, which (let's assume) has the same chemical components in terms of elements as the surrounding water, must be of a higher organization. To distinguish itself from the neutral environment, it must be different in organization and, therefore, to keep up this organization, it must be capable of exchange. One could perhaps go one step further and say: because it is of a higher organization than the environment, it is antagonistic to the environment—dependent on it and threatened by it. Thus through this positionality or boundary, in some way or another, we take account of the unavoidable possibility of dying. To keep up the boundary is always a process faced two ways. Outwardly it's active but is threatened by the impact which may come from outside and, so to speak, "break the wall" and destroy the organization which, logically, can only exist if it is of a higher level than the environment.

PROFESSOR HAAS:

I find in the paper these characters of positionality revolve necessarily around the fact of having a boundary. So that having a boundary is the more primitive notion, perhaps, than positionality.

PROFESSOR GRENE:

Surely positionality is the name Plessner gives to this *way* of having a boundary.

PROFESSOR CROSSON:

Since the characteristic of having life and positionality requires what we call metabolism, what's the advantage of not defining life in terms of metabolism? Because if positionality doesn't also entail metabolism, it doesn't involve life.

PROFESSOR GRENE:

It's not a convertible relation. Positionality entails metabolism and a lot of other things, but if you started from metabolism you wouldn't get all the other things.

PROFESSOR CROSSON:

You mean you can have metabolism without life?

PROFESSOR GRENE:

No. From just metabolism, all the other characters of life which Professor Plessner deduces from positionality would not follow as well. If you have metabolism, what would follow? I don't know what would follow. But when you have positionality, then metabolism is necessary, and so are reproduction, death, and so on.

PROFESSOR MURRAY:

Almost any system you want to consider in nature has a boundary. Society has a boundary; a territory has a boundary; every topic you discuss has a presumptive boundary, although here we've been crossing boundaries all the time. Let's say we're *supposed* to have a boundary, a boundary that will keep us within a certain area of discourse. You can't derive the nature of the system from its boundary. But you can derive the nature of the boundary from the system. Let's say we're all participants in an ongoing system of intellectual exchanges on a selected topic, with the purpose of advancing knowledge and understanding. As I see it, the nature of the boundary—the function of which is to exclude (inhibit or suppress) in each of us what is irrelevant to our shared purpose—is determined by our selected topic. Now, what Professor Plessner was saying, as I heard it, was not simply that the boundary was essential to the continuation of the life process—with which I think everybody would agree—but that the whole life process could be derived from it. This may be logical, in some sense, but it isn't applicable to the phenomena of life. How does one get growth out of the boundary, how does one get repair, reproduction, and so forth?

PROFESSOR PLESSNER:

A territory has a boundary which could also be different. A discussion has a boundary which is set by its theme. A society has a boundary which is given by the mutual concern of its members. This is a mediated kind of boundary, a mediation; there are always intermediary members which, so to speak, condition the boundary. But here, on the other hand, I mean this in a completely massive sense; I mean that certain bodies, so to speak, set themselves their own boundaries, they possess their own boundaries. You see, this is something different; this is something that is found nowhere else, and where it is found, I should say, the conditions for life are given.

MRS. PLESSNER:

It has to be bound with a species, that kind of boundary. It's an innate boundary and each individual born from this kind has the *same* boundary. The species as itself has that kind of boundary. Millions of years, and the boundaries are always the same. That's the difference between the boundaries you mean and the boundaries Professor Murray means.

PROFESSOR PANTIN:

I find what Professor Plessner has said completely convincing. But I think you can approach the matter from a different direction and arrive at the same answer. Two of the properties one can say are fundamental to living things are, first, that a living system is an open steady state (that is, a configuration with matter and energy going through), and second, that it must reproduce itself, but according to special rules. It must reproduce itself not in the way one takes repeated castings from a mold of gross matter which is subject to wear and so gradually changes, gradually wears down and down. True, the products of reproduction may *vary,* yet they must still retain the power to replicate precisely the original organism. Now if you take the first point (the open, steady state), there are many physical examples (thunderstorms, for one) which have morphological parts, but they will not reproduce. If you take the replication problem, I think the situation depends upon some very important taxonomical qualities of objects. If you take the successive levels of objects, starting with the physicist's particles, isotopes, atoms, individual molecules, there is a very sharp line between these and systems of a higher structural order. When you are dealing, for instance, with an individual animal of an individual species, you can classify it, but the rules of classification are quite different from the rules which govern the classification of carbon atoms. One of the important features of the atomic domain, the molecular and less, is that you can read nothing of the past history in an atom and you can leave no mark upon it for the future. Whereas when you are dealing with complex configurations, by looking at the bone of a creature, for example, you can tell something of its past, and you can predict something of its future. In the case of the nucleic acids alone, as we know them at present, you can have an intermediate state, because with substances like DNA you can have the whole series of molecules with very similar class properties, although the individuals themselves are not identical. That is, they stand between these two classificatory systems. And that is, I think, the condition which one sees in a thing like a virus. But a virus is not an open, steady state; it is a molecular structure of some permanence. You can crystallize it; you can do what you please with it. If you wish to replicate a virus, you need an open, steady state. For this, you must have a boundary to provide the right medium for the replication of your nucleic acid. Now, if I am right, this arrives at your conclusion by another route.

PROFESSOR PLESSNER:

Yes.

PROFESSOR MURRAY:

I think this is a fundamental issue. If you don't mind, I shall pursue it a little further. I think Professor Pantin has said in part what I thought Professor Plessner was saying, namely that the boundary is one of the essential characteristics of an organism. But as I now see it, both Professor Pantin and Professor Plessner are speaking as anatomical taxonomists, not as physiologists. They are talking about the structure of matter in the spatial sense. Is this not Whitehead's fallacy of misplaced concreteness? What is concrete and real in an organism is a temporal event which involves the interacting properties of structures, not structures per se, as one could find them in a dead organism.

PROFESSOR PANTIN:

You cannot separate anatomy and physiology. If there's a physiological problem, its conclusion is an anatomical model, for example the surface of the cell. Or if you take up an anatomical problem, its conclusion is a physiological possibility which you contest. You can call me an anatomist, but you cannot help also calling me a physiologist as well.

PROFESSOR MURRAY:

Well, then, you are both, but you might be either one or the other mainly. You might dissect cadavers, examine dead organisms under a microscope, and leave physiology and environmental transactions to others. Or you might focus on the physiological or behavioral aspect without investigating any micro- or macrostructures as such. You might study the operations of enzymes without knowing (and in many cases, physiologists have not known) their precise chemical structure. For instance, the chemical constitution of all the digestive enzymes is not yet exactly known, but their properties are known, and this is what is necessary for an understanding of the functional operations of the digestive system. The desideratum, as I see it, is a unified, theoretical system, and one can't get this out of anatomy per se. Suppose Professor Plessner and I are walking in the woods and we come upon an object with the shape of an animal lying there under a tree; it is covered with a thick fur coat—his boundary—and we recognize this coat as that of a black bear. But he isn't moving. Is he sound asleep? Is he dead? Or is this the skin of a black bear covering a sleeping child? Now I think Professor Plessner would say, "Ha, ha. I know the boundary of this species. That big, furry, black coat is my clue to what species this animal belongs to: it's a bear." So far, so good: every species has a distinguishing anatomical boundary. But Professor Plessner must be saying more than this, because the vital question is *not* what it looks like to us from the outside, but whether it is serviceable to the life processes within it. For example, is it helping to keep the organism warm? Or is the animal frozen to death?

DR. STRAUS:

Professor Plessner *started* from the macroscopic view. He asked: how do we perceive objects which we realize are living? We did not wait for chemistry or biochemistry to establish that perhaps ADP of DNA played a role. It's the other way around: chemistry may establish that the forms which we find on the earth—which we have reason to believe are living—are also related in chemistry to certain organic compounds, but Professor Plessner's topic was really the descent from the whole to the character that establishes individuality in an order of space and time in which the organism defends itself, sustains its independence against the environment, and this is what I think he tried to call the boundary.

PROFESSOR GRENE:

I might just add a note to that. I don't want Professor Murray to have the impression that this is a criterion of dead specimens in a laboratory. Professor Plessner started from the everyday question: when do you say something is alive? Apparently when it's moving in a certain way; so it is the ordinary, common-sense criterion of when you say something is living that he's starting from.

PROFESSOR FREEMAN:

I'm concerned about perhaps a similar problem; perhaps it's just another aspect of the anatomy/physiology problem. I don't understand whether Professor Plessner is dealing with what I might broadly call a *logical* problem, how *we* identify, how *we* classify living organisms, or whether he's dealing with an *ontological* problem.

PROFESSOR PLESSNER:

I would say that it is an ontological question, which, however, I have approached from a strictly phenomenological point of view. I would avoid burdening the problem, at first approach, with the full weight of an ontological thesis, because in so doing, I should be distorting the truly phenomenological approach. If I had introduced my thesis from the start as an ontological one, then I should have had to claim to give a criterion which also empirically excludes in all cases an erroneous judgment between living and nonliving. So I proceed in a strictly phenomenological way—and I have to do so, as Dr. Straus has said. I start from an elementary and simple question: what do I understand by "living"? In answering this question, in a particular case, I may be very much deceived. Certain movements make the impression of something living, and there's nothing behind them. That's why I avoided introducing my thesis from the start as an ontological one. But I am certainly convinced that it does, in effect, contain an ontological implication.

We do, after all, have the phenomenological method. Husserl invented it to clarify such elementary questions as: What do I understand by "living"?, or, What do I mean by "political"?, or,

What do I mean by "aesthetic"?, simply in this form. Therefore, my method is to start, in the first instance, phenomenologically; then I try to carry through a thesis. Here, it's the thesis of Case Two. Now I can try, whether or not I can draw any conclusions from this. If I do succeed, then my account also has an ontological significance.

DR. KOCH:

I'd like to make a regression—proceed backwards through my confusions to the point Professor Murray raised, which to me still has not been clarified, even by Professor Pantin, who I think made some progress but still left me in an unresolved condition. As I understand it, Professor Murray was saying, in effect, that if you take the Case Two, analysis of a boundary or positionality literally as given, then what you have is a necessary, but not sufficient, condition for living systems. There are many nonliving systems that can satisfy this. Then a phenomenological point (I take it) was made to the effect that no, these boundaries must have the property of replicability, and I think Professor Pantin said that these two conditions have to be taken into consideration. What I'm still confused about is the question: *Is* the notion of replicability or reproducibility or whatnot in some sense intrinsic to the notion of boundary? If it is, I don't see what the rationale can be.

PROFESSOR PANTIN:

It isn't the boundary which is replicated—it's the DNA that is replicated. I have not considered the increase and modification of the boundary—it is the DNA molecule which has the power.

DR. KOCH:

We are still dealing, I take it, with an analysis of the criteria definitive of life; this analysis says nothing about the replicability of the DNA; it says nothing about the replicability of the organism which is bounded by the boundary . . .

PROFESSOR GRENE:

No, it's not just simply another property; as Professor Pantin has shown, replicability would be impossible without the kind of boundary Professor Plessner is talking about: his Case Two.

PROFESSOR POLS:

What troubles me is that in making the distinction between the sense of boundary under Case One and the sense of boundary under Case Two, one has a difficult job grasping Case Two except by introducing various other criteria that one normally associates with biology, such as metabolism and replication and all of these things that have been put forward. I can only say, yes, you mean *boundary of a living creature;* then I understand you.

DR. KOCH:

I'm questioning what deducibility means here, too, in effect.

PROFESSOR SILBER:

I thought Professor Murray picked up his point after Dr. Straus had offered, as an attempt to clarify this problem, a statement that positionality or this immaterial dimensionality is the presence within a boundary of a higher organization than exists elsewhere. Now that higher organization within the boundary led Professor Murray to raise the point of whether it wasn't this organizing drive that was the key rather than the boundary. He is taking a Whiteheadian organismic position here. And I assume he would adduce as support for that, the kind of cell division that takes place where the boundary hasn't been created, but where the duplication of the organizational centers calls forth a boundary, creates a boundary after the duality of organizational centers has been achieved. And that ties in with the point that Dr. Koch was mentioning, because here you've got reproducibility as something distinct from boundary, as something which creates a boundary instead of being something that's derived from a boundary.

PROFESSOR GRENE:

Could I answer that? Dr. Straus said earlier that the organism must have a higher degree of organization than the medium. That is a different criterion. But I think he would already want to deduce that *from* positionality.

May I just make another point about the starting point? Actually in the book, in which he develops this at length, Professor Plessner started from some experiments of Buytendijk many years ago in which he just investigated, in a perfectly common-sense way, *when* we say something is alive. As he points out, we may be mistaken, but we do make such a predication with a somewhat irregular form, while with a regular figure, we don't. For example, if you get something like the shape of a leaf, then you say it is alive. The perceptible criterion of a living thing may be misapplied—we all know this from animated cartoons—the thing looks alive, yet we know it isn't alive. But from this criterion and just this perceptible thing (the circumstances in which, looking at an object, you say it's alive), he then deduces the criterion of higher organization, relation to medium, replicability, and so on. I don't think the Whiteheadian position is incompatible with this, but Professor Plessner is taking the analysis a step further back than Professor Murray is willing to do.

PROFESSOR KOELLN:

Positionality is defined as the condition of the possibility of organizational power, replicability, and so on.

PROFESSOR GRENE:

Yes, that's right.

DR. STRAUS:

Is not the general problem an axiological one? In chemistry it makes no difference if dynamite is in the form of a stick or if it has been exploded. There are no value differences between one system and any other system in physics or chemistry, but in biology, one condition is (to use a simple word) *better* than the other one. It is better to be alive than to be dead. It is better to be healthy than sick. So I think if one tried to find one common level for science, then, whatever DNA may contribute to life, one has already reduced the biological phenomena to something which is no longer biological. The biological problem is to find a condition preferable to many others of that thing that we call "life."

PROFESSOR SILBER:

It may be true that life is better than the nonliving. (I think it's impossible to generalize on that, at least I don't think you could state that universally. There are some creatures that are better dead than they were alive.) But I still would like to see some really careful discussion of the relation of reproduction to boundary. I would like to see how those two concepts hang together. I can conceive of a living being who, through sterilization or one thing or another, is not capable of reproduction, but I wouldn't want to call him dead. On the other hand, we also have some instances in which an individual in the process of reproducing becomes two individuals, and after having divided, these individuals—having two nuclei—exist in one boundary until they separate by the creation of a boundary between them. Now this would seem to me to show a very complex relation of reproduction to boundary, and I would like to see exactly how these two are connected.

DR. CHANCE:

I want to make a single point about the question of reproducibility or reproduction. I think Professor Pantin raised the point about reproduction of DNA, but there are in fact other forces of reproduction in cells. For example, there is the reproduction which allows an organism to become resistant. Therefore I feel the *power* of reproduction has many functional outcomes; all these functional outcomes are contained within the boundary, and certainly at a cellular objective level. I think this question of reproducibility is very fundamental, especially now that it's been found that DNA forms only part of the reproducing capacity. We must realize, I think, that reproducibility means more than a mere duplication of life.

PROFESSOR GRENE:

I want to try to clarify some of the difficulties I think people have been dealing with. I would like to introduce another example that was brought up by Mrs. Plessner to show *how* Professor Plessner has tried to deduce various other qualities from this, one that comes into his argument a little sooner than reproduction: the relation of the individual to the species. What Polanyi calls "trueness to type" is one of the earliest of the other criteria that Plessner deduces from his basic concept. If you have a shape, the kind of shape that we judge to be living, this relation of boundaries to medium—this, as he calls it, "freedom of form within form"—you have already a norm present (maybe this is what Dr. Straus was referring to). You have the relation of the individual to the type, the type which it exemplifies more or less well. And this characteristic of living things (that they do belong to species and exemplify species more or less well) follows logically from this kind of form, this relation of the body to the species.

PROFESSOR SILBER:

I disagree. The deduction that we have in mind here is not really a logical matter at all; it's a discovery, as suggested by Dr. Chance's remark about the total complexity of having a boundary. It seems to me that what he's saying is that you just don't get a boundary or a situation in which a boundary exists without also having a complex system of factors including reproducibility. It would not then be a matter of logical deduction at all, but a matter of empirical discovery that the conditions of having a boundary involve conditions which are also sufficient for reproduction. Now that would be an entirely different matter.

PROFESSOR GRENE:

It wouldn't be empirical, since that reproducibility is contained in the concept of positionality. Once we have given this kind of boundary-medium relation, then . . .

PROFESSOR SILBER:

I feel like an empiricist at a meeting of rationalists. I'll be damned if I can see how you can define your way from a boundary into the capacity for reproduction. Are you simply saying this: we now mean by boundary that which includes a reproductive capacity?

PROFESSOR GRENE:

No.

PROFESSOR SILBER:

If we don't, then I don't see how the deduction is going to take place.

PROFESSOR POLS:

I just want to reiterate the point I made before. It seems to me we're only defining this sense of boundary by saying it's the kind of boundary that a living thing has. I wonder if we're not really taking *life* as our criterion, rather than boundary.

PROFESSOR KOELLN:

I have the feeling that something doesn't come quite out of that word "boundary" that comes out of *Begrenzung*.

PROFESSOR GRENE:

Yes, I think that's part of the difficulty. Positionality is a less static, less "anatomical" concept than the term "boundary" seems to suggest to most of us.

PROFESSOR HAAS:

I want to raise a rather different question about the reduction which has taken place here of all the various criteria we have, as a matter of common sense, for distinguishing something as living from other things that are not alive. It's a reduction of these criteria to just one . . .

PROFESSOR GRENE:

It isn't a reduction. That's wrong.

PROFESSOR HAAS:

It's a kind of reduction.

PROFESSOR GRENE:

I don't think so.

PROFESSOR HAAS:

Professor Plessner says a few times that he wants to reduce the concepts needed for the purpose of doing biology to a minimum condition which would enter the theory of biology. I have the impression (I'm not a biologist; I'm just trying to follow the logical structure of the argument) that what he was saying was this: once the minimum condition is allowed to enter the theories which the biologists develop, then the rest can be done very largely by biochemistry. But this one condition is not a biochemical condition, it is one which must be superimposed, as it were, at the point at which any biochemical account of life is incomplete. Given positionality, the derivation of other qualities like reproduction can be handled by biochemical methods.

PROFESSOR PLESSNER:

The establishment of a *conditio sine qua non* cannot be called a reduction.

PROFESSOR GRENE:

No, but I do see Professor Haas's point now. He is arguing that positionality will be the *one* thing left over that biochemistry doesn't deal with.

PROFESSOR TAYLOR:

There is a question of reduction; in his paper, Professor Plessner talks about explanation in lower terms, in inorganic terms, in terms of chemistry . . . It is a matter of time, he says, but on the other hand, he says this shouldn't worry us. The properties we observe in living organisms are not in any way undermined or abolished by this. An analogy with color was given in which we understand it on one level as certain vibrations and frequencies, and on another level it's still color. But I wonder if this is very much comfort to the antireductionists. I would like to explore this further to see in what way it is so. For instance, I could say Aristotle's distinction between heavy bodies and light bodies in physics was after all saved, because we can still make this distinction; the properties are still there, although we understand it now in a completely different conceptual frame, in terms of lighter-than-air, heavier-than-air. But we no longer believe in distinctions supposedly existing between them, and therefore we have no more purpose in using this language. And, in fact, we don't use it any more, just because we have no more purpose in using it. If this is the only sense in which the properties in question are unaffected by, or at any rate, are not abolished by, explanation on another level, then it isn't very comforting. And I think the reading we have achieved is indeed the kind of reductionism which has always been claimed by a very materialistic line of thought. But I'm wondering if what is being driven at here is not another sense of reduction . . .

PROFESSOR PLESSNER:

I would say this: in one sense Aristotle has not been dethroned. It's only that we see a different meaning in what he said. Husserl already suggested this in his *Crisis of the European Sciences*. When

Aristotle says that things fall to their natural places, this is not corrected by a theory of gravitation, even though at the time people thought this was the case. But Aristotle's assertion retains a certain meaning, although a restricted one. And here, too, I would say there are certain assertions, the meaning of which has gradually become more restricted through the progress or the genesis of other sciences, but which nevertheless keep their meaning, their truth in a certain sense. Only the meaning changes. Naturally, in a very primitive sense, as people used to do in the history of science, one can say this was the Aristotelian view and it has been put out of court by modern physics and so on. But it just isn't that simple; there's another possibility here, for the meaning and truth of the statement.

PROFESSOR GRENE:

I would like to ask one more question before we go on, and I think this is on the same line as Professor Taylor's. Would you then say that the bearing of all this that you're doing ultimately is *only* for ordinary experience and that biology will be reduced to physics? You see in the case of Aristotelian physics it doesn't matter to *physics* any more; it may matter to the *Lebenswelt* but not to physics. Do you think that biology as a *science* is going to be completely reduced to physics; is that what you are saying?

PROFESSOR TAYLOR:

To which I might add that it then becomes (in a sense) a complete truism. Nonreductionism is a truism because it's like saying we'll go on being able to say, "this is living," and "that is not living," after the explanation has been reduced to biochemistry; of course no one ever wants to deny that, so in a sense we reduce the problem to a trivial one.

PROFESSOR KOELLN:

There was one element in your argument about reduction to physics and chemistry, where you compared your view to Driesch: you said that the advantage your way of description had was that it opened the way to measurable treatment of the processes. That is a point of reduction, that you make it acceptable to measurable treatment, as such, and so far to science.

PROFESSOR GRENE:

Will there still be *biology* a hundred years from now or not?

PROFESSOR PLESSNER:

Yes, certainly there will; I'm convinced of that.

PROFESSOR GRENE:

So science is not equivalent to physics.

PROFESSOR PLESSNER:

No.

PROFESSOR GRENE:

Then what did you *mean* by the statement that "it is only a question of time until all laws of biology are stated in terms of physics and chemistry"? Why do you say this if it isn't so?

PROFESSOR PLESSNER:

One can't simply translate the specific dimension of life into another language. I have no doubt that in a few years we shall succeed in synthesizing matter which has certain, perhaps even very many, of the characteristics of living substance. As far as I can see, the way things are going, there is no doubt about this. To this extent it's only a matter of time. But—that doesn't mean that I am therewith proposing a simple substitution of chemistry for biology; I am only suggesting that we shall have chemical knowledge of the peculiar compounds which constitute living matter. These compounds must be seen and analyzed in their own right.

PROFESSOR GRENE:

By the biologist as well?

PROFESSOR PLESSNER:

Precisely, by the biologist. You see this business of reductionism proceeded much too simply. What does it mean? This is what we should ask ourselves very carefully. *What* is really being reviewed? How is the expression to be understood: A is "nothing but B"? What does that mean? I believe that something is left over which resists this dissolution even though we understand it in one sense, that is, we can at any rate correlate it with the law of the lower level. That is entirely possible. But all the same, the hierarchical organization is maintained in its own structure. That's all I meant to convey in my examples of models.

PROFESSOR GRENE:

I think it should be pointed out, then, that this is a *different* case from that of the destiny of Aristotelian physics. There is a residue for science as well as for common sense.

7

MAN IN BIOLOGY

M. R. A. CHANCE

As a biologist studying the social behavior of mammals, I am profoundly dissatisfied by the absence of a framework of ideas capable of including the behavior of both man and other mammals within a single compass. As intelligent beings living in the space age, we should attempt to rectify this.

The reason why biological theory has failed to encompass man lies in our present attitude, which has been historically determined and from which it is now necessary to break away. We may consider this under the following headings:

1. Man's current ideas about himself and his behavior, in particular, originate in tradition and are the result of a process of modification which has gone on piecemeal down the ages, different aspects being considered by history, philosophy, religion, the arts, etc.

2. Partly as a result of this and partly, also, because of certain inherent difficulties about studies of our own behavior, this has been the last science to be developed. The parts of the universe which man first chose for study have been those parts furthest removed from his "self." He has worked, then, through the structure of matter (chemistry, biochemistry, physiology, etc.) toward a knowledge of himself by the study of those aspects of his nature amenable to investigation by the methods of these sciences. Hence, the science of man has eaten into his nature, rather than encompassed his nature. Hence also the prevalence of the "reductionist" philosophy, in which all explanation is sought in terms of physicochemical properties.

3. Most current academic disciplines, therefore, arise and receive their impetus from the desire to apply scientific knowledge to man in order to repair damage or supply his needs. Very little research

is carried on as part of a serious attempt to display man's nature in the order of things. Yet, in the end, this should be the aim of the whole of science. For example, many of the ideas we have about our behavior, and many of our other ideas, arise from medical research which is undertaken for its *use* value and not as a part of a major project to enlarge the scope of biology. One result is that we are too little aware of the defects in, for example, Freudian psychology; defects which would be apparent were we to make a serious attempt to bring together the knowledge implicit in all psychological schools. This type of unification of thought is, at least, a recognized objective in physics, but, so far, biologists have not displayed any interest in making progress with this aspect of theoretical biology. The purport of much of what I have to say emphasizes that there is a distortion in biology of such a serious nature that I expect a radical realignment of biological thinking in the not-too-distant future. One of the factors which will be responsible for this will be the inclusion of man within biology. This should be a prerequisite of the unification of culture.

When we have incorporated man's behavior in biology, then we shall, in fact, have encompassed the whole existing range of human experience into science, and the present state of distorted scientific awareness will become a philosophical position less easy to hold. The failure to incorporate man into biology is, therefore, the most important single defect in the structure of biological knowledge; a defect which needs rectifying in an evolutionary perspective. When accomplished, such a correction will reorient our view of what is significant in the evolutionary process. Biology can become a fully developed science only when man is included within its scope.

How are we to begin this undertaking? Just as each species, say the elephant and the giraffe, gives us examples of how the vertebrate skeleton is modified in different ways for browsing on trees, so the characteristics of man illustrate a biological feature unique to man: his *intelligence,* which, as we shall see, is the product of a highly developed faculty which has not yet reached full competence.

Intelligence

The characteristics of intelligence are not yet fully understood and are certainly much more than are assessed in the intelligence quotient procedure of Binet. The little-known work of Halstead (1947) is the best systematic investigation of intelligence. Using factor analysis, he obtained evidence of four components which may be simply described in the order of their importance for the operation of intelligence:

An exploratory drive, which brings the person into contact with a large amount of information.

A faculty of integration, which enables information gathered at different times (and available also in the inherited structure of behavior) to be freely brought together, and which has probably, in its later manifestations, contributed to what we know as imagination.

Abstraction, which involves the ability to infer a principle inherent in a mass of varied information; and, finally:

A way of conveying the outcome of all these processes in a specific expression, e.g., playing the piano, writing, etc.

I propose to take these four components as the basis for my discussion of intelligence. The recent science of ethology shows that most behavior exhibited by animals is guided by appetitive moods, the result of which is a consummatory situation and a consummatory act. In extreme forms, the information available to an animal in one mood is not available in another, e.g., in the courting and the feeding of a moth. However, since the exploratory drive is evident in the behavior of fairly simple mammals, like the rat, the mood appropriate to the more flexible handling of information (and possibly to the integration of it) may operate at the start of much behavior in animals which can only express the outcome of the way they handle information in acts linked to one mood.

A mood tends to determine the type of behavior available to the animal. Without loosening the bonds tying particular acts to particular moods, specific expression would not be possible.

What I now propose to discuss is how the faculty of intelligence could have evolved. In order for there to be no misunderstanding about the discussion of this in evolutionary terms, I want to emphasize that evolution is a theory derived from comparative studies on the behavior of contemporary species and existing traces of the fossil record.

Isolate Formation

Selective seeing is the starting point of all observation. A science begins when we not only restrict our attention but define the limits of the region within which we seek to elucidate the operation of the constituent parts. This process was aptly called "the formation of an isolate" by Hyman Levy (1947). The process of isolation has two aspects: the practical sphere of operation within which attention is restricted, and theoretical isolates or concepts which are used to identify the whole or constituent parts of the practical isolate. Hence it is the correspondence between fact and concept which we seek in scientific investigation, and different devices are required for different types of material.

What we are after is a correct description of the *underlying* structure and processes, which we get from the *pattern of events.* An isolate is, in fact, any part of the universe examined separately from its surroundings or separated physically in some way for purposes of study. Levy points out, however, that the choice of an isolate is important because, if correctly chosen, it will include a stable system, and the process of isolation will not have appreciably disturbed the system itself. It is important to realize from the start that the process of isolate formation is essentially that of defining the restriction of attention.

The principal aspect of achieving this restriction of attention requires different devices for keeping the system we have under examination in view. For example, astronomers started by confining their attention to the planets, the sun, and the moon, and isolating these from all other celestial bodies for examination. Later, as the order within this part of the system had been revealed, the isolate was increased to include our galaxy and beyond—and so astronomy came into being. The practical requirement of this work was the form of instrumentation—the telescope. By contrast, a bell jar containing a sample of gas, from which Boyle and Charles derived their laws, was a form of instrumentation which enabled them to control their system, but astronomers have no control over their isolate. Experimental control is therefore not an essential part of the process which leads to the formation of scientific hypotheses or to their validation. This is provided by the second aspect of isolate formation; the selection of adequate concepts and the construction of an adequate framework of thought. But this must, of course, go hand in hand with the acquisition of facts.

Ethological Analysis of Drive Structure

I now want to describe how we have been investigating the structure of the individual's social repertoire in a typical mammal like the rat.

Before we proceed, let us clear up any possible misunderstanding in the use of the term "social behavior." The term encompasses two different meanings: the first is the pattern of social interactions which can be seen in a group, and with which I am not here concerned; the second refers to the structure of the individual's repertoire. From this second can be deduced the underlying relationships of the social drives in that individual, who may be representative of the species.

One rat is introduced into a cage which has been occupied by another for five days (so that the home animal is thoroughly familiar with it). The subsequent encounter is recorded by two observers, after they have been trained to recognize the 50 or so postures used by rats in social encounters. Each observer watches one of the two rats and names the postures on one track of a double-track tape recorder (see Figure 1). From this record, the reaction of one rat to each act of the other can be obtained by analyzing the cross-correlation between the elements on the two tracks. But the ethologist is concerned with the frequency with which one act follows another in the behavior of each rat, because this enables him to find out the pathways of response mapped out by the most frequently

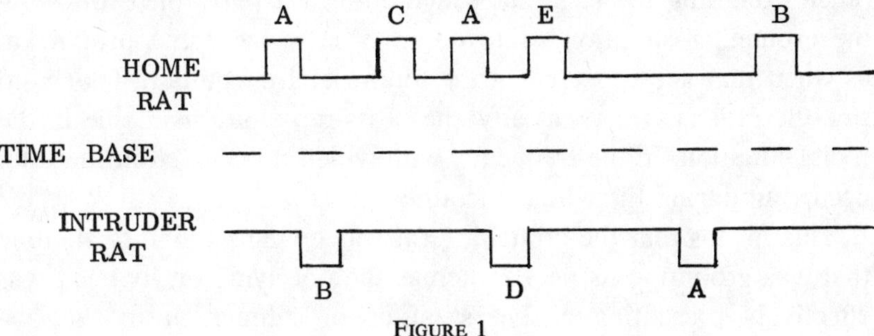

FIGURE 1

PAPER STRIP SHOWING THE TEMPORAL SEQUENCE OF TYPICAL ACTS RECORDED FROM THE BEHAVIOR OF EACH RAT DURING AN ENCOUNTER

repeated sequence of acts. For example, the sequence "sniff" at the anogenital region, "follow" the retreating rat (the sequence is the same between males as between males and females), and "mounting" are the recognizable components of the male mating behavior.

The antagonistic components are, however, less easily distinguished. If we assume that a bite is the final aggressive act and escape the final consummatory act of flight, then the whole aggressive behavior pattern is not clearly seen with males in a cage. Only cinephotos make "bite" visible; even then it is seen as a very fast nip (which may or may not be sufficiently intense to elicit a squeak); "escape" is, of course, severely limited, but retreat under the shelter provided by the food hopper takes place, if only infrequently, although it does not lead with much consistency to the separation of the rats.

Consummatory acts of social behavior are, by definition, those which lead to a cessation of that particular activity, or, more generally, to the cessation of all social activity. Hence, those acts which are infrequently followed by a return to that activity or by other social acts qualify for the role of consummatory acts.

This assumption was tested by detailed reference to the pattern presented by the analysis of the postural sequences. Inspection soon revealed that when a situation developed where one rat lay on its back straddled by another, the conditions of a consummatory act were fulfilled; a crouching rat with another grooming its neck was a situation rather similar. Whereas the social situation was completely interrupted following "one rat lying on its back with the other straddling it," each act which either rat performed following the crouching situation occurred in exactly the same proportion as when that act appeared in the total social encounter. That is to say, the rat's next act was any one of its repertoire available in the social situation, in the frequency with which it occurred in the total occurring during the whole encounter.

This means that the crouching rat was giving no sign to the one that was grooming its neck, whereas the one lying on its back was effectively presenting a sign stimulus of submission to the one straddling it. The sequences of acts leading to these two terminal situations are shown in Figure 2. From this you can see that the rats first turn their heads away (Flag) and then turn their bodies away (Evade) from the other animal before proceeding to crouch. These postures indicate that the rats are flight motivated, and if the whole encounter is carried out in a large room, then Crouch disappears and is replaced by true Escape.

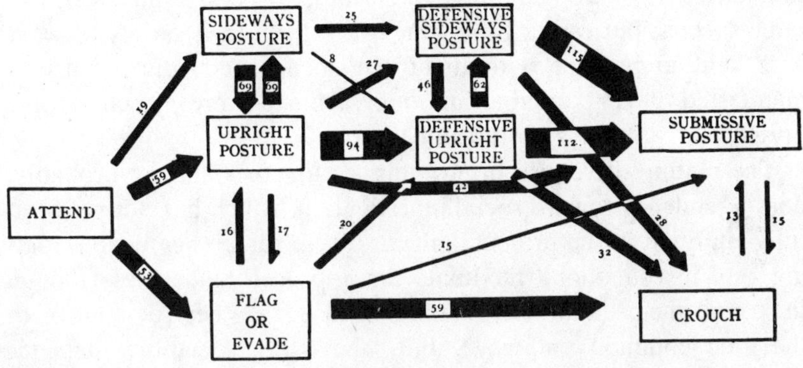

FIGURE 2

DIAGRAM OF FLIGHT PATHWAYS IN A BALANCED SET OF INTRODUCTIONS SHOWING THE NUMBER OF RESPONSES PER PATHWAY

The diagram demonstrates an escape pathway leading from attend through flag and evade to crouch, and a social submission pathway leading from attend through reciprocating sideways and upright postures to full submission (from Grant, 1963).

The printed numbers refer to the number of times each pathway is used, constructed by mapping out the number of responses between Attend and the eight flight-motivated postures.

Hence it is clear that there is a bifurcated flight pathway, with one part leading to social submission, in which the two animals remain next to each other (top pathway), and with another an escape pathway which separates the animals completely (bottom pathway), and it is also clear that these two are distinct pathways of response.

One pathway leading to escape consists of behavior arrested at stages in the turning away of one of the rats toward escape. Behavior on the other (the social pathway) consists of the upright and sideways postures, in which the rats sway back and forth between offensive and defensive social postures which, on the flight side, end up in submission and, on the aggressive side, end up in the full aggressive posture.

The aggressive rat's behavior is less stereotyped than that of the submissive rat. This means that the flight-motivated rat is determining the course of the interaction between them and that when it reaches a consummatory submissive situation itself it provides, at the same time, a consummating signal to its social partner.

Hence, the drives subserving sociability form a complex. Aggression does not, except at high intensities, disperse animals of the same species, but rather brings them together. In a variety of ways it is held in balance with flight tendencies, and this balance is manifested during combat in ambivalent postures, such as the upright and sideways postures of the rat.

The mating drive also brings animals together and so, probably, does a tendency toward social investigation, which has not yet been fully analyzed in the present context. These three (aggression, mating, and investigation) modulate the approach tendencies (though they may themselves be in conflict with each other for control of the final common pathway), but, above all, sociability depends on a sufficient availability of social submission. Otherwise, the flight tendency will be expressed in escape, and the rats separated.

This complex of submission, combined with aggression and mating, is the structure of social behavior (probably not yet completely revealed). The complex of submission, investigation, aggression, and mating can, for short, be called the SIAM structure [see Grant (1963), and Chance (1966)].

If the term "drive" is used to describe the internal state of the brain uniquely responsible for the coordination and expression of behavior in one or other of the discovered pathways of response, let us then use the term "motivation" to designate the contribution from each of the internal states of the brain toward channeling the responses into the known sequences. We can then see that some ambivalent postures, for example, can be the result of the interaction of more than one drive.

Social Drive Structure of the Rat and Mouse

The analysis of close combat has shown that the existence of a submission posture at the end of a social-flight pathway is a built-in way of terminating the behavior evoked during an encounter. This means that from the start the subordinate rat is able to terminate the encounter from time to time, and the repetition of encounters terminated by submission rapidly reduces the intensity of an encounter, so that the rat very quickly is able to set up a stable relationship between itself and other male rats in a colony, without actually terminating its agonistic relationships with other rats. It is, in effect, always testing the suitability of their relationship to its own state and that of others in the colony. We must take with caution the results of Barnett (1958), who studied the social relationships between wild rats brought into captivity, because, as he has shown, wild rats do not adapt readily to being in captivity. He distinguished very low-ranking rats, who remained immobile in the presence of other rats, and intermediate-ranking rats who adjusted their movements in relation to the dominant rats, whose movements were not circumscribed in any way by the presence of their companions. Clearly, therefore, these three categories reflect parts of a dynamic system in which, through repeated encounters, individuals test their status in rank order and can adjust to new circumstances.

In contrast to the rats, mice do not have a social submission posture, that is to say, a posture which uniquely occupies a position that terminates social encounters (Chance and Mackintosh, in preparation). Instead, one mouse flees from another, stops, and adopts a defensive upright posture for a moment toward its pursuer, who starts to adopt an attacking posture, the offensive sideways; as soon as it closes in on the defensive mouse, the defender flees again and is again chased by its pursuer. This dingdong goes on until some adventitious circumstance temporarily stops it. In the wild, this is used to chase mice back to their own territory. It is clear, therefore, that the ambivalence which is largely absent from the mouse behavior is, in the rat, associated with a submission pathway in its flight behavior.

The mating drive has long been recognized as holding individuals together, but we now see that aggression must be included, because it does not, in the rat, separate the partners, but rather brings them together into a consummatory situation where the final response of the rat under attack is submission. This act allows a flight-motivated rat to remain close to its companion in an agonistic encounter. In addition, there is some evidence of a third approach drive, that of social investigation. Hence, from the analysis of combat, we see that submission, aggression, investigation, and mating make up a structure consisting of a modified flight drive (preventing the separation of the rats) combined with three approach drives.

Mice possess a simpler structure to their social repertoire, one without an act of submission. The difference is probably directly related to their social habits; mice, given space, do not set up large communities based on stable male/male interaction as rats do, but are found in small groups of females and an occasional male associated with separated territory-defending males (Mackintosh, in preparation).

There is a different twist to the escape pathway of baboons and macaques which turns them back and makes them move toward a more dominant monkey. They in fact escape toward the dominant. Kummer (1957) has found this true, especially of the female Hamadryas baboons, and it is equally, if not more, characteristic of the males constituting the rank order of breeding male macaques. Kummer says:

> During expression of fear, the frightened individual does not remain where it was threatened. Either it flees from the cause of its fear, or it seeks out another animal of the highest possible rank. When fear is intense, the latter invariably happens. It seeks out the highest-ranking of the animals present, though this individual has himself been the cause of its fear.

Kummer has also shown how this comes about: the young baboon, from a very early age, habitually seeks out its mother and, for much of the time, clings to her or is embraced by her. Early in life both the young macaque and the young baboon seek out their mothers as refuges, that is, they escape toward their mothers; Kummer has now worked out in detail how this escape behavior is transferred from the mother to a sibling and then to a more adult male, ultimately disappearing in the male Hamadryas baboon society (in which the adult males form a single center for the social unit), but remaining in the female. The reflected escape, as we may call it, is retained in the adult male macaque, forming the basis of the behavior of the subordinate males, who run toward the dominant or alpha male.

The final link in the succession of events which forges the social bond between the growing monkey and the other members of the colony seems to be that, with advancing age, the elements of behavior in the young in their relationship with their mothers do not vanish, but project themselves upon ever higher ranking individuals, forcing the recipient of threat to go toward the center of the society and, when adult, to congregate in the region of the dominant males. The bond uniting the society would therefore appear to be the complete suppression of escape or avoidance, leaving the other two tendencies derived from aggression and mating to draw the subordinate animal closer to the high-ranking animals. The switching of attention up the hierarchy, together with the suppression of the motor elements of escape, would be enough to explain this behavior, but the evidence from young monkeys suggests more than this. In addition, Harlow's (1958) evidence shows that the young macaques regard their mothers as refuges rather than as sources of food.

Comparative Morphology of Social Drives

The comparative morphology of social behavior is now apparent. As the need for more persistent sociability increases, it is achieved not by increasing the strength of the approach drives, but, in the first stage, by blocking escape by means of submission built into an agonistic social repertoire. Later, this is supplemented by turning back the residual escape toward the aggressor, and so converting a withdrawal tendency into an approach drive. This latter, however, could not have been achieved without a submission posture first being provided for agonistic situations since the reflected escape drive increases the frequency of agonistic social situations. This comparative morphology is expressed in Figure 3.

Thus far the evidence has enabled us to draw a picture of the way in which social behavior orients an individual toward or away from a companion when different social propensities are brought into operation. With rising social excitement, of whatever type, the attention of one monkey becomes fixed on a more dominant one. This not only provides the mechanism for keeping the society together, but also, since the breeding performance of the individual males (or females) is related to their success in reaching a high position in the rank order, and since in every social situation the result is dictated by the reciprocal action and reaction of the partners, the ability to predict the outcome of a particular course of

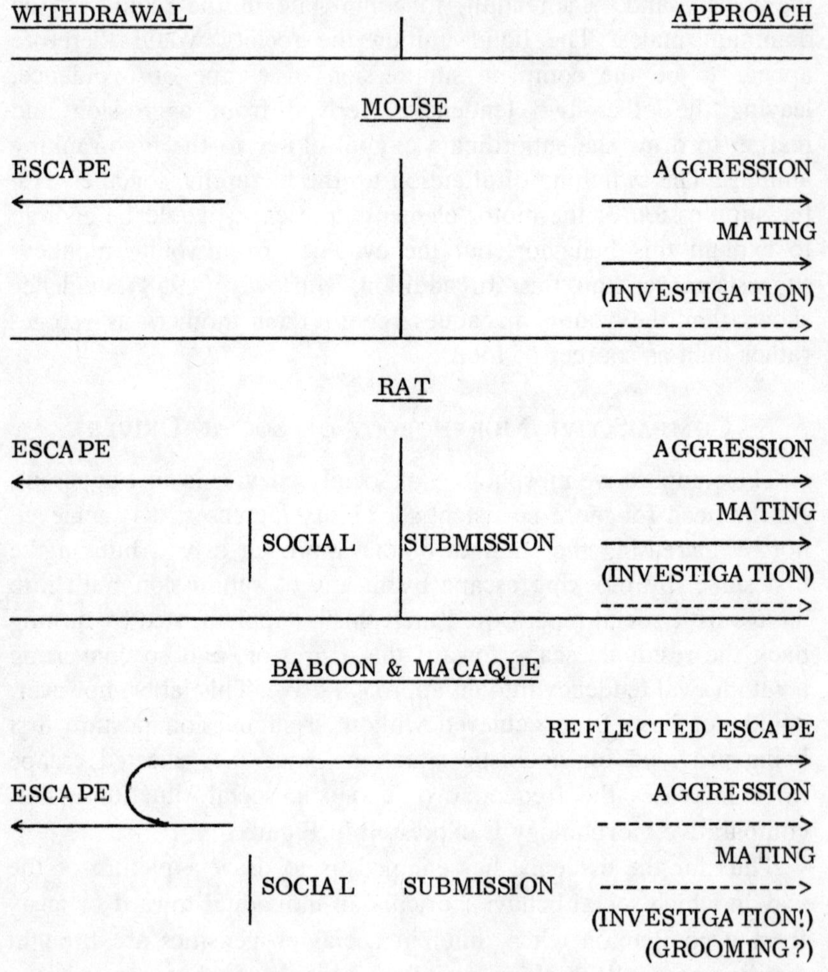

FIGURE 3

DIAGRAM TO ILLUSTRATE THE WAY IN WHICH SOCIAL ORIENTATION IS BROUGHT ABOUT IN DIFFERENT SPECIES

action by the subordinate will enhance its chances of success in life and ultimately be rewarded by a breeding premium.

Despite the fact that the ultimate orientation of the subordinate individual is maintained toward a more dominant male, the behavior of the subordinate animal which comes close to a more dominant one under these influences shows evidence of conflict, such as "displacement activities," "ambivalent movements" toward and away, and sometimes screeching behavior. These activities are evidence that it is torn between some tendencies to withdraw and some to approach and that the reflected escape brings the subordinate back toward the alpha animal by the way in which its attention is fixed on that animal. Negative and positive tendencies are therefore still present but are held together in a new orientation.

This situation is developed out of the requirement of safety under predation in open territory. It has also, in the circumstances of their lives, developed a compulsive quality. This is especially evident when one realizes that, even when the threat is directed at a subordinate by a more dominant animal, the subordinate animal is under a compulsion to move toward the source of this threat. Little wonder, therefore, that in this situation of conflict for the individual, many stereotyped forms of behavior appear which have, in part at least, the function of temporarily preventing the animal from precipitating an open attack upon itself.

In captive colonies, where this relationship is intensified, and presumably in any comparable situation in the wild, a great deal of time is spent in such stereotyped activity. These activities have virtually no functional outcome other than to prevent the conflict from becoming uncontrollable, and the amount of time involved seriously restricts that available for other activities. In these circumstances, therefore, anything that can reintroduce flexibility of action will be of advantage. The situation resulting in reflected escape, then, is a focal situation in which a number of different behavioral attributes interact and one which would be of great interest for further study if it could be correctly isolated. It should be possible to some extent to predict the elements of behavior which, in the relationship of a subordinate to a more dominant monkey, would have a selective advantage.

One feature of the situation in which the maturing subordinate monkey finds himself is that, while his attention remains predominantly fixed on the dominant male during periods of social arousal, he is unable to consummate any of his social drives in the way that most other animals are able to do; the result is that, unless he is able to reduce this social arousal in other ways, he will become caught in the situation.

One possible way to escape the situation is to introduce stereotyped acts or postures which deflect his vision from the object of his attention. I have called these "cut-off" acts (Chance, 1962). This is likely to result in a reduction of the arousal component possessed by all social signals. It is also clear that what ethologists have described as displacement activities play some part in achieving the same result.

There are different categories of behavior involved in this social conflict: elements of awareness and actions. A way out of the difficulties involved would be to loosen the links in the structure which compel an animal to complete a series of actions in a fixed manner once started on a particular course. (We saw this kind of compulsive behavior in the pathways of response in the rat.) This would give greater control over its motivation.

Another major category of behavioral elements could also be loosened with advantage and would have a complementary effect on the control of motivation. This would be a reduction of novelty or complexity, for both these elements (according to Berlyne, 1960) increase arousal and, hence, make transition from one motivation to another more difficult. Recognizing a persistent familiar element in a changing situation is equivalent to abstraction and will reduce the novelty of the over-all situation. It may also be expected to increase the predictive power of the subordinate animal.

Integration of a number of past and present experiences is also made easier thereby. Integration and abstraction are two of the four factors of intelligence formulated by Halstead. The social relationship, therefore, between subordinate and dominant monkeys contains the primordial situation in which intelligence may have a selective advantage. It would appear that the loosening of the behavior structure in the ways described is an essential prerequisite for the development of skills, such as the exploitation of objects as tools or weapons and their eventual fabrication. It seems also that it would be an advantage in cooperation between individuals in hunting if a prior resolution of differences enabled them to take up different roles in the hunt.

Let us return to the enhanced control of motivation. Reducing the general level of arousal is one way of making a transition from one type of motivation to another. Despite the growth of intelligence, it is obvious that *we* gather information and do not necessarily readily transfer it to situations appropriate to other moods. (We can say that this is the moth in us.) Therefore, additional devices for assisting the mobility of conceptual awareness across moods will assist the process of loosening the behavioral elements; this looser structure we can now see is the foundation of intelligence.

Combinatorial Competence

Now let us turn to the possible significance of the nature of intelligence seen as a mode of adaptation. It is clearly an example of the recombination of information obtained from the environment—not a simple combination, but a structured rearrangement of the elements of awareness, which gives an ability to predict and control on the one hand, and to construct and create on the other. Has this any deeper significance for the general concept of biological adaptation? I think it has: it seems perhaps the most highly developed example of what we may call combinatorial competence, following the scheme outlined by W. M. S. Russell (1961). This condition is the outcome of a process of combinatorial selection, which, he has postulated, can be identified at three different levels, as in the following table.

TABLE 1

THE INTERNAL ANALOGIES OF ORGAN EVOLUTION

Level	Combinatorial Selection	Loss of combinatorial selection
Microevolution	Genetic homeostasis	Loss of homeostasis
Mesoevolution	Selective radiation without isolation	Speciation
Macroevolution		
1.	Selective radiation in the life cycle	Developmental fixation
2.	Progress	Specialization

In a search for the general principles governing evolution at different levels in the genetic and ontogenetic aspects of the individual, Russell is looking for isomorphic systems at each level, and makes the following statement:

> If two systems can be mapped upon each other so perfectly that their behavior is indistinguishable, they are said to be *isomorphic*. Without being isomorphic, two systems may have enough in common to permit a mapping which, provided we ignore some of the behavior of each, makes the remaining behavior identical: such systems are said to be *homomorphic* [p. 83].
>
> The discovery of these mappings showed me an invigorating spectacle: one fundamental principal of Darwinian mechanism is repeated again and again, at many levels, on many time-scales, in many contexts. At all these levels, on all these time-scales, in all these contexts, we see one type of process which means success, and the loss of which, unless corrected at another level, means failure. I call this process *combinatorial selection* [p. 84].

He goes on:

> At the micro-level, we have the process called by Lerner genetic homeostasis. . . . This process, by favoring wide recombination, *exposes alleles to a variety of genetic environments,* by combining them in a variety of genotypes: the fruits of this combinatorial selection are re-assembled in a gene pool at each generation. Homeostasis may be lost by various means, such as excessive linkage, fixation of alleles, population decline, and in-breeding. . . .
>
> At the meso-level, we have the process called by Sewall Wright cellulation, or more generally, selective radiation. This process, by scattering sections of a population over a number of ecological situations, *exposes alleles to a variety of external environments in space*. The fruits of this combinatorial selection are re-assembled in the gene pool by migration between sub-populations. The advantages of selective radiation are lost when speciation occurs [p. 84].

In 1959, before I was aware of Russell's work, I attended a conference on "The Social Life of Early Man," organized by the Wenner-Gren Foundation for Anthropological Research, from which I came away with one clear impression. This was that, during the late Pliocene and early Pleistocene, conditions on the continent of Africa provided a wide variety of niches (in the tropical forest, open savannah, and the fluctuating border between them) into which hunting man could deploy in small communities and yet remain as one breeding unit.

Leaving aside for a moment the question of macrolevel evolution 1., it is possible to see that intelligence carries on the operation of combinatorial competence at the level of thought. The great emphasis which biologists put on the specific adaptive features of species deflects attention from the combinatorial elements of the individual and concentrates attention on the niche-bound features of the species. By contrast, in man we have the peak product of combinatorial selection. By recognizing this it is possible both to ascribe to man a unique position in the scheme of living creatures and, at the same time, to retain him as an integral part of the evolutionary process. In this context, the uniqueness of man does not place him outside biological reference, but, indeed, firmly within biology, opening a new way of comparing him with other living creatures.

Bibliography

Barnett, S. A. (1958), An Analysis of Social Behaviour in Wild Rats. *Proc. Zool. Soc. Lond.,* 130:107-152.

Berlyne, D. E. (1960), *Conflict, Arousal and Curiosity.* New York: McGraw-Hill.

Carpenter, C. R. (1942), Societies of Monkeys and Apes. *Biol. Symp.,* 8:177-204.

Chance, M. R. A. (1962), An Interpretation of Some Agonistic Postures: The Role of "Cut-Off" Acts and Postures. *Symp. Zool. Soc. Lond.,* No. 8:71-89.

——— (1966), Resolution of Social Conflict in Animals and Man. In *Conflict in Society; A Ciba Foundation Volume,* ed. A. V. S. DeReuck & J. Knight. Boston: Little Brown, pp. 16-35.

——— & Mackintosh, J. H. (in preparation), The Social Behaviour of the Laboratory Mouse.

Grant, E. C. (1963), An Analysis of the Social Behaviour of the Male Laboratory Rat. *Behaviour,* 21:260-281.

Halstead, W. C. (1947), *Brain and Intelligence.* Chicago: University of Chicago Press.

——— (1951), Brain and Intelligence (shortened version of Halstead, 1947). In *Cerebral Mechanisms in Behavior,* ed. L. A. Jeffress. New York: Wiley.

Harlow, H. F. (1958), Development of Affection in Infant Monkeys. *Proc. XVth Internat. Congr. Zool.*

Koestler, A. (1964), *The Act of Creation.* London: Hutchinson.

Kummer, H. (1957), Sociales Verhalten einer Mantelpaviangruppe. *Beiheft Scheiz. Z. Psychol.,* 33:1-91.

——— (in press), Tripartite Relations in Hamadryas Baboons.

Levy, H. (1947), *The Universe of Science,* rev. ed. London.

Mackintosh, J. H. (in preparation), Territory Formation in Laboratory Mice.

Russell, W. M. S. (1961), Evolutionary Concepts in Behavioral Science. III. The Evolution of Behavior in the Individual Animal, and the Principle of Combinatorial Selection. *General Systems,* 6:51-92. Ann Arbor, Michigan: Society for General Systems Research.

Weiss, P. (1958), in Concepts of Biology, symposium ed. R. W. Gerard. *Behavioral Sci.,* 3:89-215.

DISCUSSION

PROFESSOR GRENE:

Dr. Chance gave us what he called a comparative morphology of animal behavior and then asked: how can we see how the human level fits in, in analogy with—and I think he also wants to say in a different way from—the other levels? Of course with this aim I am wholeheartedly in sympathy. My objection is simply that I don't see how one can account, in terms of adaptation, for the human level until one has made it clearer what that level is. If Russell's scheme is just a way of saying that there are different levels, all right, but it certainly is presented as a good deal more than that. If that's what it is *meant* to be, then I think one has to object that really all it does is to set conditions in terms of which the human level is possible; it does not begin to cope with the morphology of the human level. That is, the whole business about this kind of selection and that kind of selection gives one an account of the *conditions without which* a higher structure, the human structure, of social behavior couldn't have arisen, but it doesn't tell us what this higher structure is. Dr. Chance has given us some hints about intelligence and creative activity, and these are what I'd like to see specified further, without so much use of this very ambiguous adaptational kind of language. That's really the problem, I think. What we want to do is to take his diagram of the three animal levels and build another level on top of it.

DR. CHANCE:

Perhaps it will clarify the situation to say something about the outcome of some recent research. As you probably know, ethologists have been speaking about the behavior of animals in terms of their drives, and the schema I have been using was constructed of that way of seeing things. But the whole thing comes down to the structure of *attention*. Both drive structures and intelligence control attention, and the problem is converted into a description of the attention structure of the individuals rather than of drives. I have begun to reorganize the research in the department on the idea that we should investigate the attention structure of animals—that is to say, not only the attention structure in relation to individuals, but in relation to the whole environment. Since we have computers and other devices with which to handle immense quantities of information, there is technically no reason why this can't be done.

PROFESSOR POTEAT:

Why then, Dr. Chance, do you speak of drives if these are intentional phenomena?

DR. CHANCE:

The drive has always been a bone of contention with the ethologists, but the point is . . . I define it here as I see it. It is defined by a sequence of acts which leads to a consummatory situation, a situation which breaks off the continuity of an activity. That does come out of the material, but it is only, so to speak, the scaffolding. Now that we've got the structure, however, we can describe the structure as we see it, and the structure as we see it is an attention structure.

PROFESSOR GRENE:

Then what happens to the drives? Are they still *there?*

DR. CHANCE:

They are still presumably operative, controlling to some extent the attention of the animal.

PROFESSOR GRENE:

The drives are ruling the attention, or the attention structure is channeling the drives?

DR. CHANCE:

Well, in animals, the drives are fixing the attention. But in our case, probably, we are capable of controlling attention by manipulating the drives. This is where I think we are different from other animals; we have obtained a more independent attention structure.

As a matter of fact, this is interesting because both cases seem to occur in man. I think a lot of pathology is due to the fact that some people operate at the macaque level. For instance, we studied one group of schizophrenic women who had lived together for a long time. They set up a social structure which I could hardly have predicted better from the monkey situation, although I did not know how it would manifest itself. And this is the point: that at a certain level of development we undoubtedly can get stuck at this macaquelike stage, where the drives are all-important in orienting our attention. Whereas, in effect, when we are fully developed, the drives are subsidiary to the activity in which we are involved.

PROFESSOR POTEAT:

If I may introduce a philosophical question: are you not rearranging the logic of such concepts as "action" and "intention" in a way which throws into question every traditional conception of biology? Now to this I have no objection whatsoever; in fact, I applaud it. But when you have done this, you have not only moved from biology in the reductionistic sense, but you have begun to rely upon a psychology which is equally nonreductionistic. I wonder, therefore, if the stress of your paper isn't, in part at least, somewhat misleading. Let me make this final point to illustrate what I mean: it would appear that the reductionist in general wants to say that human intelligence is really just like animal intelligence, and therefore if you want to understand human intelligence, you study animal intelligence. Then you reduce animal intelligence to stimulus and response, which is to say not intelligence, and then you go back and say: therefore, human intelligence is not intelligence. And you don't subscribe to this at all.

This leads me to a second philosophical point, thinking of Professor Grene's question; namely, it's not merely that you are specifying the necessary conditions for these adaptations that take place, but you are also, if not specifying, at any rate suggesting, that there must be sufficient reasons for these adaptations to take place even if at this point it's very difficult to say what they would be.

DR. CHANCE:

I was led to this view because of the complete inadequacy of psychotherapy—I mean by that, in the traditional psychiatric sense. The entire adequacy of the psychoanalytic procedure for *some* persons seems to me to be evident. But I mean the complete inadequacy, for example, of electrotherapy, which, as far as I can see, simply brings the person back, as someone said the other day, "to bump into fewer objects." It makes him socially less intractable and easier for other people to live with. It doesn't enlarge his capacities; he hasn't any more control over himself than he had previously. This was illustrated to me when we took a tape recording of a discussion in which a woman gave a fantasy of her world of problems, which was quite easy to understand if you once got the symbolism right. After she had electroshock, she was always talking about getting out of the hospital and doing a few odds and ends like cooking meals and so on; she didn't have another thought in her head. It seems to me that she was really much more concerned about the real things that mattered to her when she was in a sick condition. That is what should have interested the psychiatrists.

PROFESSOR GRENE:

I think this bears on my uneasiness with Dr. Chance, if I may come back to that point about your presentation. Most people would say this woman was *better* adapted afterward, because she could go home and cook the dinner and not worry, yet this seems to me to be one of many cases which show that our superior intelligence, our ability to direct our attention out of immediate relation to our drives . . . I might even put this in existential terms: the negativity which separates us from the world, the gap between ourselves and the ordinary biological ongoings even in ourselves, these are not just a question of adaptation. It makes us very maladapted, as it did in this woman's case when she was ill, but it's what makes us human and we want to keep it; we don't want to get rid of it. That's why you're dissatisfied with this kind of therapy. So these concepts of adaptation and preadaptation simply are not congruent to the problem with which we are trying to deal.

DR. CHANCE:

Well, they are only congruent to the mode of phylogenetic origin.

PROFESSOR GRENE:

Perhaps. But then I would want to quote Professor Plessner, a statement of his in the little book, *Vom Lachen und Weinen*. I don't know quite how to translate this: *"Um zu begreifen, wie etwas wird, muss man aber erst begriffen haben, was es werden soll"* (Plessner, 1961, p. 25). And I think we haven't yet described clearly enough what the human level is, so we just mix things by trying to ask about phylogeny before we've worked out what levels we are talking about.

DR. STRAUS:

These days the astronauts are up in outer space, and it seems to me rather difficult to consider this adventure and accomplishment as an adaptation. Adaptation means to respect the given in nature and, so to speak, creep into the bed which nature has made for the individual. But man just steps *out* of the situation which has bound him to the moment and the environment where adaptation would be possible. For instance, besides the fact that it demands an active process to achieve it, the adaptation of temperature control, which is linked to that of homeostasis, guarantees to the warm-blooded animals *the possibility to act.* It makes them to a great extent independent of the variations of temperature on the outside, and therefore they are able to go on. So homeostasis, if we take temperature control as the model, as I think one can do, does not really take us down to the lowest level (which is the Freudian idea involving the discharge of energy, or Kinsey's outlets and so on), but it guarantees the possibility of acting. And I think the human situation is to increase tensions, to be curious, to look for things, to go to France; not to be satisfied just with the local environment.

PROFESSOR POLANYI:

This situation fits in with the fact that we have a sociology which identifies moral demands with conformity at a time when the only moral principle which is effective in our civilization is nonconformity, which is very odd. But in any case, this is obviously a way of reducing something, so that by its explanation we destroy its meaning.

DR. CHANCE:

But is there actually any contention about the question of adaptation? It is true, of course, that I introduced this line of argument because I was trying to find how such a situation could have come about.

DR. STRAUS:

But this evolving may mean two different things. I think many biologists have a tendency to say: whatever his present condition, man was something like a monkey; therefore, look at the monkey, and we will understand man. We have to bring back his past. The other way is to try to understand how the past developed into something *new,* which first has to be understood in its own right, and then perhaps we will be able to relate the present backwards.

PROFESSOR GRENE:

So that it may be, using ourselves as a model, we try to understand the monkey?

DR. STRAUS:

No, using man as a model, we don't do that. But we could try to understand Homo sapiens (if that is still a permissible term) to try to see the world in which Rhesus macaque lives. We have to bring the monkey with his world into our world. We have to see *his* environment as a structural relation to him in our own world and environment. And therefore, I think in some way, we must *know* our environment in a way that is not merely reacting to stimuli in order to survive.

PROFESSOR TANSEY:

In other words, man has the power to *change* his environment, to guide his own adaptation to it, and he is continually doing just that. Thus, for example, in the technological revolution, we change, we really change the shape of the world; we guide our own adaptation.

PROFESSOR WIGNER:

I wonder if the word "adaptation" isn't used in a twofold sense. It is clear that we adapt always to surroundings, but the usual meaning of the word is that the purpose of the adaptation to the surroundings is the survival of ourselves and our progeny. Now there also may be adaptations to surroundings to satisfy other desires, such as curiosity, understanding, and what are usually called the higher purposes of life. That I think eliminates some of this paradox which was alluded to.

PROFESSOR POLANYI:

No, we cannot formulate the decision of Socrates to remain in prison and die as an adaptation. It just doesn't work.

PROFESSOR WIGNER:

Of course, you protest against the use of the word "adaptation," and you may be right. But what I'm trying to say is that man has desires which are not directly connected with his survival and the survival of his progeny. And natural selection, or *some* other development, enabled him to satisfy these other desires also. Man doesn't live by bread alone, so to speak, not even if we add the bread of his progeny.

DR. STRAUS:

I would like to propose one example of, let us say, human thinking. This is geometrical demonstration and proof. We start from the proposition, and then we go into a series of further statements and end with the theorems, with what was to be demonstrated. This is a sequence in time, and we may allow it to be a very long sequence in time, but we understand that these propositions, the first, second, whatever propositions we used, have no temporal difference. The final proof is not later in time than the first proposition, and so with the intermediary steps. I think this is one of the human possibilities: while acting, moving, perceiving in time, we can see relations which are not *temporal* sequences, but, as in this case of geometrical proof, *logical* sequences. Though not completely logical sequences, because supposedly at least one of the things I'm working with is already familiar to me. And there is, perhaps, in the abstract demonstration of mathematics, some kind of personal involvement. But there are certainly two temporal orders: the sequence printed in a book, which is no temporal sequence, and the procedure of our understanding. Of course, the mathematical demonstration is only *one* example of what we *are* doing on the human level. Such a procedure cannot be described on the "survival" level.

PROFESSOR TAYLOR:

Let me come to Dr. Chance's defense. I think what is to be learned from lower levels of behavior is much more than some people have said. I want to give a view of this, see why it is so, and see what Dr. Chance and other people think about it. There are certain human behavior patterns and capacities which are obviously closely parallel to those of animals, and the higher we go in the animal kingdom, the more parallels we develop. But this itself is the question: which patterns are and which are not parallel? Some *obviously* are. Now one of the basic differences we first notice between ourselves and the animals, who lack the specifically human desires, arises from the fact that men are always thinking about what the object of a particular desire is. You find in different human beings, in different cultures, different conceptions of what the goal is, and therefore different ways of working out the desire. For example, in man there is an immense number of ways in which sexual desire is worked out, whereas in a given animal species the approach is relatively monotonous. But there's of course a reflection in human beings about which is the right way, or the best way, to fulfill a particular desire. However, we can learn something from the animals, though not in the simple-minded reductionist sense that since it all started there they must have the right answer. We might think, if we didn't look at animals, that a great deal of social behavior in man is something which rises at a specifically human level. In the 17th century people thought society rested on some kind of clever ideal that someone had thought up to make us healthier, happier, saying, "Let's all get together and sign a social contract." But this misses the psychological depth of the social instinct in man completely. You rapidly get over this illusion when you look at the social instinct in animals. We can learn by comparing animal behavior and human behavior a great deal about what really *is* specifically human. We can also learn a great deal by looking at all this in the light of adaptation, because it helps us to understand the phenomenon itself, to know and to see it as something which has arisen. Therefore, I don't think we can dispense with this level of understanding until we have seen what the phenomenon is *in itself*. For we are almost bound to get it wrong if we don't look at a wider range of behavior.

DR. CHANCE:

I agree. There is a whole realm of information that comes from this kind of study which I think, frankly, is going to make an immense difference. There are, for example, certain habits which operate in almost every group of people. I haven't fully demonstrated this, but as soon as I mention it to psychologists they say, "Oh, yes, that happens all the time." These habits are what I call *cut-off acts*. That is to say, if you're in a conflict which you can't resolve, one thing that is happening, and one reason why you can't resolve it, is that your arousal seems to be going on and on, so your attention is fixed on the conflict more and more. But you can get out of it if you drop your arousal. An easy solution is not to be involved in this problem any more at all. But the stimulus, the problem, contains both information content *and* arousal content. So if you turn away from the problem in order to get rid of the arousal content, you also give up the information content. Birds do this in courtship, because they first meet their partners as intruders in their own territory. Whether it's male or female, the first reaction is always that it is an intruder. So they are antagonistic, let's say flight motivated, at first. The courtship procedure is partly a device to drop the antagonistic arousal so that feelings of mating can come to the fore. This is now known: courtship behavior is not only fluffing up the beautifully colored feathers at the opposite sex to attract them; it's trying not to run away from them and not to be aggressive to them.

PROFESSOR POLANYI:

I'm also very keen on tracing back the higher functions of imagination and creativity to experimental responses of animals. I have done so, or tried to do so. I think that the emotional involvement of the discoverer, of the person who is involved in a problem —that indispensable emotional involvement can only be understood in a physiological way, in so far as its roots are concerned. This, I'm sure, is in harmony with what Dr. Chance has given us and suggested to us. We should try to make this line go back as far as possible in the phylogenetic laboratories of men. But I do think there is something which must appear to us from the beginning as different from what he has represented in using the term "adaptation." May I put it a little paradoxically: I wouldn't be surprised if the time came in which we would acknowledge that development (phylogenetic development) has taken place, and then the problem would be how to adapt oneself to the fact of that development. This certainly corresponds more closely to what we human beings are concerned with in our lives, our most important form of existence. But I don't really think we have an adequate understanding of the descent of man, and therefore the particular idiom in which we now talk about it naturally leads to paradoxes and objections on the part of those who want to emphasize that we really *don't* know how this thing came about nor how much an adaptation is evolutionary rather than controlling evolution.

DR. CHANCE:

You made a point about this in a discussion with me before; you thought that adaptation, or rather that evolution in our sense, was merely the elimination of incapacities rather than the selection of specific adaptations.

PROFESSOR GRENE:

That's the right side of Russell's chart: it's the elimination of undesirables which leaves the specialized, highly adapted alternative. But what is he saying in the left-hand side? Just that where you have phylogenetically what Professor Pantin calls emergent properties, where you have something new arriving, there is flexibility. That is, there has to be the material available. The fish that started to develop lungs from his air sac and make himself into some kind of hydromechanic system had to have the genetic material available for that to happen. And that's all the left hand says. It still doesn't give any account of how it happened. I would agree with Professor Polanyi that it is a mystery, and if you call this left-hand side "selection," you're just stretching a word. Then you make some sort of anthropomorphic statements, the way, for instance, Simpson does: no matter how little we can see in the difference that happens over a million years in such and such a situation, "selection sees much more." Well, what *is* this selection? Let's just compare the structures that are involved and not pretend that we know much more about what it is.

DR. CHANCE:

I feel that this combinatorial element has been left out of your criticism of the idea of combinatorial selection, where one has a number of different aspects of the species, or of a population, being adapted to a number of different niches and, at the same time, all breeding back into a single population.

PROFESSOR GRENE:

This is just saying that you have to have a good deal of variability, if you like, "preadaptation," but I don't see the advantage of calling "preadaptation" adaptation. Why not just say, "there must be something there out of which the emergent property can emerge?" To say it's a preadaptation is either to sneak in some kind of a mysterious end, such as the selectionists won't admit, or just not to say anything except that obviously the conditions must be available. It's not an explanation.

PROFESSOR SILBER:

I think, in connection with that point, it would be worth while to notice the argument put forward by L. Whyte in order to direct schematic attention to internal factors in evolution. He has stated many of the logical properties necessary to that theory of evolution, and he is pointing out elements on the left-hand column of Russell's chart, in a way that is not finalistic, but in a way that talks about a selection that is not predicated upon external conditions in the world . . .

PROFESSOR GRENE:

I wouldn't be objecting to it even if it were finalistic, if it were *admitted* that it is finalistic, but it's pretending not to be finalistic . . .

DR. CHANCE:

I want to relate a remark made by Taylor to the idea of the attention structure: why is it that we can learn so much from animal prototypes? Because their attention is constantly fixated in a number of predetermined ways. Now, it is undoubtedly true that we pass through phases in the ontogeny of our lives in which we *do* have very similar fixations. We recognize at any rate that our direction of development is toward broadening our ability to pay attention both to a wider and wider field of awareness and to various aspects of that wider field. This is why I was excited when I discovered that this analysis based on drives was ultimately more simply described and, in fact, *was* an analysis of the attention structure.

PROFESSOR GRENE:

Then let's call it that, rather than an analysis of changing "adaptations."

[*Levels of reality:* A pervasive problem which arises in connection with almost all our discussion is that of explanation in terms of hierarchies of structure as against a single principle of physicochemical explanation. A somewhat different version of this problem arose in connection with Dr. Chance's paper, that is, the problem of the relation of the concept of adaptation as an explanatory principle to that of organizational levels in biology. A statement made by Professor Polanyi about his approach to this general problem may help to clarify some of the issues involved.]

PROFESSOR POLANYI:

Professor Pols[1] has introduced, though in rather different language from mine, a conception of levels of reality which seems to me fundamental to the problems we are discussing. I think it would help us if I introduce here a statement of my own on this matter, since it relates this problem to what I said earlier about tacit knowing, and it also bears on the problems raised in the papers which deal with biological topics.

I want to talk briefly about what I call "the principle of boundary control." Behaviorists and other reductivist thinkers ask: Is not the material substance of all higher entities governed throughout by the laws of inanimate matter? Does it not follow, then, that it must be possible to represent all their workings in terms of these laws? Yes, this would follow. If I claim that these higher entities are irreducible, I must show that they are governed in part by principles beyond the scope of physics and chemistry. I shall do so. I shall show first that a number of different principles can control a comprehensive entity at different levels; I have repeatedly presented

[1] For the topic of Professor Pols's paper, see the Introduction, p. 4, and the Program for the 1965 meeting of the Study Group, p. 4.

this theory in more particular terms. It will be developed here on general lines.

There exist principles that apply to a variety of circumstances. They can be laws of nature, like the laws of mechanics; or principles of operation, like those of psychology, as for example those controlling muscular contraction and coordination; or they can be principles laid down for the use of artifacts, like the vocabulary of the English language or the rules of chess. Not all important principles have such wide scope; but I need not go into this, for it is enough to have pointed out that some principles exist that do.

We can go on to note, then, that such a principle is necessarily compatible with any restriction we may choose to impose on the situations to which it is to apply; it leaves wide open the conditions under which it can be made to operate. Consequently, these conditions lie beyond the control of our principle and may be said to form its boundaries, or more precisely, its *boundary conditions*. The term "boundary conditions"—borrowed from physics—will be used here in this sense.

Next, we recognize that in certain cases the boundary conditions of a principle are in fact subject to control by other principles. These I will call higher principles. Thus the boundary conditions of the laws of mechanics may be controlled by the operational principles which define a machine; the boundary conditions of muscular action may be controlled by a pattern of purposive behavior, like that of going for a walk; the boundary conditions of a vocabulary are usually controlled by the rules of grammar, and the conditions left open by the rules of chess are controlled by the stratagems of the players. And so we find that machines, purposive actions, grammatical sentences and games of chess are all entities subject to *dual control*.

Such is the stratified structure of comprehensive entities. They embody a combination of two principles, a higher and a lower. Smash up a machine, utter words at random, or make chess moves without a purpose, and the corresponding higher principles—that which constitutes the machine, that which makes words into sentences, and that which makes moves of chess into a game—will all vanish, and the comprehensive entity which they controlled will cease to exist.

But the lower principles, the boundary conditions of which the now effaced higher principles had controlled, remain in operation. The laws of mechanics, the vocabulary sanctioned by the dictionary, the rules of chess, will all continue to apply as before. Hence no description of a comprehensive entity in the light of its lower principles can ever reveal the operation of its higher principles. *The higher principles which characterize a comprehensive entity cannot be defined in terms of the laws that apply to its parts in themselves.*

On the other hand, a machine does rely for its working on the laws of mechanics; a purposive motoric action, like going for a walk, relies on the operations of the muscular system which it directs; and so on. The operations of higher principles rely quite generally on the action of the laws governing lower levels.

Yet, since the laws of the lower level will go on operating, whether the higher principles continue to be in working order or not, the action of the lower laws may well disrupt the working of the higher principles and destroy the comprehensive entity controlled by them.

Such is the mechanism of a two-leveled comprehensive entity. Let me show now that the two-leveled logic of tacit knowing performs exactly what is needed for understanding this mechanism.

Tacit knowing integrates the particulars of a comprehensive entity and makes us see them forming the entity. This integration recognizes the higher principle at work on the boundary conditions left open by the lower principle, by mentally performing the workings of the higher principle. It thus brings about the *functional structure* of tacit knowing. It also makes clear to us how the comprehensive entity works: it reveals the meaning of its parts. We have here the *semantic aspect* of tacit knowing. And since a comprehensive entity is controlled as a whole by a higher principle than the one which controls its isolated parts, the entity will look different from an aggregate of its parts. Its higher principle will endow it with a stability and power appearing in its shape and motions and usually produce also additional novel features. We have here the *phenomenal aspect* of tacit knowing.

And finally, we are presented also with an ontological counterpart of the logical disintegration caused by switching our attention from the integrating center of a comprehensive entity to its particulars. To turn our attention from the actions of the higher principle, which defines the two-leveled entity, and direct it to the lower principle controlling the isolated parts of the entity, is to lose sight of the higher principle and indeed of the whole entity controlled by it. Thus the logical structure of tacit knowing covers in every detail the ontological structure of a combined pair of levels. In the so-called "mechanistic" tradition it was argued (at least I suppose this must have been the argument) that since a machine works without interfering with the laws of physics and chemistry, it must be determined by the laws of physics and chemistry. However, it is not so determined. Laws of physics and chemistry leave open, just as Professor Wigner mentioned, the boundary conditions, the initial conditions of their setting. And this is precisely the area over which control is exercised by another principle. Now perhaps one could say that the structure of a machine and the working of a machine are not to be defined as a principle in the same sense in which you would admit that the control of the moves in the game of chess constitute a principle in conducting the game. But I think it must be so recognized because, for the game as for the machine, one can define this principle in very general terms. This is always done if you want to take out a patent on a machine. You must define the principles of the machine which you are patenting, irrespective of its physical and chemical composition. Besides that, it is not physics and chemistry which constitute this principle—you can recognize this by the fact that it invariably and necessarily involves a purpose. I had an amusing experience illustrating this point: I defined a watch and said that it is defined by a mainspring which uncoils under the control of a hairspring and a balance. Now since then I have bought a watch in which there is no mainspring—the movement is electric; and then I saw a watch in which there is no balance. The only thing it still does is to show the time. A watch that doesn't tell the time, of course, can never be a watch. So you see this is very essential to it—it is constituted by a purpose and a very limited one; it is only human interest which keeps it alive. So it cannot by any stretch of the imagination be derived from the laws of physics and chemistry. And therefore I would maintain that this general fallacy should be corrected, that one should cease to talk about mechanisms as being explanations in terms of physics and chemistry. In which case, however, the whole discussion about organismic and mechanistic explanation turns out to have been misplaced, because it is no more difficult to explain nonphysical and chemical principles which produce a mechanism than nonphysical and chemical principles which operate organismically. So, as you see, it changes the perspective, and it's quite essential. Therefore I insist on having this structure of the boundary control, because without it I think that the confusion would be perpetuated and the situation hopeless. Whereas if we do accept it, we can build up hierarchies which lead us from the meaningless atomic topography—from the Laplacean vision, which is then overcome—to an increasingly meaningful range of living biological functions leading right up to that of consciousness.

Now let me introduce, further, a particular application of this principle—its application to the mind-body relation. The question is whether the functioning of living beings and of their consciousness is in fact stratified. Is it subject to the joint control of different principles working at consecutive levels? Now, to begin with, the laws of physics and chemistry do not ascribe consciousness to any process controlled by them; the presence of consciousness proves, therefore, that principles other than those of inanimate matter participate in the conscious operations of living things.

There are two other fundamental principles of biology which are beyond the scope of physics and chemistry. The structure and functioning of an organism are determined, like that of a machine, by constructional and operational principles which control boundary conditions left open by physics and chemistry. We may call this a *structural principle*, lying beyond the realm of physics and chemistry. Other functions of the organism not covered by physics and chemistry are exemplified by the working of the morphogenic field. Its principles are expressed most clearly by C. H. Waddington's "epigenetic landscapes." These show that the development of the embryo is controlled by the gradient of potential shapes, in the way the motion of a heavy body is controlled by the gradient of potential energy (see Waddington, 1957, p. 167). We may call this principle an *organizing field* or speak of it as an *organismic principle*.

Most biologists would declare that both the principle of structure and of organizing fields will be reduced one day to the laws of physics and chemistry. But I am unable to discover the grounds—or even understand the meaning—of such assurances, and hence I will disregard them and recognize these two principles as actually used in biology today.

Living beings consist in a hierarchy of levels, each level having its own structural and organismic principles. On the mental level, explicit inferences represent the operations of fixed mental structures, while in tacit knowing we meet the integrating powers of the mind. In all our conscious thoughts these two modes mutually rely on each other, and it is plausible to assume that explicit mental operations are based on fixed neural networks, while tacit integrations are grounded mainly in organizing fields. I shall assume also that these two principles are interwoven in the body, as their counterparts are in thought.

I shall now proceed to explain the relation between body and mind as an instance of the relation between the subsidiary and the focal in tacit knowledge—the distinction which I introduced in the discussion of my paper. The fact that any subsidiary element loses its meaning when we focus our attention on it explains the fact that, when examining the body in conscious action, we meet no traces of consciousness in its organs. We are now ready to complete this project.

We have seen that we can know another person's mind by dwelling in his physiognomy and behavior; we lose sight of his mind only when we focus our attention on these bodily workings and thus convert them into mere objects. But a neurophysiologist, observing the events that take place in the eyes and brain of a seeing man, would invariably fail to see in these neural events what the man himself sees by them. We must ask why the neurologist cannot dwell in these bodily events, as he could in the subject's physiognomy or intelligent behavior.

We may notice that the latter kind of indwelling, for which we appear to be equipped by nature, enables us to read only *tacit* thoughts of another mind: thoughts and feelings of the kind that we may suitably ascribe to organismic processes in the nervous system. We can get to know the *explicit* thoughts of a person—which correspond to anatomically fixed functions of the nervous system—only from the person's verbal utterances. The meaning of such utterances is artificial; though ultimately based on demonstrations pointing at tacit experiences, such utterances have no direct appeal to the native mind. The facility for indwelling can be seen to vary also when prehistoric sites, unperceived from the ground, are discerned from the air. Our incapacity for experiencing the neural processes of another person in the manner he experiences them himself may be aligned with these gradual variations of indwelling.

We arrive thus at the following outline. Our capacity of conducting and experiencing the conscious operations of our body, including that of our nervous system, lies in the fact that we fully dwell in them. No one but ourselves can dwell in our body directly and know fully all its conscious operations; but our consciousness can be experienced also by others to the extent to which they can dwell in the external workings of our mind from outside. They can do this fairly effectively for many tacit workings of our mind by dwelling in our physiognomy and behavior; such powers of indwelling are fundamentally innate in us. By contrast, our explicit thoughts can be known to others only by dwelling in our pronouncements, the making and understanding of which are founded on artificial conventions. Objectivization, whether of another person's gestures or of his utterances, cancels our dwelling in them, destroys their meaning, and cuts off communication through them. The nervous system, as observed by the neurophysiologist, is always objectivized and can convey its meaning to the observer only indirectly, by pointing at behavior or at reports that we understand by indwelling.

The logic of tacit knowing and the ontological principles of stratified entities were derived here independently of each other, and we found that our tacit logic enables us to understand stratified entities. It shows us then that the higher principle of a stratified entity can be apprehended only by our dwelling in the boundary conditions of a lower principle on which the higher principle operates. Such indwelling is logically incompatible with fixing our attention on the laws governing the lower level. Applied to mind and body, as to two strata in which the higher principles of the mind rely for their operations on the lower principles of physiology, we arrive at three conclusions:

1. No observations of physiology can make us apprehend the operations of the mind. Both the mechanisms and organismic processes of physiology will ever be found to work insentiently.

2. At the same time, the operations of the mind will never be found to interfere with the principles of physiology nor with the even lower principles of physics and chemistry on which they rely.

3. But as the operations of the mind rely on the services of lower

bodily principles, the mind can be disturbed by adverse changes in the body or be offered new opportunities by favorable changes of its bodily basis.

PROFESSOR POTEAT:

You've suggested that if we violate the controlling principle of a comprehensive entity, we destroy the comprehensive entity, but the laws governing the particulars in themselves continue to hold. Now I wonder about the application of this which you have just made to the mind-body problem. Does this application put you in the position of having to claim that the alleged existence of psychosomatic illness, or psychogenetic illness, is ungrounded or that we misunderstand what this is?

PROFESSOR POLANYI:

If I may say so, even more fundamental questions arise—whether the mind can control the body, what does that mean? Perhaps the answer is still that the psychosomatic phenomena are a comparatively small corner of the fact that the mind *is* in control of the body; I mean, this is the big thing. And what I have derived from what I have here communicated is that if the mind (as I believe) is in control of the body, it does not, thereby, interfere with any laws of physics and chemistry.

PROFESSOR POTEAT:

Does it interfere with any laws of biology?

PROFESSOR POLANYI:

No, it interferes with none of the laws of lower levels.

PROFESSOR POTEAT:

For example, the integrity of the organic structure, or a part of an organic structure, cannot be invaded by the action of the mind.

PROFESSOR POLANYI:

I think that is true, yes. I see your problem, and I agree it is a difficulty.

[Unidentified speaker]:

Is the definition of the boundary given in terms of the higher principles or in terms of the phenomena embodied by the lower principles?

PROFESSOR POLANYI:

The particular boundary which any particular higher principle controls cannot be identified except in terms of that principle. If you ask yourself, what are the boundary conditions (if I may use that term, after all) for the conduct of a game of chess, only if you *know* something about a game of chess can you identify what the limitations are which are imposed on moving chessmen on the board in playing a game of chess. And similarly, you can't say, in general, what kind of limitations a machine imposes, what kind of boundary conditions it controls, unless you know what it is you are controlling. But I do think that what Professor Poteat has said shows that there is a complication here. So far as I'm concerned, I can't answer your question. It is something which is different, you see, from the ordinary physiological behavior of the organism which I have so far sketched.

PROFESSOR HAAS:

One thing that disturbs me: as soon as you speak of mental phenomena, we seem to be asked to assign them separate status as a new kind of entity.

PROFESSOR GRENE:

No, I don't think that's implied. Do you mean to imply that mind is a separate entity?

PROFESSOR POLANYI:

No. I think I know what Professor Haas means. The ontological principle, I think, appears in his conception of it in a somewhat different light from what I attribute to it. The point is this: I am sure we both agree that games of chess exist, that books exist, that human beings exist. Whether you then regard this as a level of reality, as I would prefer to do, is really a matter of terminology. That it has an ontological claim I don't think you are inclined to deny; certainly it seems to be manifest.

PROFESSOR HAAS:

I accept the whole logic of boundary conditions, levels, and so on. Only then, somehow, you claim we have reached a different kind of stuff; that we have on the one hand the body, which is governed by one kind of principle; and on the other hand, there is a new kind of entity emerging—not just a control by principles which are added to principles of a lower level, all controlling the same kind of reality, but some kind of new entity emerging. I just don't understand what more is being said here . . .

PROFESSOR GRENE:

But we *have* emerged; here we are!

PROFESSOR POLANYI:

You have defined the situation correctly. It's a dual control, and thereby arise entities like you and me and all the rest of us . . .

PROFESSOR GRENE:

I think the difficulty arises when one talks about mind *and* body. There are levels which are governed by physical laws *and* biological laws *and* psychological laws; but that there are separate things at each of these higher levels which have got cut off from the lower ones, this I don't think you want us to say.

PROFESSOR HAAS:

There is then just the same thing which is characterized in a number of ways?

PROFESSOR GRENE:

Yes, in a sense, but also it is involved in a number of levels of reality, even though as you get to a higher level you don't have new kinds of things that you can cut off from the lower ones. Or better, you do have new kinds of things, but they still depend on the lower levels; and it does *sound* as if one were denying this when one talks about "mind" as separate from "body."

PROFESSOR POLS:

Speaking of it as a new kind of "stuff" emerging is what is perhaps the difficulty. If you think of a new mode of *agency* or a new mode of acting, you emphasize an aspect that the notion "entity" is designed to bring out.

Bibliography

Plessner, H. (1961), *Vom Lachen und Weinen.* Bern & Munich: Francke.
Waddington, C. H. (1957), *The Strategy of the Genes.* London: Allen & Unwin.

PART IV

NEW APPROACHES TO PSYCHOLOGY

The exclusive reliance on mathematical physics as a model for science as such, which has exacerbated the foundations problems of all the biological sciences, has borne hardest of all, perhaps, on the science of psychology. It is especially important, therefore, that the Study Group should concern itself with the problem of reductionism and its alternatives in the behavioral sciences. The 1965 meeting included two papers which approached the problem from very different points of view. Dr. Erwin Straus showed us, both in his paper and in his contribution to the discussions throughout the week, how fruitful the phenomenological approach can prove itself in dealing with psychological issues. Dr. Sigmund Koch consolidated his opposition to behaviorism in a paper which suggested ways for handling, more adequately than experimental psychology has so far been able to do, the vast area of human behavior inaccessible to the techniques of classical motivation theory or to the experiments devised under its auspices.

8

EMBODIMENT AND EXCARNATION

ERWIN W. STRAUS

The material for this study was obtained as a by-product of experiments arranged with the intention of refuting the "reflex theory" of action. I use this term as a collective name for a variety of schools unified by an "article of common faith," as Lashley called it. This "article of faith," presented some years ago to the participants of the Hixon Symposium, stated that "all phenomena of behavior and mind will ultimately become describable in terms of the mathematical and physical sciences." Lashley's credo required as a scholium the thesis that all experience and behavior can and must be reduced to the "underlying neural processes." If a tender-minded fellow should so desire, he may add, to the otherwise complete physiological account, the fiction of some data of consciousness coordinated with the actual cerebral events. Whether he does or not is of no consequence; for the theory limits consciousness, in all circumstances, to the role of a detached observer who only registers in the strange code of sensa the events occurring in the nervous system with which consciousness is connected and disconnected at the same time.

Yet the scientists who boast that they "have perfectly succeeded in developing a coherent science based on behavior, taking no account of consciousness," act in a strange self-forgetfulness. They ignore the elementary fact that any science—coherent or not—is founded in the conscious knowledge of the scientist himself and that in their own case that knowledge had to be acquired through observations in which an observer, reaching beyond himself, was concerned with an observable object. Grotesquely unaware of their own situation, many scientists replace intentionality completely by causality; objects are identified with stimuli; the reflex schema rules tyrannically over the interpretation of purposeful action.

Since afferent and efferent impulses and their synaptic links are located within the nervous system, since the experiencing organism supposedly had no direct relation to an object qua object, "it follows," to quote William James, "that voluntary movements must be secondary, not primary functions of our organisms." A few lines later James added, "But if, in voluntary action properly so called, the act must be foreseen, it follows that no creature not endowed with prophetic power can perform an act voluntarily for the first time" (James, 1890, Chapter 25). Phrases like "it follows . . . this act must . . . no creature can perform"—this whole terminology clearly indicates that James's interpretation of the will was not based on observation of human conduct. At the time when James wrote *The Principles,* he was still spellbound by the Western tradition with its radical contempt for sensory experience, its ontological destruction of the *Lebenswelt.* In James's vocabulary the term "experience" does not refer to a creature which, in seeing, hearing, touching, acts upon and reacts to things encountered in its environment. "Experience" is understood as a completely passive process, a change suffered by an organism under the impact of stimuli: "The nerve centers are so organized that certain stimuli pull the trigger of certain explosive parts; and a creature going through one of these explosions for the first time undergoes an entirely novel experience." Of course if the intentional relation to visible objects is replaced by the effect of invisible optical stimuli, then no field of action can be retained. An output—to be sure—cannot act upon an input. Action is directed forward, or more appropriately: in my action I am directed forward, toward something which I encounter, something which I can approach, put my hands on, or leave alone. With the same stroke of reduction which forecloses the field of action, the whole area of observation, description, experimentation, measurement, demonstration, communication has been sacrificed. Experience is not a specious shadow, a sham product of physiological events (see Straus, 1956, especially Part 3).

Through sensory experience an authentic relation is opened for experiencing beings, a relation to the everyday life world, the common domicile for all of us: young and old, men and women, laymen and scientists.

Since it had been my intention to vindicate the *Lebenswelt* and to reveal its unwritten constitution, I decided to demonstrate (contrary to James's pontifical dictum) that anyone can "perform an act voluntarily for the first time." If these experiments should prove successful—as they actually did—the situation would be completely inverted in its logical sequence. From certain premises James had reached an apodictic conclusion. Yet the conclusion was not confirmed by observation; indeed the opposite was found true. Therefore, if James's syllogism was correct from the point of view of formal logic, if the conclusion followed the premises with necessity, the refutation of the conclusion compellingly invalidated the premises.[1]

It was during these experiments that, while watching the subjects and studying the film records, we realized that we had received, as a bargain, precious protocols of the expression of thinking. I shall now describe the setting of the experiments and comment on the findings.

During the first period of the experiments we placed the subjects with their backs to a blackboard, put a piece of chalk in their left hands, and asked them to write without any optical control three capital letters: USA. Volunteers from all branches of the hospital staff served as our subjects. Among them not a single one had been known for prophetic powers; but all of them, without exception, were able to comply with the assignment. Their performance required a completely new set of movements, containing more than a single addition to the repertoire of learned skills. This type of writing, with the left arm and hand, was in sharp contrast to the accustomed procedure, acquired in early youth and fortified many thousand times throughout later years. Yet all the well-established circuits and feedback systems did not interfere with the new mode of writing, which is strongly at variance, not only with habitual movements, but also with the typical organization of stimuli. In writing everyone is used to seeing his hand, the pen, the pad, and finally the script. Our subjects did not see any of these, but there was no lack of optical stimuli, because the subjects had to face an open

[1] *The Principles of Psychology* was published more than 70 years ago. Nevertheless, I consider James as a contemporary thinker rather than a historical figure. The charming terms, input and output, widely used by many physiologists and psychologists today, leave no doubt that they all still share James's interpretation of will and action.

room flooded with light, necessary for filming (see Straus, 1959).[2]

Neurologists like to repeat Wernicke's remark: "When once writing has been learned it is possible to write with the left hand, with either foot, or by moving the head while holding a pen between the teeth" (R. Brain, in Wilson, 1955, Vol. 3, Part 7). In search of an explanation, Russell Brain and others play with the idea of some sort of remote control of certain cortical areas, by the so-called graphic motor schemata, a hypothesis which, however, is physiologically absurd.

Wernicke and his many followers failed to acknowledge that a novice in the writing craft has to learn two lessons in one: he must familiarize himself with the graphic characters, the letters of the alphabet, and he has to acquire the skill of reproducing them. While the motor execution is usually trusted to the right hand and arm, the knowledge of the graphic characters is not limb connected. The spread of the ability to write, from the right hand to the left, to feet or mouth, is not due to a transfer of motor skills but is an unrehearsed application of the knowledge of letters. Any child of kindergarten age, still untutored in the art of writing, could draw with his big toe a line, a circle, in sand; he could perhaps even combine circle, or oval, and line forming the Greek letter ϕ, while the best scribe in Pennsylvania could not write the name of its old capitol in Greek letters had he not learned them beforehand.

Certainly, a transfer of graphic motor schemata would have been of little help to the participants in our experiments. The assemblage of movements required in their situation was in sharp contrast to all established habits. Indeed, not a single one among all our subjects attempted a motor solution of the assignment; no one started with tentative random movements. Not preoccupied with any theory, our subjects set out to work in the nonbracketed world of everyday life. There they all followed the same pattern; one could almost say all of them applied the same method in the true sense of the word. Their operation clearly passed through two phases: a preparatory phase of contemplation, where they stood almost motionless in open-eyed attention, followed by a quick and decided performance. Watching them at work, one would get the impression that their hands were gliding along a track laid beforehand in imagina-

[2] Films of these experiments were shown at the meeting.

tion. The letters were not a more or less accidental result of trial-and-error movements, but their motor actions were obviously directed by planned and anticipated production.

While all the subjects—more than 20 people participated in the first series—were able to perform such action the first time, not all were equally successful. Technical errors occurred; among the three letters USA the "S" was the one most frequently distorted. With some slight variations of the initial assignment, we easily demonstrated that such mistakes were due to an error in design and not in execution. We decided, therefore, further to divide the experiments into two groups, with the intention of either increasing the demands on unrehearsed motor performance without complicating the design, or making the task of designing more difficult without adding to the motor requirements. In this section we then discovered a true gold mine, providing rich material for the study of the expression of thinking.

In the second set of experiments, the subjects were seated behind a small table or on a high chair, directly facing the camera; in their left hands they held a small blackboard in horizontal position. They were instructed to write on the reverse side, removed from optical control, four digits so that the numbers would appear in normal position either to the photographer or to any other person in his place, when the blackboard was raised and turned toward him, or so that the numbers would be "in order" when the blackboard was raised toward the writer himself. In the first case the subjects had to start at the right margin of the blackboard and continue writing from right to left, drawing the figures as in mirror writing; the second assignment compelled them to start from the left, as usual, but to draw the numbers upside down. The film shows the subjects "deep in thought," eager to find a solution. When the subjects believed that they had discovered the right answer, then once again the motor execution would follow promptly. Due to the capricious shape of Arabic numerals, each figure required individual treatment, so that the whole procedure of writing four digits frequently ran in a staccato movement, alternating between designing and executing. In spite of the unrehearsed maneuver, the motor performance as such never created any difficulty or delay, nor was the procedure changed, accelerated or retarded, when the opaque blackboard was replaced by a sheet of transparent plastic.

The third set of experiments was even more difficult. No one ever succeeded with just one stroke of genius. We returned once again to the large blackboard, but this time we let the subjects face it. On the blackboard we drew a rectangle, subdivided into four rectangular fields. This diagram was supposed to represent in an outline a printer's case, which would permit a printer to set the letters for a four-page pamphlet. We assumed that the printer had at his disposal only small sheets of paper covering just one half of the case. Therefore, after having printed the first two pages, the printer would have to turn the sheet over in order to complete his job of printing before folding.[3] Our subjects were asked: (a) to indicate in the printer's case the location of each of the four pages; (b) to mark on each page the corner where one would start reading the text; (c) to draw in these corners the initial letters of a word (in capitals), indicating how these letters would appear to the printer.

In theory there are four possible solutions. We did not ask for more than one. Since the execution of these assignments did not require any unusual motor skills, some of our subjects were quick in allotting numbers to the pages, and just as fast in erasing them again, when they thought the matter over for a second or third time. In the two first tests (USA and numerals), designing, executing, and checking the results occurred in different positions. The subjects had to turn around or turn the little blackboard to check the results. In the third group of experiments the consequences of the first decision became immediately visible. Having selected one of the four fields as page one, the subject would quickly realize that—and how—he had tied his hands in advance. But instead of expanding these introductory remarks any longer, I will resume a discussion of these differences later, together with the description and analysis of the results.

Each individual experiment began with a prelude during which the subjects received their instructions. These instructions were not given like a recorded announcement; the subjects were told in a casual manner what we expected them to do. There was an interplay

[3] A printer actually proceeding in this manner might not stay in business for long. However, in formulating our problem we did not feel bound by the actual conditions of a print shop.

of questions and answers, a conversation during which the subjects would turn to the experimenter, face him, and often express their willingness to cooperate, opening up with a friendly, receptive smile. However, the moment the subjects had apprehended the assignment there was a sudden change of climate; they turned away from the observer, the smiling lips now closed tightly. The subject became a recluse, fitting for the situation. Although a dialogue is an excellent medium to present an argument, we feel pretty sure that even Plato did not write or dictate his dialogues in "dialoguing." The advantage of a written dialogue is that the poetical author, all by himself, puts words and cues into the mouths of his characters, presenting his own argument as a response to their arguments. Whether a theme is wide and ramified, or a problem is narrow and precisely formulated, the final solution must be solved and found in solitude. Our subjects could not withdraw into a private room; we all remained together in the same wide clearance of the laboratory. Just because we remained so closely together, their withdrawal was the more marked and significant. There was no break of diplomatic relations; their attitude was not hostile; social contacts were but temporarily suspended. The subjects withdrew from the social environment (*Mitwelt*); they also withdrew from their physical environment (*Umwelt*): they did not turn around and inspect the area selected for writing; in fact they would not focus their eyes on anything in their immediate neighborhood. We observed three quite typical attitudes: (a) while pondering how to produce the USA letters, standing with their backs turned to the large blackboard, the gaze was directed upward and sidewards to their right or left. Usually the direction of the gaze was diagonally opposed to the writing hand. (b) Seated and holding the little blackboard, each would stare at something without seeing it. While the gaze was directed forward, the eyes did not converge. The raised eyebrows and the furrowed brow emphasized the contrast between gaze and sight. (c) In contrast to the open-eyed attitude, subjects concerned with a solution of the second assignment—and especially of the third (the printer's case)—would lower their heads and close their eyes before starting the execution. These three basic attitudes were not mutually exclusive; the same subject might pass through a number of variations, which, we assume, were all variations of the same theme.

Since we had arranged the experiments and had given the instruction, we knew that our subjects were thinking, and we even knew what they "had in mind." Yet, when our films were shown without any forewarning of what to expect, the spectators nevertheless judged correctly that our actors were busy thinking. We are, therefore, perfectly justified in assuming that the expression of thinking is not due to an accidental acquisition of habits but that there is, that there must be, a meaningful relation between the act and the expression of thinking.

Our subjects were silent; their statuesque immobility sharply contrasted with their attentiveness. Obviously, they were directed toward something not to be found in their immediate neighborhood; they were not looking at something but for something not, or not yet, directly present. It is quite understandable that some of them closed their eyes, virtually removing themselves from the scene. We are accustomed to call absent-minded one who walks around deep in his thoughts, unaware of his environment; perhaps we may just as well call him absent-bodied, because he does not dwell in the actual here and now; he performs an "ekbasis."

To comply with their assignment the subjects had to start from the expected result and work their way back to the initial situation. They had to resign their own viewpoint and imagine how the letters would appear on the large or on the small blackboard to an observer facing them. The subjects had to visualize the laboratory not as they actually saw it, namely, from one point, in one direction, in perspective, under a certain visual angle, and in fragments, but as a whole, without perspective arrangements, comprising directions and counterdirections at once. A ground plan conceived in thinking is not copied from past experience, not computed from particular impressions, not achieved by elimination of details. To be sure, past experiences are used, but in radical transformation. A ground plan represents a room, a house, a street, as it is "per se," not as it is accessible to us. Things are not comprehended as actually seen at their particular places "over there" but in an unsubstantial weightless schematic order, permitting geometrical representations drawn to scale. In thinking, we break down the barriers of a concrete position, we comprehend the visible fragments as parts of a whole in its own right, but not from our particular viewpoint. In this whole, then, we can eventually mark our own position. When our subjects had completed the design, then they could return, as it were, to the driver's seat and resume the performance. But first they had to eject themselves and had to perform an ekbasis. This ekbasis is expressed in the position and gaze of thinking.

The last assignment was the most difficult, because of the amazing discrepancies between the initial stage and the final product. To give just one example: On the folded pamphlet, the text of page 1 begins at the left upper corner with the margin of the lines near to a sharp page edge; the pages 1 and 4 are separated by the inner pages 2 and 3; the first word of page 1 and the first word of page 4 are diagonally opposite to each other. In the printer's case, however, the pages 1 and 4 are on the same side of the fence; the text of page 1 begins next to the mid-line; there is full symmetry between pages 1 and 4. To reconcile the discrepancies, to bring the final and the initial stages in line, the participants had to use all the power of thinking at their disposal. It is not surprising, therefore, that the repertoire of expressive movements was considerably enlarged during the third assignment. In those experiments where higher demands on motor execution had been made, the unfamiliar exertion led to a total mobilization of the motorium. The actions of the performing hand and arm were accompanied by practically useless motions of the other limb, and by grimacing efforts of forehead, jaw, and tongue. While the assignment of the printer's case did not provoke such total mobilization, the frequently rash, but unsuccessful, attempts released signs of frustration and impatience until the subjects finally renounced their trust in a quick solution and consented to thoughtful deliberation.

In the last phase of our studies the subjects, confronted with the schema of the printer's case, not infrequently exhibited another characteristic attitude. After several futile attempts to solve the problem in a quick attack, they changed their tempo of action from an *allegro* to a *molto sustenuto*. While standing in front of the blackboard, they no longer looked at it; instead they closed their eyes, lowered their heads, and rested their chins in one hand—this supporting hand and forearm buttressed in turn at the elbow by the other hand which had crossed the mid-line. In short, they imitated —even while standing on their feet—the well-known attitude of *The Thinker,* a name almost too exclusively associated today with Rodin's well-known sculpture. Yet Rodin had had his forerunners in Michelangelo and other sculptors and painters, in the Occident as well as in the Orient. Here and over there the attitude presented is always the same: the thinker is seated, his trunk bent forward; the head is lowered and slightly turned to one side; the chin sunk into the cup of one hand which at the elbow has somehow found its support. The thinker gives the impression—in art and in nature—that in meditation upright posture cannot be freely sustained, that head and trunk have become too heavy a burden, demanding some support from outside. Even so, the attitude of Michelangelo's and Rodin's *Thinker* is quite different from that of Dürer's brooding *Melancholia*. The thinker is not oppressed, he does not succumb to gravity, he does not collapse under the burden of his own weight; he yields to a certain point; in sitting down he renounces upright posture, though not completely. While locomotion is arrested, the tightly closed lips, the furrowed brow, indicate that the thinker is active in his repose.

The expression of thinking is not found on Darwin's list of the "expression of emotions." Nevertheless, it belongs to the standard equipment of every stage actor and to the rank and file of expressions in daily life. The expression of thinking is a fact, but this fact presents a kind of anomaly: it does not fit into a conceptual system where expressions are interpreted—to put it rudely—as motions manifesting emotions. Within such a system the expressive motions are easily arranged together with the emotions in antithetical pairs like pleasure and pain, hope and despair. Thinking, however, has no single counterpart, not even in Roget's *Thesaurus*. The expression of thinking does not belong in the same category as the expressions of emotion. It is at variance with all the familiar attitudes.

We do not want to interpret the thinker's attitude as an outward sign somehow connected with some "inner events"; we do not consider him an individual in isolation; we do understand his attitude as a different mode of being-in-the-world, as the mien of someone who in his corporeality comports himself toward the world. The characteristic loss of tone, yielding as it were to "heft," becomes more conspicuous when we compare the position of the thinker with the erect position of a guard, or of a spectator watching a horse race through his binoculars, or of someone listening to an unusual noise. The counterexample to the thinker is probably reached with the comportment of a soldier who stands "at attention."

Etymology and metaphorical usage testify that language has

taken cognizance of the peculiar role and function of "heft" (weight) in the exercise of thinking and perceiving. We will follow language's example; but not content merely to state the fact that it is so, we will try to understand why it must be so.

Since yielding to heft follows rising against it, since the expression of thinking counters the upright attitude, since thinking follows sensory experience, I will call your attention first to some essential characters of sensory experience ignored as a rule in theoretical interpretation:

1. The film made of these experiments may serve as a starting point. Though its theme is a very special one, the film belongs to the well-known class of moving pictures, as they are seen every day by millions of people all over the globe. To see and to enjoy a film as such requires no special training; no effort is involved; nobody in a typical audience lays claim to an unusual accomplishment. The millions of movie-goers demonstrate—as through a gigantic experiment—that the capacity to see such pictures must be a character inherent in visual experience. Effortless in practice, it nevertheless strikes with wonder.

Calling a film a moving *picture,* we silently acknowledge that the actors seen are not present in person, that the laboratory in which they worked is not a part of the theatre. Yet we see the actors and see them with our own eyes. The *physiological* conditions that enable us to follow their performance do not, in principle, differ from our seeing the theatre, our neighbors, the screen itself before and after the show. The people on the screen were acting. There was a temporal sequence, a beginning and an end of their actions, but the time of their actions was not that of our own present. Still photos, like those printed in newspapers every day, also show something that happened somewhere else at some other time in the past. Obviously, when we recognize pictures as pictures, two temporal orders must be conjoined: one, our personal present and act of seeing; the other, the temporal order of things and actions seen. We witness past events as past, although we witness them in the present. From such observations we conclude that sensory experience has a polar structure: it comprises my own act of seeing and the things seen. In other words, sensory experience must not be identified with the appearance of sensa or images in consciousness, causally related to stimuli of some sort. In sensory experience I experience myself, embodied, in relation to things, not one without the other, not one before the other. In sensory experience we are affected; nevertheless, in and through sensory experience, we are directed to objects existing independent from us, but on the same plane together with us. The polar character of sensory experience is an indispensable, although by itself not yet a sufficient, condition that enables man to see pictures as pictures, i.e., to detach the effigy from the continuum of accessible space and actual time.

2. When I close my eyes this room disappears from my sight; when I open my eyes it reappears. The room itself reappears, not stimuli, sensa, or images. The room remains visible, lasting, enduring, indifferent to my acts of seeing. True, when I close my eyes the intensity of stimulation approximates zero; when I open my eyes its energy increases—though, of course, with another set of photons. Nevertheless, this disappearing and reappearing, related to my sight, does not mean that—in my experience—this room vanished into nothing and was recreated out of nothing. The room itself became visible again to me, who remained seated—incarnated—here in this field of gravity that harbors both the room and myself. This sequence of seeing now, seeing no longer, and seeing once more, is but one of the many manifestations of the experience of repetition. Whenever we see or do something for a second time, the first time must be past, yet if it were completely gone there could be no second time, no *re*currence. An interplay of continuity and discontinuity of clock time and historical or personal time characterizes all the variations of the theme "again," such as *re*peating, *re*hearsing, *re*turning.

On working days I leave my lodgings in the morning and return home at night. Coming back from my office in the hospital, I see my street and my house again. There it stands, well constructed, founded on solid ground. While I moved around, always carrying my "here" with me, the house did not change its position among its neighbors. My acts of seeing are repeated, in contrast to the visible things that last. It is not the act of seeing again which endows them with the character of stability; it is their stability together with my mobility which makes "seeing again" possible. Had I on my way home decided on a detour through streets never passed before, had I visited a friend and seen his house for the first time, all of this would not change the character of permanence of streets and houses.

My "seeing again" is not an unalloyed optical phenomenon; it is inserted in the history of my encounters with the world.

Whether I leave or return home, this house itself faces me, this building of red bricks. When I open the front door, enter the hall and rooms, I do not step into sensa, impressions, percepts projected outward. Although on my way through the house the vistas of its partitions follow each other in time, in my experience the rooms appear immobile, side by side. Walking through the house, garden, and street, I am *in* the world, moving in the embracing space of terra firma.

3. The film shown and seen could serve us once more as an example. But we may do better replacing the film with a live performance, say an opera. Up there is the stage with its dramatic action and down here the audience seeing and hearing the opera. The audience comprises a group of individuals; whether their number is small or large, each one sees and hears for himself, alone; nevertheless, all of them see and hear the same performance, together. The view is one, the actions of looking and listening are many. The view is "public" while the sights are "private." If I want to hear Miss Callas sing, I must go to the Metropolitan; I must attend the opera in person; no one else can replace me. Only if I obtain a ticket will I be admitted; a particular seat will be assigned to me. Prices differ greatly, because the spectacle presents itself in different perspectives; even from the best seat the view is never complete, never perfect. But in spite of all the variant perspectives, we in the audience attend one and the same performance. I need not consult my neighbors to make sure that they and I are witnessing the same spectacle. Just the opposite! "Intersubjectivity" is found in the polarity of sensory experience which opens to each one the world as the common ground of individual existence.

Although polarity characterizes sensory experience throughout, the balance between public and private, distance and nearness, between the experience of objects and that of my own bodily existence, varies with each modality. The trills and coloratura of Miss Callas's arias and the smell of popcorn munched by my neighbor—both are public, both affect me, though in different ways. If my neighbor annoys me by jabbing his elbow into my side in his outbursts of enthusiasm, this is an affair between him and me, exclusively; while the public character is confined, polarity still prevails. In the tactile sphere, activity and passivity, touching and being touched, are intimately related. Even in an active, gnostic, tactile exploration of things, the area is restricted to immediate contact. If the room becomes too hot, my attention shifts from things to my own body. My irritated throat, my attempt to suppress an attitude of coughing, is no longer a public event. It isolates me in my bodily existence from the community. Yet if I drop my program and my neighbor starts to pick it up, he thereby demonstrates that the two of us see one and the same thing, a thing heavy enough to fall to the floor and to be lifted from it.

4. It should be noted, however, that in passing the sheet of paper from his hand to mine, he also makes it plain that we see, touch, hold, and move that white *thing,* not the white *color*. Obviously this sheet of paper is an object accessible to various senses, yet it is not a "common sensible" in the Aristotelian sense: sight and touch do not perceive motion, rest, number, shape, and size indifferently. I am related to *one thing,* which presents itself in different modalities, though with characteristic differences. Among all the modalities, vision has a privileged status, a special kinship to permanence. The spoken word originates and perishes with the sound. One of the merits of writing is to transpose transient sounds into lasting letters and thereby to preserve the word. But this is not the place to analyze the spectrum of senses any further.

In everyday life the senses and sensory experiences are appreciated as one of the most precious gifts bestowed on man and animal. In everyday life we realize that with and through sensory experience we reach out far beyond the border of our own physical existence. Philosophy and science, however, have assigned the role of Cinderella to sensory experience. It has been discredited as deceptive, berated as purely subjective, denounced as a mere phantasma, censured as a multitude of confused ideas. Redundance has been turned into a deficiency.

Since the days of Democritus, sensory experience has been interpreted as a kind of ingestion. Through the eidolon theory Democritus tried to account for a correspondence between the perception of things and things perceived. Modern theory, following Galileo, has abandoned all attempts to establish such correspondence. In theory the receptors, stimulated by physical agents of some sort, conduct excitations to the cerebral centers, where supposedly some kind of magical transformations occur: (1) the purely physical event is transformed into sensa; (2) the sensa are assembled by experience into more or less permanent structures; and (3) this assemblage is finally "projected outward." Ultimately some correspondence between "inside" and "outside" is re-established, for the outward projected images remain—it seems—also "inside." *Credo quia absurdum.*

The theory, however, still requires one essential exception: it must not be applied to the scientist himself. The physiologist who examines and describes the brain of an octopus or the structure and function of the human retina is convinced that he sees the brain or the retina as they are and that they are as he sees and describes them.

Sensory experience is enigmatic, because of its transitive character, expressed in statements like "I see you" or "I just heard the bell ringing." How could it be that I, in my position here, could have access to something over there, register it here "within myself," and nevertheless leave it as it is, over there? Since theory cannot accept this paradox, it forces the phenomena into the smaller of the two Procrustean beds. The joker in this game is that science actually presupposes what it denies: the objectivity and validity of sensory experience.

I will try to "save the phenomena" in the sense of classical astronomy. If I want to save the phenomena I have to accept them as they present themselves. I will try therefore to explore sensory experience in its relation to man and animals as living creatures and thereby, after a long but unavoidable detour, return to the topic of weight and the lived body.

From here on I must proceed in seven-league boots:

A. 1. Sensory experience is a distinctive mark of living creatures. Only man and animals share the privilege; plants do not participate; therefore I will center my further discussion on man and "the beasts of the earth."

2. If we ask what is—in addition to vegetative functions like metabolism, growth, reproduction—the characteristic endowment of all the members of the animal kingdom, our answer is: motility.

3. Yet, we must not forget, or rather, we must be fully aware that the word motility is a global term, denoting three types of movement: (a) That which is related to vital functions (circulation, breathing) persisting through sleep. (b) Locomotion in the widest sense (including the motions of individual limbs), which is confined to the waking state. (c) Rising from the ground against gravity, which is also confined to the waking state.

4. While the mechanisms of standing (the myotatic reflexes, the "magnet" reaction, etc.) have been thoroughly explored in physiology, the philosophical implications of rising from the ground have been ignored almost completely. Yet rising from the ground is the prerequisite of all locomotion and also of sensory experience, as I am going to show. Rising from the ground is not just one type of locomotion; it first constitutes loci.

B. 1. In rising from the ground—pulling, as it were, all roots from the soil—men and animals conquer gravity, though not completely; we and they remain bound by it. The result is that the *zoon* establishes itself as an independent part, but as a part still belonging to the *totum*. The freedom gained in rising from the ground and, thereby, the emancipation from the environment, are not complete. The situation created by rising from the ground may be characterized as: belonging in opposition. (The German word *selbstständig* characterizes the situation well.) In rising from the ground a Lilliputian faces the universe. But it is from the vantage point of this position that I am able to visualize and comprehend the totality to which I belong. (To speak in the first person pronoun is unavoidable in this discussion.)

2. In getting up and constituting my "here" I find myself in opposition not only to the supporting ground but to the world in its totality. I will use the term "Allon" for this totality, which includes all other human beings and animals as partners (friendly or hostile). Rising against gravity establishes the I-Allon relation.

3. The position gained in getting up is an achievement of the individual organism as a whole. Not the individual cells and cell combinations, not even the individual organs like bones or muscles are upright, but only the organism as a whole. The I-Allon relation is of a *macroscopic* order (varying with the species); therefore it cannot be explored with analytical methods exclusively.

4. Rising against gravity, belonging in opposition, the motile animal body makes sensory experience possible and determines its structure.

C. 1. In rising against gravity I establish my "here" as the starting point for all my activities in the world, i.e., in terrestrial, gravity-dominated space.

2. I experience the Allon as an integral part of it and therefore from within; unlike Leibnizian monads, experiencing creatures do have windows; but even this is a misleading expression; for they do not stare through windows into external space.

3. The I-Allon relation is permanent, enduring, although in the actual situations, here-now, the *totum* is never explicitly given but only in temporal fragments. (The particulars, however, do not present primary, nonproblematic data.)

4. The I-Allon relation is a power relation. Standing "here" I place myself within the Allon over against it. I must maintain my position in continuous effort and vigilance, supported, but also threatened, by the ground from which I arose. Therefore awakeness, getting up, and sensory experience are closely related to each other.

5. Sensory experience, founded in the I-Allon relation, is not a compile of neutral information. Personally involved, we experience our own existence threatened or assured. Swinging between the poles of annihilation and preservation, sensory experience is permeated by physiognomic characters. The Allon appears dreadful or propitious. Since dread is coeval with the experience of the world, the struggle against the power of the Allon, the effort to gain security, to assuage dread, to appease the Allon never ends.

6. In getting up, in constituting my "here," I experience my own body as mine in an eminent sense. The body-subject is the possessor of all possible possessions. The precise meaning of the term "my" and "mine" varies, therefore, when these words are used in reference to my body or in relation to anything else that belongs to me.

7. Yet, since in opposing the Allon I remain a part of it, I may, nevertheless, perceive my own body as belonging to the Allon also. I hear my own voice, I see my own hand, I put down my foot, and last but not least I incorporate, with breathing and eating, parts of the Allon in my body. The body *I am* may also be experienced as the body *I have*.

8. In all this the senses serve me, not as instruments mounted on a mobile apparatus, which they start, break, and direct, but as organs. My eyes don't see, but I do (see) with their help. My gaze is directed from here to distant points over there. Yet the "here" itself is not seen; though an indispensable component of the act of seeing, it is not an optical datum but is established with my opposition to the Allon. In the century-long discussions about the "third dimension," the eye was considered as an instrument. The third dimension, however, is but one limited feature of the astounding fact that we are aware of the space which encompasses us—a fact understandable only within the I-Allon relation.

9. Sensory experience guides the individual organism in particular situations, serving the satisfaction of its needs and working for its self-preservation; things appear comforting or frightening, appealing or repulsive. From this pathic relation man—and man alone—can detach himself and consider things in their own right in a gnostic survey instead of tending toward or avoiding them; for the emancipation from the ground approaches its climax in man's upright posture. Animals move in the direction of their digestive axis. Their jaws, snouts, trunks, beaks, are placed in the "visor line"; bite is subordinated to sight. The interest of animals is limited to the proximate; their attention is caught and held by that which is within the confines of reaching or approaching. Man in upright posture does not move in the line of his digestive axis; he moves in the direction of his vision; sight becomes insight (see Straus, 1952).

D. 1. In animal experiments, a dog, a rat, a monkey, is directly involved in the situation. Searching a solution for its "problems," the animal learns to turn, through its own action, the given situation into a preferred one; to exchange one particular condition for another particular one.

2. *Il Penseroso—The Thinker*—is not concerned with problems of this order. The techniques applied to deal with those are not the methods used by him in his meditations. The conception of the heliocentric system provides a perfect illustration for our topic.

When Copernicus conceived and elaborated the heliocentric system, he did not watch the skies; he thought about cycles and epicycles. The heliocentric system deals with the relation of sun and stars, envisioned as if it were from a point outside of the solar system and certainly from a position removed—in thought—from the earth, which Copernicus had cut loose from its moorings and enlisted in the company of other planets. The Copernican system contradicts, or at least seems to contradict, the testimony of the senses. Yet although Western man knows the sun is at rest, all of us—astronomers not excepted—see the sun move, rise, and set.

The gift of sensory experience is available only to motile creatures which, in rising from the ground, establish a position opposite to the ground and thereby gain a relation to objects qua objects within the open horizon of the world. In this truly fundamental situation, the senses serve men and animals first of all in their basic task of orienting them toward their environment. The primary frame of reference for our motosensorium is the earth and firmament, resting in their own weight. Against this background we actually see the sun, the moon, and the stars moving, and I daresay we see it correctly as far as seeing is concerned.

The Copernican system does not correct erroneous sensorial impressions. It transcends the realm of sensory experience. Though contemplated on earth, it is not visualized from the earth. The observer is transferred to Erehwon, to nowhere; he is removed from his terrestrial point of viewing and freed from its limitations. The astronomers consider planets, sun, and earth in one view of imagination; they comprehend the whole of their circuits; they comprise in one geometric figure all the possible positions of the earth and its path around the sun, passed in the course of one full year. With the aid of a mathematical model, indifferent in its proportions to the natural conditions of place and time, size and weight, the scientist does not simply provide a correct description of natural events, he outdistances nature. The ellipses in Kepler's laws are conceived as closed geometrical figures in their totality. Using such an ideal frame of reference, which reaches far beyond the momentary actuality, the transitory positions can be determined.

Seeing and thinking are two different modes of being-in-the-world. The distance between sight and thought cannot be reduced to the difference between certain cerebral functions nor to the differences between "impressions" and "ideas." In sensory experience we are in direct contact with things; they stand before us, and we, before them. In thinking, the relation is an indirect one; the *noëma* mediates between the thinker and the target of his imagination. Conceptual thinking requires a radical ekbasis from any particular position. We may say that because man can perform such ekbasis from his social and his physical environment and finally from his own corporeal existence, he is able to think. The characteristic attitude of the thinker expresses this "excarnation"—the price man must pay for his intellectual and spiritual achievements.

BIBLIOGRAPHY

James W. (1890), *The Principles of Psychology*. New York: Holt, 1918.
Straus, E. (1952), The Upright Posture. *Psychiat. Quart.*, 26:529-561.
——— (1956), *The Primary World of Senses,* 2nd ed. New York: Free Press, 1963.
——— (1959), Human Action: Response or Project. *Confinia Psychiat.*, 2:148-171.
Wilson, S. K., (1955), *Neurology*. Baltimore: Williams & Wilkins.

DISCUSSION

DR. KLEIN:

I was reminded, as Dr. Straus spoke, of Polanyi's model of discovery, and I should like to know if others see the parallel between Polanyi's theory and what Dr. Straus was saying. It also struck me that the behavior of his subjects seemed analogous to that of the dreaming person in the fact that they seemed to be removing themselves from the situation, enveloped in images perhaps, and, in a sense, derealizing the present situation. One of the important characteristics of the act of thinking is getting away from the immediate reality, and this, of course, is true in the extreme in the dreaming experience. This might indeed be one of the conditions for the vividness of the dream experience and of its identifiability as a perceptual experience as the dream is being dreamed.

The area of psychology in which Dr. Straus's ideas about the body and sensory experience are most helpful is one that is in a primitive stage of development: the phenomenology of varieties of experience, the different modes of experienced contact with objects. This is a subject on which there is practically no experimental literature. There is only one experiment that I know of which has tried to distinguish the properties of an image and a percept, although that would seem to be one of the primary requirements of a perceptual psychology. Most psychologies of perception start from an assumption of the experience of contact, but the very experience of contact, which is unique to perception and which distinguishes it from an imagery or from a memory experience, we know practically nothing about. I think this is what Dr. Straus's work is partly about.

The only experiment which I know to be analogous to this one was done in Titchener's laboratory in 1917, by one of his students, Cheves Perky; she wanted to know the conditions under which a person will accept an experience as one of perception or of an image. Briefly, the experiment presented this situation to the subjects:

There was a dimly projected picture of an apple or a pear on a screen—so dim that it was subliminal, that is, below the level of reportability. Focusing on the screen, the subject was asked to imagine an apple or a pear. Then, without the subject's knowing it, the picture of the apple or the pear was gradually brightened, and the experimenter wanted to know at what point the subject would report either "I have an image of a pear," or "This is not my image, you are *showing* me something."

Perky's study is the only one I know which attempts to make this distinction experimentally. I think her experiment raises a question about the way in which the experience of reality obtained with an image compares with that of a perceived content. These two modes of experience are critically different, and the difference is a basic one for survival. You don't try to eat an imaged banana. You may do so if you *perceive* one. I'd like to hear how the principle Dr. Straus proposes of the cleavage between body and object could be applied to accounting for the experienced distinction between an image and a percept. There is, of course, the further problem of how these experiences are distinguishable from a memory experience. The fact that in perception we have an experience of contact given in a mediated way through a sheaf of light rays, that a transformation occurs which gives us the distinctive quality of being in contact with something—all this we know very little about.

What we do know a great deal more about is how conception plays into perception. That has been a prominent theme in perceptual psychology for the last 50 years. I'll illustrate it briefly with an example reported by Professor Boring. He had collected a lot of microscope drawings before the discovery of the chromosome, and there were no chromosomes to be seen in the drawings, but after the chromosome concept had been discovered, you could see plenty of chromosomes in the drawings.

Dr. Straus touched on another problem which is also a mystery; it concerns what I would call a process of *derealization* that has to occur in the carrying out of an intention, that is, the elimination of sensory experiences that go counter to the intention. I'd like to illustrate the problem through an experiment that we have done which I think is the converse of Dr. Straus's. I think it makes the same point he is making, but from another direction. In our experiment, based on a procedure developed by a Danish psychologist, Torsten Nielsen, the subject confronts a box with an aperture and looks through it. His gloved hand, which holds a pencil, is inserted through the aperture. The subject is told to look down at his hand and to trace a straight line, to move his hand up a straight line. Then, on another trial, the experimenter, who is back of him, drops a mirror which occludes the subject's sight of his own hand. The experimenter inserts his hand, also wearing a glove and wielding a pencil. Now the subject sees this hand and thinks he perceives his own hand. Again he is told to draw a straight line. This time, however, what he sees is the gloved hand drawing a line veering off on an arc from the vertical. What does he do? It's an instance of thwarted intention, where the subject knows *where* he wants to go, fully intends to go there, but his sensory experience tells him that he is failing. There are many fascinating reactions to this, but one I think is particularly pertinent. This is the case when a subject recognizes that the hand is not his own; he makes a test and finds that the movements don't coincide. However, what he nevertheless persists in doing, even though he knows it isn't his hand, is to draw a compensating movement which he thinks will pull the line back to the vertical. It makes no sense, he knows, but he is unable to get away from the sensory experience that the hand is alien yet somehow subject to his control. This I think is a counterpart of what Dr. Straus was talking about. In the pursuit of intention here, the subject would have to disown the alien movement. Not only disown it, but act in terms of disowning it; he has to derealize it, if you will.

DR. STRAUS:

I cannot agree with the similarity of the thinker to the dreamer. After all, the dreamer is sleeping, and the sleeper is one who has resigned his upright posture. He has succumbed to gravity and is, therefore, in a different position. If the conditions for seeing the film had been better, you could have seen that these people were not sleeping, but concentrating. You could have seen the activity of the furrowed brow, the closed mouth. I don't think there is in thinking an expressive similarity to dreaming.

You asked about my idea of the image and of intention. The image is no longer bound—that's just the point—to the here and now. It's without weight and without substance. I can take the images with me wherever I go. I may take your image downstairs now. If I understood the background of your question about intention (if you mean intention to act), you place the intention still within the creature in isolation. If I walked to the wall over there, what I see from here over there is already given as my goal. The door over there is a point to be reached in the future. It's not a temporal point which extends here from me, but it already carries with it all the future possibilities, not only of walking over there, but of performing an action, of changing the conditions. So, of course, the temporal aspect would be another one which needs a bit of discussion.

Those experiments you mentioned are against my nature. They are so complex and put the poor creatures first with an eye toward a slit—I don't think they really give you genuine information about sensory experience. Professor Polanyi also mentioned the Innsbruck experiments with inverting spectacles. Subjects wore prisms which turned things upside down; after a while they become adapted to it. I think this adaptation is possible only because the vertical (i.e., gravity) is predominant and finally forces even optical experience into the normal situation.

PROFESSOR CROSSON:

I'm going to raise some philosophical points, having relied on Dr. Klein to raise the psychological ones. First, Dr. Straus says that by denying the conclusion of William James, he denies his premises. Strictly speaking, in logic he denies only the conjunction of the premises, which means that at least one of them is wrong, but perhaps he means both. And the other is simply a suggestion. He says that the antithesis of the thinker's attitude is perhaps the soldier standing at attention. I've seen some very distracted soldiers at attention: I would suggest the soldier *in enemy territory,* because soldiers standing at attention might not be very wary or watchful.

But the main thing I want to do is draw together some themes for my own satisfaction and the group's profit. One of the basic questions is the relation between parts and wholes, between individuals and society, between subordinate and supervening levels, and the problem of behaviorism in psychology is only a particular form of this. Here I want to pose a methodological problem, a problem of how to pose the problem—whether to analyze down or up, whether to ask how hierarchies emerge from the lower levels or to ask how lowerarchies, so to speak, emerge from the higher levels. That is, with respect to evolution, it may very well be true that it is a question of the supervening or higher levels coming out of the lower, but culturally it is the other way around, that is, with respect to the history of psychology and philosophy as well. The paradoxical question is: how the subsidiary clues to the comprehensive entity which is the person could come to be taken seriously by philosophers and psychologists as *signs* needing to be interpreted. There is an objective point of view that's adopted, and Dr. Straus has commented on it in his concept of excarnation. But the objective viewpoint does not result from simple cessation of action. That is, there is a kind of withdrawal or pause from action which is like the Greek notion of *theoria.* I can try to make that clear by taking first, say, Plato's *Republic,* which asks questions about society: he withdraws from society, refuses to enter politics, but he poses questions about society in the terms in which they are posed in action. "What is the good thing to do?" "What is the bad thing to do?" On the other hand, if we contrast this with the kind of speculation or observation exemplified by Rousseau, we find that Rousseau's point of view transforms the question as it is posed in action. For Rousseau the question is: how these notions of good and bad ever came about. How does this thing we call society come to emerge, and so on. In the latter case, there's a transformation of the meaning that is being investigated.

More particularly, for Dr. Straus's paper, I take it his main purpose was to argue with respect to the first of his theses that there is not a transfer of training, but rather that there is, in the examples that he showed us, unrehearsed application of the knowledge of letters. One can certainly cite other examples of this. That is, it is not a motor schema by which these subjects are activated, but rather a terminus of action at which they aimed and which itself crystallized a motor schema. He suggested that there was exemplified in the action of these subjects a withdrawal from the *Mitwelt* and from the *Umwelt,* that is, from the social world and the surrounding world. They closed their mouths; they stopped looking at the person who gave them the instructions. After a while, perhaps, they glanced aside, closed their arms, and in the most difficult problem, they finally closed their eyes. I want to raise two questions about this. One is, the interference it suggests between the levels in which man lives, and the second is whether there isn't a similar kind of withdrawal in Köhler's description of apes, in *The Intelligence of Apes.* I remember the description of Sultan, for example, who, after his first try at solving a problem, Köhler says, would not socialize for a while. In other words, there may be times when the pattern of withdrawal from the *Mitwelt* in the case of other organisms, too, exemplifies something approximating thinking behavior.

Dr. Straus referred to the role of imagination in the heuristic process, the problem solving of his subjects, and described it as the attempt to—he didn't quite use these words—evoke or induce a solution, a schema of motor action you might say, by keeping the end in view. That is, he stressed the fact that there was not a tentative motor essay, but that the motorial aspect of it was laid out at once, after a certain imaginative contemplation of the end which was desired; the person thought about the goal. Perhaps it would be better to call this a heuristic role of imagination, rather than a creative role of imagination, though it is a first-time phenomenon, so perhaps there is something creative about it.

The I-Allon relation, constituted by rising up: it seems to me in his description of this that it's difficult not to recall Professor Plessner's paper: his concept of positionality, and the boundary opposing the living unit to the environment. I'd like to get comments if I could from both these gentlemen. That is, is positionality, one might say, a yet more general *Lebensform,* of which the I-Allon relation is a particular one? What is the relation between these?

Dr. Straus's comment on Copernicus, I would like to question.

When he says that Copernicus could not have derived his ideas from direct observation, it seems to me that he goes too far; it may well be that there is an overpowering gestalt, or structure, that imposes itself on us, so that we almost ineluctably tend to see the sun rise up, but the alternative seems to be possible. I can mention one personal and one experimental, or what seems to me experimental, indication. You stand at the seashore and look at the horizon as the sun rises. It seems to me that there are three possible things that one could see. One is to see the sun rising. The other is to see the earth falling. This is perhaps easier if you've ever been on a large ocean liner, where the deck goes back and forth and where for a time you have the problem of deciding whether it's the horizon going up and down, or the deck that's going back and forth. But I think that I was capable of seeing the sun still and the earth going down. The third is that one simply sees the space between them increasing. This would be a completely neutral observation, and perhaps one that wouldn't be possible until these two alternatives had emerged.

The experimental analogy here, it seems to me, would be the Ames experiment of the distorted room, where again there is the overpowering effect of the room as horizon, which forces, as it were, this paradoxical size equivalent of the child and the adult, but in which it's possible to reverse the figure-ground structure.

One last general comment, coming back to my earlier remarks. Wittgenstein in the *Philosophical Investigations* says something to this effect—I wish I could quote it exactly—when I act toward someone as having a soul, I am not of the opinion that he has a soul, but my attitude toward him is the attitude toward a soul. I think I could paraphrase him: it's not a question of a hypothesis used to interpret signs; it's a question of attitude (he uses this word and I would like to relate it to Husserl's notion of *Einstellung*, or fundamental attitude), in the sense of existing or living a meaning of the world, living the world as a theophany, for example, as the garden of God, if you like, living the natural world, the world of the natural sciences, of objectivity, living the cultural world—using "living" here in a kind of transitive sense, living the world, living a meaningful world. It seems to me one should distinguish this very clearly from the question of opinions or hypotheses or inferences. And I would like to relate this comment of Wittgenstein on the one hand and Husserl's *Einstellung* on the other to Professor Polanyi's analysis of the structure of tacit knowing, particularly the semantical and ontological elements of it. That is, I want to relate here what Professor Polanyi calls the ontological element in the structure of tacit knowing and something like what the existentialists call "existing the world," or living the meaning of the world. It seems to me necessary to include both the poles (to use the phenomenological terms), both the *noësis* and the *noëma* of the experience.

DR. STRAUS:

In my paper I tried to deal first with sensory experience, the one which all hypotheses, Wittgenstein's and other methodological hypotheses, presuppose. Every science is built on the naïve realism of everyday life. This may be shameful, but it is so. The question, then, is whether we should go the other way round, start with doubts, which in practice nobody ever has. Just to doubt is no method. We must have reasons for our doubts. So I would say that really my whole enterprise was not on that high level of hypothetical assumption which you assumed. Whether Köhler's apes, looking for the banana and the box, were thinking or not, I leave to others to decide. Maybe they were, but I don't think that leads us very far, because their problem was still a concrete one to be solved, here at this moment: how to reach that thing there. It is not the same problem as how we can understand, for example, the apparent irregularities of the planets, which caused the classical astronomers, convinced that the movements must be regular, to try to "save" the phenomena.

I was myself pleased when I read Professor Plessner's paper; I also felt that the idea of the boundary and this rising and belonging position certainly have an affinity.

But about Copernicus. I think in rising from the ground and getting up, we experience—and this has no logical grounds but is our factual reality—the world as stable, as resting. That we can make experiments with a rolling ship, I grant you, but the floor on which we stand itself is no longer the ground on which we would see the sun rise and set. The third interpretation with the relative size of the increasing space, I think, has nothing to do with seeing the movement of the sun, when the earth in relation to us remains the invariant. One of the great accomplishments of Copernicus was that he was able really to step out from the concreteness of sensory experience and see it from that whole, the Allon, which we tried to explore in order to understand our particular position.

PROFESSOR TANSEY:

I just want to say about Dr. Straus's statement that the problem of the external world is an artificial problem, that maybe it isn't a problem; it doesn't have to be a problem; it can be an I-Allon relation. All the Allon outside my body, and to all intents and purposes the world of objects outside of me, is for me an external world, although I know perfectly well that I'm in it; again you have that strange paradox of being in it and yet having everything in it outside of you.

DR. STRAUS:

All this about the "external world": after all, this is a charm which has come down from Cartesian dualism, where the *res cogitans* in some way looks through an undescribable periscope into an external world to which he doesn't, as *res cogitans,* belong. There is this hypothesis of a mind external to the *res extensa,* and then, the never-answered question of how they are related is somehow nevertheless evaded. But that's not the situation I was describing. Of course this piece of wood here is outside me—I could eat it. "External world" in this sense denies that we are on the same basis as the other things on which we set our feet. My own body is also a part of that outside world. What I said about gravity is an attempt to account for how experiencing, first of all sensory experiencing, can be *related,* instead of being *in contrast,* to the living body. I think in some way this whole presentation really deals with the centuries-old problem of dualism, or of the one-and-a-half-ism which is the usual epiphenomenal approach. It really gives an answer, maybe never complete, but indicating that the living body is the condition from which sensory experience (i.e., consciousness) alone can develop.

PROFESSOR TANSEY:

When Copernicus steps out from the here and now, you must mean, as I would, that in abstract thought we could do that.

DR. STRAUS:

True. If Copernicus had kept his mouth shut, nobody would have known. They would have taken it for granted that the sun sets at night and likewise the sunrise is visible to all of us. In fact this world, this world against which I get up, is the one in which I find my partners. I think that this approach also answers the so-called problem of intersubjectivity, which is really a bad dream, a nightmare, for philosophy—how to get out of this solipsism—while I think there is here a possibility of seeing the other person as my partner.

PROFESSOR PLESSNER:

May I just add something which seems to me very important: the concept of excarnation is exactly what I mean by "eccentric positionality." This I believe to be a monopoly of man and not shared with the animals. We can see everything from "outside" and from a point which is precisely nowhere—from nowhere; this can furnish us with, among other things, localization and also the principles of map-making. Now, in my view, this position of excarnation can also produce something which you have questioned: namely the possibility of being self-contained, the possibility which we may call a fallacy given by our organization of seeing everything in ourselves. *Everything*. From this stems the problem of solipsism. The problem we attribute to Descartes is, I believe, in a sense given with the human mode of existence as a latent possibility of error. This fact is important for certain kinds of self-knowledge, for certain philosophies, and indeed, for certain types of mental illness. I can, so to speak, isolate myself within myself. Then I can say: but in reality I am out there; in reality this within and without doesn't exist at all. But it does exist. It does exist, but as a recurrent, testable, controllable difficulty. The difficulty is that we keep having to jump over our own shadow. We stand in the way of our own vision; we are our own barrier, though a transparent barrier. With this is connected the possibility of understanding pictures.

PROFESSOR GRENE:

A question about two parts of Dr. Straus's paper. First of all, we had the demonstration of people thinking, and actions, and so on, which, I take it, is excarnation; then it was pointed out that we had risen twice: first of all as animals from the ground and then stood upright. I got the impression that excarnation was an extension of this, and then I wondered, if we can abstract, take a position, how this weight business, this kind of thing comes into thinking? On this analogy, one would expect that we would start to fly when we think, that we would get further up. But why do we have this reversion to the ground, to heaviness?

DR. STRAUS:

Perhaps I did not mention one important aspect of sensory experience: namely that every sensory experience has a double aspect. There is one which I call *pathic:* emphasized in the so-called lower modalities, with appetite, smells, and what not (though also present in the higher ones, hearing and sight). But hearing and sight are pre-eminent in the uniquely human situation in the second rise of the upright posture. This second aspect of sense experience I call *gnostic;* it consists in seeing things as already independent from us in their own right. *Facing* things, I think, is characteristic for us and demands the upright posture—to get up, to awaken. This is intimately related to sensory experience, but in its gnostic aspect. So in this thinking attitude, first, I have to get up from my immersion in the pathic and then come down from that position, preserving the gnostic situation as it has been developed. It is perhaps good to keep in mind that after all art and science have developed only in the field of the visible and the audible.

PROFESSOR PANTIN:

I should like to suggest that it's significant in this posture of deep thought that the rate of change of proprioceptive information is reduced to a minimum. And this cutting off of a very important source of irrelevant information is extremely important. In the same way, this is not the only position in which one thinks deeply. You can also go for a walk, if you walk like an automaton, deep in thought. And there again, although the rate of change of proprioceptive information is not reduced to a minimum, it is absolutely regular; it can easily be allowed for.

PROFESSOR SILBER:

I think that this point about proprioception also relates to a more systematic question about this entire method. May I express a couple of doubts about the phenomenological method? It seems to me that, while recapturing the facts, recapturing the complex concreteness of human experience, is very important, it should never be confused with an explanation if it. We haven't explained what we are trying to explain by recapturing it and by reminding behaviorists or reductionists that they have left something out. I think Husserl very often supposes he has somehow solved the problem, and I think Dr. Straus does too, simply by recapturing the initial facts. Secondly, it doesn't prove that the initial stages of the final phenomenological achievement never occurred. We find, for example, a statement that John Doe need not consult his neighbors to find that he and they are witnessing the same spectacle. I would qualify that by saying that John Doe need not *now* consult his neighbor, but if there had never been any consultation, then I doubt seriously that he would be aware in this way. I'm not at all sure we disqualify these genetic interpretations of how things developed simply by insisting on the concrete complexity of the things once they are done. I don't think that all the philosophical problems that arise here are simply bogus. Unless Berkeley got his facts wrong in his report of the experience of congenitally blind men who, on receiving sight, reported colors and things pasted on their eyeballs, it is obvious that they had to learn something about the interpretation of the *Mitwelt* and the *Umwelt* that they didn't have just by being there without processes of orientation. And the same point can be made about dreaming. Most bad dreamers never understand why people make a point about it, but many people have vivid and coherent dreams, and they do understand the point. I well recall mending a crack in my ceiling and the bags under my eyes quickly disappeared while I tried to figure out how to get rid of it. I did it the right way, gouging it out and filling it with expanding plaster and resurfacing it. I thought I'd done a superb job. A few days later, the hairline crack had reappeared, and I complained bitterly to some of my friends how I had failed to do the job properly. One of them came over for a drink that afternoon and I showed it to him, and there was no crack. I then decided that I had dreamed it, that it was just an anxiety dream. A couple of days later, I looked up, and there was the crack again. This time there was no nonsense; I got on the telephone, called a friend and said, "Look, there's a crack in my ceiling." I finally noticed there was a correlation between humidity and the presence and absence of the crack. But there wasn't anything about my orientation in the *Umwelt* that solved this problem. I think that there are many times when we simply cannot rely upon these phenomenological data. If problems are genuine problems, they do call for explanations, and those explanations are not given simply by talking about the marvelous capacity of men to orient themselves in their experience.

DR. STRAUS:

If John Doe, as a baby, had had to learn there was something else besides him in the world, he could never have learned it, because his experience of the other is presupposed in this. To whom could he talk? To himself? If he talks to someone, he already has the whole phenomenological situation fullfilled.

PROFESSOR SILBER:

He doesn't begin to talk to anyone until he's talked to. I think that Hegel's analysis of this in the *Phenomenology* is in many ways more instructive because he does have a recapitulation theory, that the self develops because it's already been encountered by a human being. I think the one point to remember is that although other people don't exist for John Doe as a newborn baby, John Doe doesn't exist either as John Doe when he's a newborn baby. There is a mutual process of developing self and world. Now I can sympathize with you in saying something went radically wrong in philosophy when we started having individuals on their own and then created the problem of a world, because there is no greater problem in finding a world than there is in finding individuals. But to talk about their interdependence does not in any way make irreducible or infallible the content of phenomenological experience. And consequently, I don't see that we go very far by phenomenological descriptions alone. It seems to me that the most we derive from phenomenological descriptions is a reminder that we don't want to lose concrete factual complexities in the development of our theories. We want to avoid the fallacy of misplaced concreteness; we want to preserve the phenomenon. But I don't see any reason to suppose that the phenomenological description is in any way a substitute for a theory.

DR. STRAUS:

It's not a substitute; it's the thing itself.

PROFESSOR SILBER:

"It's the thing itself": *what* thing itself? It's neither reality nor is it theory, it is a description of something.

DR. STRAUS:

If you speak about our dog, for example, you ought to believe that we have some communication and we understand each other as partners. My dog communicates with me, and I don't think he has to learn this. The thing which every animal has to learn, every child has to learn, is that there are things which do not respond. The nonpartnership is the thing which has to be learned and had to be learned in the course of human history. All the mythologies see the trees as alive, and one is able to talk with them. What we really learn is the grim, cold, nonresponsiveness of the world which surrounds us. For the child, the responsive world is usually his mother (I didn't bring in this term here, but I call it the *hetairos,* the other one who lives with him, but the mother as *hetairos* represents also the Allon at that time). And when the child grows, he discovers the world which is no longer responding and therefore is a fearful world, and from this fearful world he runs toward his mother where he finds protection. I think the responsiveness, the I-Allon, is primary, and what is learned is that there are unfortunately huge parts of this world which do not respond. I think history and science have expanded this cold world enormously.

9

VALUE PROPERTIES: THEIR SIGNIFICANCE FOR PSYCHOLOGY, AXIOLOGY, AND SCIENCE

SIGMUND KOCH

I. The Predicament of Psychology

The predicament of psychology is—in a word—behaviorism. Yes, still. That recent years have seen an increase of nonbehaviorists does not matter. Whether neogestaltist, phenomenologist, existentialist, Zen Buddhist or Reichian, the nonbehaviorist is twisted, cheapened by the quirk of history that makes his first calling that of *anti*behaviorist. He gives too much of himself to protest; too little to constructive performance. Worse, he is forced to promise too much that is too easy to a colleagueship and a world that has too long fed on total answers of utter simplicity.

I have given half a career as psychologist to the detailed registration of scholarly horror over the phenomenon—and strange time course—of behaviorism. It has been a tiresome role which I gladly relinquish to my partners in dissidence, even to the philosophers amongst them. I am tired of "demonstrating" that the main thread of continuity in the wildly erratic 50-year course of this "school" is a misinterpreted version of an epistemology which even in its "proper" philosophical formulations was monstrously deficient; that philosophers themselves have been regarding this epistemology (originating in the "logical atomism" of Russell and Wittgenstein and achieving its canonical form in the logical positivism of the early thirties) as an embarrassment for at least three decades; that although behaviorism in its actual theory and research was never consistent with its "objectivism," it was always biased toward the selection of nonsensical or trivial problems, and indeed solutions, by its efforts to seem consistent; that a 50-year accumulation of expertise at the accommodation to such constraints has produced a "science" which denies its subject matter in principle and insults it in practice.

I *now* think it more important to ask: what does behaviorism mean? I mean in a human way. The answer is really very simple: behaviorism is the strongest possible wish that the organism and the person not exist—a vast, many-voiced, poignant lament that anything so refractory to the assumptions and methods of 18th-century science should clutter up the worldscape.

Classical behaviorism (1913-1930) implemented this wish by the simple expedient of acknowledging only stimulus (S) and response (R) events, and their associative "connections." (Skinner, closer to the classical position than any other currently influential behaviorist, has cleaned out that residue of the organism suggested by "associative connections.") The *neobehaviorism* (1930-circa 1950) of Hull and others gained an apparent ability to cope with certain aspects of "complex behavior" by interpolating between S and R certain "intervening variables" purporting to offer an *objectively* grounded mathematical algorithm for computing the behaviorial effect of factors (e.g., past learning, motivation, inhibition) contingent on the dread possibility that some focus of biological activity intervened between stimulation and response.

Liberalized neobehaviorism (*neo-neobehaviorism;* early '50's onward), as practiced by people like Neal Miller and Osgood, became uneasy over the circumstance that "fields" like perception and cognition had been bypassed in earlier behaviorism. What to do? Make room for central process, but not for the untidy vehicle thereof (the organism?). Solution: acknowledge a class of "central" or "mediating" responses (and correlated stimuli) functionally equivalent to "percepts," "ideas," "images."[1]

The final development to date (Miller, Galanter, and Pribram, 1960) calls itself—with a dedication to doublethink far more sincere than that of all earlier behaviorism—*subjective behaviorism.* So long as you will acknowledge that the brain is a fairly sophisticated binary digital computer, the votaries of this school will talk

[1] The historic phases of behaviorism are dealt with more laboriously in Koch (1954, 1959, 1961, 1964).

manfully about plans, ideas, thoughts, even "will," if you will. Indeed, one of its proponents (a neurophysiologist), in a tender moment of humanist largesse, issues to his colleagues the methodological caution (in a footnote) that it may be well to bear in mind that the brain is rather more a species of "wet software" than of "dry hardware."

The concept of the machine has indeed been extended! How right are such celebrants of this happy metamorphosis as Toulmin. To "subjective behaviorists," and all other devotees of the transistorized ganglion, may I suggest the following paradox: Only a genuinely irreducible human being would passionately insist that he was a machine or devote his career to an attempt to prove himself one. If a fully successful robot were achieved, it can confidently be predicted that it would resent any allegation that it was a machine and, indeed, invent a consoling rationale to the effect that it was utterly and irreducibly human.

II. Value Properties and Motivation

So much for protest. Many psychologists are now disposed to work free of behaviorism. Yet the past is not easily sloughed off! Any science which for 50 years has enforced misphrasings and even denials of subject matter will have so corrupted all concepts in the public domain that the "past" can somehow subtly survive every proclamation of its demise. It is to an examination of one of the more subtle contexts in which the reality-defiling schematisms of psychology's past live on that we now turn. The "field" of *motivation* has seen much ferment, and indeed genuine progress, since the early '50's. Despite this, one is impressed at how much even those who most genuinely wish to embrace human phenomena are hampered by the restrictions of an inadequate conceptualization. To the extent that we can dig out from the influence of behaviorism, to that extent we clear the way for work in psychology that might have a chance of making significant contact with human phenomena. But the aim of my analysis will be more specific than that, and in two senses:

1. The analysis will show, I think, that major psychological problems cannot be addressed except at levels of experiential sensitivity cultivated in the past only in the humanities.

2. More specifically, the analysis will show that any phrasing of phenomena called "motivational" which does not blight them demands recognition of an utter interpenetration between what philosophers have been wont to call the "realms" of "fact" and of "value." The resulting concept of "value properties" will, I think, make it difficult to doubt that differentiated value-events occur as objective characters of experience, are related in lawful ways to the biological and, ultimately, "stimulus" processes of which experience is a function, and that such value events are, in perhaps the typical instance, *not* need dependent, as would be demanded by most motivational theories in psychology or by "interest theories" of value in philosophy.

The above promises would indeed be as febrile as they may sound if I were proposing to go any appreciable distance toward their fulfillment. I propose nothing of the sort, but merely to point to the feasibility of an important line of inquiry, one that can never be completed. And even this last verges on overstatement, for this line of inquiry will prove to be one which every human being has already commenced.

Twentieth-century theories of motivation have generated a gigantic mass of words. But most of those words presuppose and elaborate a single, simple schematism. This schematism—which I shall here call the "extrinsic model," sometimes "extrinsic grammar" —seems to be deeply embedded, at least in the West, in certain of the interpretive categories of "common sense," and this for a sizable stretch of history.

In the common-sense epistemology of the West, there has long been a tendency to phrase all behavior and sequences thereof in goal-directed terms: to refer behavior in all instances to ends, or end states, which are believed to restore some lack, deficiency, or deprivation in the organism. I have called this presumption a kind of rough-and-ready "instrumentalism" which forever and always places action into an "in order to" context. In this common-sense theory, behavior is uniformly assumed predictable and intelligible when the form "X does Y in order to . . ." is completed. In many instances in practical life it is possible to fill in this form in a predictively useful way. Often, however, a readily identifiable referent for the end term is not available. In such cases we assume that the form must hold, and so we hypothesize or invent an end term which may or may not turn out to be predictively trivial and empty. For instance: X does Y in order to be happy, punish himself, be peaceful, potent, respected, excited, playful, or wise.

Precisely this common-sense framework—or syntax, if you will—has been carried over into the *technical* theories of motivation of the modern period. In the technical theories, the central assumption is that action is always initiated, directed, or sustained by an inferred internal state called variously a motive, drive, need, tension system, or what-not, and terminated by attainment of a situation which removes, diminishes, "satisfies," or in any other fashion alleviates that state. The model is essentially one of disequilibrium-equilibrium restoral, and each of the many "theories of motivation" proposes a different imagery for thinking and talking about the model and the criterial circumstances or end state under which such disequilibria are reduced or removed. Matters are rendered pat and tidy in the various theories by the assumption that all action can be apportioned to (a) a limited number of biologically given, end-determining systems (considered denumerable, but rarely specified past the point of a few "e.g.'s" like hunger and sex), and (b) learned modifications and derivatives of these systems variously called second-order or acquired motives, drives, etc.

My proposal, I think, is a quite simple one. In essence, it points up the limitations of referring *all* action to extrinsic, end-determining systems, as just specified; it challenges the fidelity to fact and the fruitfulness of so doing. At the most primitive level it says: if you look about you, even in the most superficial way, you will see that all behavior is *not* goal directed, does not fall into an "in order to" context. In this connection, I have presented (Koch, 1956) a fairly detailed descriptive phenomenology of a characteristic sequence of "creative" behavior, which shows that if this state of high productive motivation be seen by the person as related to an extrinsic end (e.g., approval, material reward, etc.) the state becomes disrupted to an extent corresponding to the activity of so seeing. If, on the other hand, some blanket motive of the sort that certain theories reserve for such circumstances, like anxiety, is hypothesized, one can only say that the presence of anxiety in any reportable sense seems only to disrupt this creative state, and in precise proportion to the degree of anxiety.

If such states seem rare and tenuous, suppose we think of a single daily round and ask ourselves whether *everything* that we do falls into some clearcut "in-order-to" context. Will we not discover a rather surprising fraction of the day to be spent in such ways as "doodling," tapping out rhythms, being the owners of perseverating melodies, nonsense rhymes, "irrelevant" memory episodes; noting the attractiveness of a woman, the fetching quality of a small child, the charm of a shadow pattern on the wall, the loveliness of a familiar object in a particular distribution of light; looking at the picture over our desk, or out of the window; feeling disturbed at someone's tie, repelled by a face, entranced by a voice; telling jokes, idly conversing, reading a novel, playing the piano, adjusting the wrong position of a picture or a vase. Yet *goal directedness* is presumably the *fact* on which virtually all of modern motivational theory is based.

The answer of the motivational theorist is immediate. He has of course himself noticed certain facts of the same order. Indeed, much of motivational theory is given to the elaboration of detailed hypothetical rationales for such facts, and these the theorists will have neatly prepackaged for immediate delivery. There will be a package containing the principle of "irrelevant drive"; others, "displacement" and other substitutional relations. An extraordinarily large package will contain freely postulated motives with corresponding postulated end states, as, e.g., "exploratory drive" and its satiation, "curiosity drive" and its satisfaction, perceptual drives, aesthetic drives, play drives, not to mention that vast new complement of needs for achievement, self-realization, growth, and even "pleasurable tension." Another parcel will contain the principle of secondary reinforcement or some variant thereof like subgoal learning, secondary cathexis, etc. Another will provide a convenient set of learning principles which can be unwrapped whenever one wishes to make plausible the possibility that some acquired drive (e.g., anxiety, social approval) which one arbitrarily assigns to a bit of seemingly unmotivated behavior, *could* have been learned. Another contains the principle of functional autonomy. There are indeed a sufficient number of packages to make possible the handling of any presumed negative instance in *several* ways. Why skimp?

The answer to all this is certainly obvious. The very multiplication of these packages as more and more facts of the "in-and-for-itself" variety are acknowledged, makes the original analysis, which was prized for its economy and generality, increasingly cumbersome. But more importantly, it becomes clear that the *search* for generality consisted in slicing behavior to a very arbitrary scheme: the result was a mock generality which started with inadequate categories and then sought rectification through more and more *ad hoc* specifications. In the end, even the apparent economy is lost and so, largely, is sense.

The positive part of my proposal would commence with an analysis of what seems involved in behavior which is phenomenally of an "in-and-for-itself" variety as opposed to clear-cut instances of the "in-order-to" sort of thing. Take "play" to start with. I would resent being told that at any time I had a generalized need for *play* per se. I do not like to think of myself as that diffuse. I never liked cards, nor even chess, and I rarely entertain urges toward the idle agitation of my musculature. My play "needs," or activity "needs," etc., have been such that, if described with any precision at all, we soon find ourselves outside the *idiom* of "needs." I have been *drawn toward* certain specific activities which—because they fall into no obvious context of gainful employ, biological necessity, or jockeying for social reward, etc.—could be *called* "play." But I have been drawn to these activities, and not others, because (among other reasons) they "contain," "afford," "generate" specific properties or relations in my experience toward which I am adient. *I like these particular activities because they are the particular kinds of activities they are*—not because they reduce my "play drive," or are conducive toward my well-being (often they are not), or my status (some of them make me look quite ludicrous), or my virility pride.

Do I like them, then, by virtue of nothing? *On the contrary,* I like them by virtue of something far more *definite,* "real," if you will, than anything that could be phrased in the extrinsic mode. Each one I like because of *specific* properties or relations immanent, intrinsic, within the given action. Or better, the properties and relations are the "liking" (that, too, is a terribly promiscuous word). The determinants of such properties and relations in any ongoing activity can be thought to be dated instances of aspects of neural process which occur each over a family of conditions. Similar properties or relations would be produced (other factors constant) the next time I engaged in the given activity. And no doubt there are families of activities which share similar properties and relations of the sort I am trying to describe. Thus there may be a certain consonance (by no means an absolute one) among the *kinds* of "play" activities that I like. But, more importantly, properties or relations of the same or similar sorts may be generated within activity contexts that would be classified in ways quite other than play: eating, aesthetic experience, sexual activities, problem solving, etc.

I call such properties or relations *value properties,* and the (hypothetical) aspects of neural process which generate them, *value-determining properties.* Values or value-determining properties to which an organism is adient, I call "positive"; those to which the organism is abient, "negative." Adience and abience of organisms are controlled by value-determining properties (or by extension, value properties) of the different signs.

It can be instructive to consider from the point of view just adumbrated any of the types of "in-and-for-itself" activity to which it is common gratuitously to impute extrinsic, end-determining systems with their corresponding end states. Thus, for instance, one can only wince at the current tendency to talk about such things as "curiosity drives," "exploratory drives," "sensory drives," "perceptual drives," etc., as if the "activities" which are held to "satisfy" each of these "drives" (if indeed they are distinct) were just so much undifferentiated neutral pap that came by the yard. I am inclined to think that even the experimental monkeys who learn discrimination problems for the sole reward of being allowed visual access to their environments from their otherwise enclosed quarters, are being maligned when it is suggested that what their "drive" leads them to seek is "visual stimulation." Could it not be that even for the monkeys there are sights they might prefer not to see? Be this as it may, when explanations of this order are extended, say, to visually mediated aesthetic activities in man, the reduction to a paplike basis of those particulate experiences to which many human beings attribute intense (and differentiated) values, can only be held grotesque.

To make such points graphic and further to clarify the notion of "value properties," it may be well to take a second, slightly more formal example. I take the hypothetical instance of a person looking at a painting:

X looks at a painting for five minutes, and we ask, "Why?" The grammar of extrinsic determination will generate a lush supply of answers. X looks in order to satisfy a need for "aesthetic experience." X looks in order to derive pleasure. X looks because the picture happens to contain Napoleon and because he has a strong drive to dominate. X looks because "paintings" are learned reducers of anxiety. Answers of this order have only two common properties: they all refer the behavior to an extrinsic, end-determining system, *and* they contain very little, if *any*, information. Anyone who has looked at paintings as paintings knows that if X is *really* responding to the painting, then any of the above statements which may happen to be true are trivial.

A psychologically naïve person who *can* respond to paintings would say that an important part of the story—the essential part—has been omitted. Such a person would say that *if* the conditions of our example presuppose that X is really looking at the painting *as* a painting, the painting will produce a differentiated process in X which is correlated with the act of viewing. The fact that X continues to view the painting or shows "adience" toward it in other ways is equivalent to the fact that this process occurs. X may report on this process only in very general terms ("interesting," "lovely," "pleasurable"), or he *may* be able to specify certain qualities of the experience by virtue of which he is "held" by the painting.

Suppose we assume that there are certain immanent qualities and relations within the process which are specificially responsible for any evidence of "adience" which X displays. Call these "value-determining properties." We can then, with full tautological sanction, say that X looks at the painting for five minutes because it produces a process characterized by certain value-determining properties. This statement, of course, is an empty form—but note immediately that it is not necessarily more empty than calling behavior, say, "drive reducing." It now becomes an empirical question as to *what* such value-determining properties intrinsic to the viewing of paintings may be, either for X or for populations of viewers.

Though it is extraordinarily difficult to answer such questions, it is by no means impossible. The degree of agreement in aesthetic responsiveness and valuation among individuals of varied environmental background, but of comparable sensitivity and intelligence, is very remarkable indeed.

It becomes important now to note that even in cases where the extrinsic model seems distinctly to fit, it may still yield an extraordinarily crass specification of the activities involved and either overlook their subtle (and often more consequential) aspects, or phrase them in a highly misleading way. Thus, for instance—though I shall not take the time to analyze the large class of activities imputed to so extensively studied a drive as hunger—I know of no account which gives adequate attention to the facts that in civilized cultures cooking is an art form and that the discriminating ingestion of food is a form of connoisseurship. There is no reason in principle why value properties (or classes thereof) of the sort intrinsic to eating processes may not yield to increasingly accurate identification. Further, though we should not prejudge such matters, it is possible that certain of the value properties intrinsic to eating processes may be of the same order as, or in some way analogous to, value properties involved, in, say, visual art-produced processes.

Because these ideas are often found difficult, let us take the case of another activity class which can be acceptably, but only very loosely, phrased in a language of extrinsic determination: sexual activity. On this topic, the 20th century has seen a vast liberation of curiosity, scientific and otherwise. Yet the textbook picture of sex, human sex, as a tension relievable by orgasm—a kind of tickle mounting to a pain which is then cataclysmically alleviated—is hardly ever questioned at theoretical levels (at least in academic psychology). When it is, it is likely to be in some such way as to consider the remarkable possibility that some forms of "excitement" (e.g., mounting preclimactic "tension") may themselves be pleasurable, and this may be cited, say, as a difficulty for the drive-reduction theory, but not for some other drive theory, say some form of neohedonism like "affective arousal," which recognizes that the transition from some pleasure to more pleasure may be reinforcing. But our view would stress that sexual activity is a complex sequence with a rich potential for value properties; for ordered, creatively discoverable combinations, patterns, structures of value properties, which are immanent in the detailed quiddities of sexual action. Sexual experience offers a potential for art and artifice not unnoticed in the history of literature, fictional and confessional, but rarely even distantly mirrored in the technical *conceptualizations.* (The technical *data language* is another matter, but even here the "fineness" of the units of analysis involved in much empirical work is aptly symbolized by Kinsey's chief dependent variable, namely the "outlet" and frequencies thereof.) The vast involvement with this theme at private, literary, and technical levels has produced little toward a precise specification of experiential value properties, certainly none particularly useful at scientific levels.

Sex, eating behavior, activities written off to curiosity, play, perceptual drives, creative behavior, etc., are contexts each with a vast potential for the "discovery" and creative reassemblage of *symphonies* of value properties. Doubtless each such context offers a potential for different ranges of value properties, but it is highly likely that there is marked overlap among such ranges. Indeed, formal or relational similarities in experiences that "belong" to quite different contexts of this sort suggest that nature sets a fairly modest limitation on the number of "fundamental" value properties implicated in activity. There is much reason to believe, from the protocols of experientially sensitive and articulate people, as well as from the observation of action, that certain of the value properties intrinsic to such varied contexts of events as the perception of (and directed behavior toward) a picture, a poem, a "problem" (whether scientific, mathematical, or personal), a "puzzle" in and for itself, are of an analogous order and in some sense overlap. And, as we have just tried to show, it is reasonable to believe that the so-called consummatory aspects of hunger or of sex "contain" relational qualities not dissimilar to some of the value properties immanent in "complex" activities like those listed in the last sentence.

Once the detailed phenomena of directed behavior are rephrased in terms of intrinsic value properties, it becomes possible to reinspect the extrinsic language of drives and the like, and determine what utility it might actually contain. For *some* behaviors clearly are brought to an end or are otherwise altered by consummations, and organisms clearly show both restless *and* directed activities in the absence of the relevant consummatory objects.

Questions about the relations between what one might call *extrinsic* and *intrinsic grammar* for the optimal phrasing of motivational phenomena are among the most important for the future of motivational theory.

Whatever is viable in the drive language is, of course, based in the first instance on "organizations" of activity sequences which converge on a common end state. Each such organization, if veridical, would permit differential (but overlapping) ranges of value properties to "come into play." No doubt *primary* organizations of this sort, when veridical, are related to deviations of internal physiological states, the readjustments of which play a role in the adaptive economy. When such deviations are present, it is probable that certain value properties, or ranges thereof, are given especial salience and effectiveness with respect to the detailed moment-to-moment control of directed behavior. That all activities, however, must be contingent on such deviation states, seems on the face of it absurd. Behavior will often be directed by value properties which have nothing to do with gross organizations of this sort, and which may in fact conflict with the adjustment of the concurrent deviation. Much of what is called "learned motivation" will consist not in "modifications of primary drives"—whatever that can mean—but rather in the building up of expectations and expectation chains which terminate in anticipated processes with value properties. "Learned drives," whatever that means, would be built up as systems of anticipation of value-property constellations and sequences.

This, however, is not the place to develop whatever exists of the more detailed aspects of the formulation. The purpose was to suggest a line of thought which might bring psychology into contact with phenomena of fundamental concern both to itself and to the humanities. If I have established the barest possibility of such a development, that is all I could have wished.

III. Some Consequences for Aesthetics

Some such conception as "value properties" is perhaps more likely to obtrude upon an inquirer while surveying phenomena called "motivational" than other conventionally discriminated fields of psychology. For one is here compelled to think about factors which determine the "directedness" of experience and action: the characters of events which organisms tend to strive toward, maximize, prolong, savor, prize, cherish, etc., and those which in specific ways the organism tends to flee, take precaution against, avoid, terminate, dislike, loathe, pass on from, minimize, reject. Even if one begins analysis in the extrinsic mode, one is soon forced into contact with those characters which, by criteria of the directionality of action and experience, may be said to be in some sense "good" and in some sense "bad." And as soon as one can discern that organisms are oriented not in reference to "good" and "bad" as global generalized states of affairs, but rather in reference to a plurality of particulate "goods" and "bads," having differentially specifiable effects, one is fairly close to a conception like "value properties."

Once in possession of the notion of value properties, however, it is clear that they are not specifically "motivational" (whatever that can mean), but rather that such relational features of experience and action as are discriminated by that concept will be ubiquitous in psychological functioning. Any analysis of experience or action, then, which does not slight or, for some practical reason, "suppress" its fine-structure must at some level take cognizance of value properties. If one thinks in terms of functionally isolable psychological processes of the sort loosely bounded by major "fields" of psychology, it will immediately be obvious that, for instance, concrete value-property distributions will be of the warp and woof of all *perceptual* processes. Every percept will contain relational characters "corresponding" to value properties; indeed, immanent within percepts of differing degrees of articulation and complexity will be correspondingly different value-property structures. Obviously, the intention is not to assimilate *all* "terms" and relations of a percept to a constellation of value properties; rather, the relation of analytically discriminable "parts" of a percept to whatever value properties are immanent is a many-one relation.

Any conceivable percept, then—whether a simple "abstract" contour or an exquisitely articulated and richly meaningful painting, whether an isolated noise or tone or a symphony, whether a punctiform patch of white pigment on a dark ground or a delicately expressive and mobile human face—will project a particulate distribution of value properties. Consider also something already implicit in certain of the preceding examples: that if one thinks of the psychological processes of *meaning* in *perceptual* terms, then any given dated occurrence of a meaning—whether of a word or phrase or other linguistic unit, whether of a work of art, a gesture, a social "response," a historical event—will also "contain" a unique value-property distribution. Again, perceptual "feedback" from one's *own* activities, and inner processes and states, must also be thought to "contain" value properties. And certain classes of value properties may be thought to emerge from interactive relations as among "multidimensional" organizations of formal, meaningful, and actional suborganizations (to the extent to which these may be discriminable for analytic purposes).

Differentiated value events, then, are omnipresent in psychological function. If fact and value are ontologically disparate or in some sense separated "realms" or aspects of the universe, I do not know what the *psychological* evidence could be. I do not in fact see how one can conceive of any such monster as an axiologically neutral fact, or, for that matter, a factually neutral value.

Perhaps we have come to the preceding conclusion too rapidly, but I do not see how it can be resisted—nor indeed that much further argument is required, once the concept of value properties emerges. Those, however, who may initially find such a conclusion too great a wrench upon their previous beliefs, may find that it gains plausibility as we consider certain of its consequences. Since brief exploration is all that can be undertaken at this place, I shall move rapidly and more or less at random over a scattering of themes.

The reader will no doubt wish that his first payment on the promissory note issued by the preceding analysis will be concrete illustrations of the "value properties" which have been talked about with such indirection. The reader's wish is unfair! Much as I would like to oblige, I cannot accomplish in passing what several thousand years of human, humanistic, and scientific analysis have failed to do. In the case of visual art-produced experience, the typical kinds of things that the aestheticians, articulate artists, and art critics have been able to come up with in millenniums of analysis have been such global discriminations as harmony, symmetry, order, "significant form," "dynamic tension," "unity in variety," the "ratio of order to complexity," etc. By "value properties" I have in mind far more specific relational attributes of experience. They could, to borrow a cue from Gibson, be contingent upon subtle relational invariants in arrays of stimulation, as distributed over space and cumulated over time. They are almost certainly related to what Gibson would call "high-order variables of stimulation" and are themselves high-order relational variables within experience. The isolation of such value properties will not be accomplished within any specifiable time limit, will require learning to use language in new ways, and will require most of all the efforts of many individuals of exceptional and specialized sensitivity in significant areas of experience.

Certain of the difficulties that one faces in any attempt, even in a loose first-approximation way, to circumscribe value properties may perhaps be suggested by an informal example. For several years I have been impressed with an elusive common property of many perceptual "manifolds" in highly diverse contexts—a property which seems one of the marks of "elegance" or a certain kind of "sophistication" (in some special, "valuable" sense of the term). I suspect the quality in question—which is quite specific and can be only loosely suggested by any word currently in the natural language—to be intrinsic, in some fairly rudimentary sense, to simple perceptual contours having certain canonical properties. But how specify these canonical (value) properties? It is not easy!

The most effective presently available method (at least for me) would be by "differentiated ostension" via a large range of perceptual materials "possessing" the type of contour which I believe to have the canonical properties in question. If the addressee could then independently pick out further appropriate examples—perhaps localizing the contours with the canonical properties by finger tracing, or some such differentiated ostension—the presumption would be that he had at least in some degree disembedded the intended referent, and thus that communication had in some measure been achieved. Naturally, whether the addressee found the property or property complex in question to enter into similar relations within *his* experience to those I find in mine; whether he too found the property in some sense "attractive," etc., would be open to determination. Naturally, also, we could agree on a name for the property, either by selecting an available one from the natural language or by invention. Such a procedure would give some knowledge of this hypothetical value property, but not much.

Finer knowledge would be achieved if, say, a skilled artist could disembed the relational invariants constitutive of the percept properties in question sufficiently well to "create" instantial contours, so to say *ad libitum*. The artist, of course, might not be able, especially initially, to *specify* the relational invariants which "guide" his drawings. Should he (or anyone else) succeed at any level in making these effable, a still finer level of knowledge would be achieved. A further level of fineness might be achieved if now it became possible to relate this specification of the "critical" invariants to such a mathematicophysical metric for specifying "higher-order variables" of stimulation as has been conceived (very programmatically) by Gibson. Bearing in mind, of course, the limits of knowledge, analysis, language—not to mention the embeddedness of the phenomena at issue—it should be clear that even our ultimate encroachments upon "value properties" must be thought to be loosely approximative. But it should also be clear that the limiting precision cannot be established a priori, and that even small increments of precision are worthwhile.

If I were at this moment asked to specify verbally my "bounding" of the percept properties constitutive of what I have loosely called "elegance," I would have to be extremely vague. Consider imaginatively characteristic examples of "high fashion" costumes, aristocratic faces, fine *gran turismo* motor cars, "sophisticated" furniture (of any era), a range of highly stylized "schools" of art (e.g., Art Nouveau). Contrast these (to keep things simple, in terms of contour) with characteristic instances of grossly "nonsophisticated" forms of the relevant categories. For me, one fairly conspicuous difference is that in the "elegant" or "sophisticated" case the forms tend organically to encompass, yet transcend and subdue, a certain specific "awkwardness," "ungainliness," "disruptive tension," "distortion." A certain specific *range* of such "awkwardnesses," of course, each given instance being unique and "appropriate" to the contour in which it is encompassed. The awkwardness must have a special and in some sense meaningful relation to the form in which it is housed. The whole must conquer it, be victorious over the tension set up by the awkwardness. But the awkwardness must be such that the whole is enriched and given style, quiddity, bite, wit, life, depth (not necessarily in the spatial sense), interest, by its presence.

Now this description leaves me highly thwarted: it misses what I have in mind by a light-year. But if the reader can accept that what I have in mind is not entirely illusory, we can forget, for purposes of the *example,* whether even minimal justice has been done to the "value property" at issue. We can nevertheless note a number of interesting things:

Note first that in talking about this fairly specialized value property, the description presupposes that the "elegant" or "sophisticated" forms are more "complex," contain more "tension" or "conflict," have a different "ratio of order to complexity," and a more "significant form" than the negative cases. But all of these timeworn counters of aesthetic-perceptual analysis are so utterly general that, no matter how sensitively or discriminatingly applied, they could tell us next to nothing about the specialized "property" that we are after. Though not one of these counters is nonsignificant, they could be applied and reapplied for several millenniums (and some have) with no refinement or even cumulative increase of analytic knowledge. It is my contention that not only aesthetics and the humanities but, for reasons which I hope by now to be obvious, psychology, will remain in a very bad way indeed if we cannot do better.

Another thing worth noting is that once the search for such a relatively specific X as the one at issue has begun, possible interconnections with a very broad range of other psychological phenomena begin, if only vaguely, to suggest themselves. If, say, we begin with some such loose mapping of our X as "overcoming an awkwardness," it is clear that the nature and subspecies of the "awkwardness" would invite (and indeed require) analysis, as would the *mode* of "overcoming." Interpreting the "awkwardness" as a somewhat "repugnant" element which enriches the whole that conquers it, one can immediately think, say, of certain perfumes, the subtlety of which is much dependent on specific interplays against "unpleasant" olfactory components, certain exquisite examples of culinary art which depend on such subduals of the inappropriate or slightly repugnant (e.g., a certain Central European pastry blends a many-layered sweet crust with an intensely salted filling of cabbage). One thinks, further (and perhaps more loosely), of a large class of contexts which involve the "overcoming" of recalcitrant, gross, rough, crudely textured, or otherwise "inappropriate" *materials* ("content") by a specific over-all *form:* e.g., use of folk dialect or slang, or even an arbitrarily restricted language like that of symbolist poetry—in literature; use of "trash" and bric-a-brac in modern sculpture, "paintings," and collages. Keeping in mind the over-all range of these examples, it is already obvious that no single "value property" would give an equally apt description of every "case" (or indeed, any two "cases"). But it is equally clear that some degree of kinship which is yet more specific than whatever might be described by the traditional aesthetic counters (e.g., tension) is in principle achievable. More importantly, what seems to be suggested in that value properties will fall into similarity classes, the comparative investigation of which may in fact throw light on differentiations which would never have emerged if not for the superordinate similarities. One can thus look toward an anatomizing of the variables implicated in perceptual, motivational, and related psychological processes of a sort that might give truly differentiated, yet general, insight into the fine-structure of experience and action.

It will perhaps seem natural to think of value properties as being relevant to the "formal" aspect of art, as divorced from representational "content," "meaning," etc. But such an impulse can only stem from certain of the traditional vagaries concerning the significance of "content." For, as has already been briefly noted, if one follows the proposal that we think of "meaning" in a perceptual mode, then a distribution of value properties will be as much a "parameter" of the *meaning* of an aesthetic (or any perceptual) object as of its "form." This, incidentally, is implicitly recognized in much traditional aesthetic analysis in the tendency to apply global value-property categories of the order already illustrated (e.g., "unity in variety"; "tension," "conflict" and their dynamic resolution; "harmony") indifferently to phenomena of formal or contentual character: e.g., "conflict" in relation, say, to the interplay of formal elements in an abstract design, or in relation to the clash of motive in the drama; "complexity" in relation to the differentiation of form in visual art, music, or literature, as against complexity of any "representational content" that may be said to be conveyed by specific objects in any of those areas.

In the terms of the present conception, then, to the extent that "form" and "content" are analytically separated, there can be said to be separate value-property distributions corresponding to each. The total effect of the aesthetic (or other perceptual) object, in so far as mediated by value properties, can then be said to be a joint function of (1) value properties of the form, (2) value properties of the content, and (3) (very importantly) value properties which can be conceptualized as relationally determined by interactions of the formal and contentual ones. These latter "resultant" value properties would, of course, be implicated in the entire range of phenomena that aestheticians and critics consider in relation to such matters as "appropriateness" of formal to contentual aspects of the art object, and to the many controlled effects in the arts which are based on stresses or other modes of interaction, often ones which dynamically change over time (e.g., in poetry), as between formal and contentual "elements."

One general consequence for aesthetic theory of such points as have just been urged might be mentioned in passing. A familiar topic of aesthetic and critical speculation bears on the differential potentialities of the different primary "art forms" (e.g., painting, sculpture, music, architecture, poetry, the novel, etc.) and the various subspecifications of these into subforms of greater particularity, depending upon "medium," "genre," "intent category," some such dimension as "scope," "style" (in some collective sense), etc. A more or less standing premise of criticism is that the work of art be assessed relative to criteria appropriate to the genus (*cum differentia*) to which the work is allocated. When, however, the characteristics of the different art categories are considered or, say, when some question arises as to the absolute evaluation of a work of art, independently of its "category," analysis tends to become highly indeterminate and often to proceed in terms of some such diffuse notions as the differential "complexity," "richness," "depth," "scope," permitted by the different art forms.

Assuredly the present pretheoretical speculations offer no pat or immediate solution to such problems. But they do suggest these problems to be open to continuing and increasingly determinate analysis. For in the present terms, the differential characteristics of the various art forms, media, styles, etc., which will determine the potentialities of each for aesthetic experience, will depend upon the differential ranges of value properties which may be engendered within the resources of each. It is certainly reasonable to expect that the specialized value properties mobilizable by, say, painting versus architecture, by oil painting versus water color, by epic poetry versus lyrical, by differing prosodic forms in general, by poetry versus the novel, the novel in its different forms, the 12-tone scale versus the normal scale, and so on and on, differ markedly in range, though no doubt there is much overlapping. It should be possible ultimately to specify such differences not merely in a neutral jargon of "complexity" and the like, but in a far more illuminating way.

Such knowledge would obviously have important consequences not only for the theory and practice of criticism, but for more general questions. Among the latter is an issue which has long been treated rather superficially: that of whether art (in contradistinction to science) is "noncumulative." This "issue" is, of course, shorthand for a disorderly family of questions, none of them resoluble in passing. But the present line of thinking does suggest that there is one fairly determinate sense in which art may be said to be cumulative: i.e., artists of different sensibility and objective will inevitably "explore" (whether by intent or no) the potentialities of the "form," "medium," etc., within which they work; the very "uniqueness" attributed by all to the artist's "methods" and achievements will thus ensure within the history of any given "form" that much will be learned about its distinctive potential for the mobilization of value properties. Critics to some extent acknowledge this state of affairs by their frequent (and often glib) diagnoses of the demise through "exhaustion" of one or another form, tendency, genre. From the present point of view, then, there is a definite, if limited, sense in which it is "more" than metaphorical to talk about "experimentation" in reference to art and even to expect that "findings" (though most will remain implicit) cumulate. The great and self-conscious emphasis on "experimentalism" evidenced in most of the arts during the 20th century can thus be seen to be founded on something more substantial than merely a chic image—even though some of the passion behind the use of this image has an extra-aesthetic origin.

Though I believe that many more consequences of programmatic importance for aesthetics tend to follow from any such notion as "value properties," it is no part of my intention to continue a story which lacks all of its central characters. The immediate purpose of the above brief references to aesthetics was further to explicate the hypothetical notion of "value properties." But in so doing, we are thrust up against considerations that clarify the force of a point which thus far has been made only in passing. Recognition of the importance of increasingly fine specification of value properties not only opens a bridge between psychology and the humanities—more particularly, it points to a special and necessary kind of dependence of psychology on certain research resources that can only be made available by the humanities. The chief research "instrument" for disembedding value properties can only be human discrimination—and not just the kind of discrimination practiced by the most readily accessible sophomore but, rather, discrimination as informed by finely textured and relevantly specialized *sensibility*. In this of all areas, psychology must finally abjure its long cherished belief that "observer characteristics" are of minor importance (if indeed observers are granted *any* relevance to observation whatsoever!). To make significant progress toward the isolation of value properties will require the observational efforts not merely of individuals who are equipped by training with stocks of discriminations appropriate to the given area in which value phenomena are sought, but individuals of outstanding discriminal and even creative capacity in those areas. And it should be added that individuals from every field within the scholarly and critical humanities, the creative and performing arts, would be appropriate for the type of research here being envisioned.

IV. Coda: Philosophy, Science, and Value

Here we shall peer into this threatening jungle but briefly and hesitantly. The following few pages are offered only to punctuate the utter divergence between any analysis which sees the world so fulsomely inhabited with value phenomena as the present one and recently dominant views of the proper domain of axiological study, the relations between "value" and science, and thus more generally the place of value in the context of "knowledge." If the analyses of this paper are in any measure correct, then fundamental reconstruction is called for in the sweeping connections just mentioned.

The dimension of the reconstructive task that would have to be joined can be revealed only by reference to a view, some form of which dominated axiological thinking from the late '20's until quite recently: the "emotivist theory." This was the more or less official view of logical positivism, but its imprint can be seen as well in some of the more sophisticated thinking of the analytical philosophers. It is easily summarized. Recall that the meaning cosmology of classical logical positivism is exhausted by (1) formal tautologies, and (2) verifiable empirical statements. Question: Are value judgments tautologies? No—or at least *some* are not (and, be it noted, if "sin is evil" is a tautology, it is not a "good" one, not the kind that falls into the class of logical and mathematical propositions). Question: Are value judgments verifiable by observation? No: "conceit is sinful" seemed to these observers to have no clear-cut linkage to an "observable thing" definition base. Strictly, an ethical or aesthetic judgment is *meaningless.* Or it is at least "cognitively" meaningless. What then are ethical or aesthetic utterances? They are exclamations (or, if you prefer, ejaculations, imprecations, or some such emotional "expression"): they are expressions of approving or disapproving feeling, affect, emotion. Such a view was stated very sharply and simply by Ayer in the mid-'30's and has been elaborated in varying degrees of detail by others (rather fulsomely by Stevenson, 1944). Let us assure ourselves as to what this view is really saying. As A. C. Graham, an analytical philosopher, has recently pointed out (1961, pp. 13-14), the view in effect is saying that "There can be no fruitful dispute over questions of value except in terms of tastes and goals which the disputants happen to share. Moses blew off his emotions about murder by saying 'thou shalt not kill'; and if a killer from Auschwitz happens to feel differently, *de gustibus non disputandum.*"

Within the ambiance of analytical philosophy, the emotivist view soon shaded over into (or was supplemented by) the "imperativist" view, which holds that value judgments, pronouncements, standards, etc., are in effect commands. Since analytical philosophers had stressed the multiplicity of "use" functions in language, it was no longer to be maintained that value utterances are *meaningless,* but rather that being commands, they "behaved" in a very different way than did factual statements. As Graham puts it: "With this change of viewpoint it becomes possible to admit that moral and aesthetic standards do not say anything true or false about entities called 'goodness' and 'beauty' or about inclinations in taste, and yet to hold they are as meaningful as statements of fact" (pp. 14-15).

Analytic philosophy is currently extricating itself from the almost incredible simplism of such positions in the work of people like Hare (1963), Kerner (1966), and von Wright (1963). But it is too optimistic to believe that views of this order no longer have currency in philosophy and, what is worse, they live on in large segments of the scientific community and of the culture at large, into both of which contexts these views sifted, against little resistance, a long time ago. Indeed, there is a sense in which such views existed in science and the general culture considerably before they were reborn as technical philosophical formulations. Of course, "emotivism" and "imperativism" must also be seen in the line of subjectivistic views of value in philosophy and, to some extent, psychology, of which they are perhaps the supreme vulgarization. Subjectivistic theories agree in seeing value "constituted" in relation to the needs, motives, purposes, interests, wants, wishes, of individual men or organisms: values are thus regarded as ends or goals of systems of motivation to which they are extrinsic in the very sense described in our earlier analyses of the "extrinsic grammar."

Though sustained analysis in the philosophic mode is not here possible, a few remarks may perhaps clarify certain consequences of the present position. Suppose we start with some such proposition as "That picture is exquisite" or "That action is noble." It is hardly necessary to explain that from the present point of view these propositions are not equivalent (or fairly transformable) to "Picture, wheee!" or "Action, uhhuh!" (the "emotivist" interpretation) or to the imperativist's "Look at that picture!" (or "buy it" or "copy it"), or "Emulate that action!" From the present point of view, such statements are just as much "factual" as, say, "That picture is large" or "That action was rapid." In some sense more "factual" (if one be permitted degrees of "facticity") in that explication, even at relatively gross levels, of the "value properties" which *"in fact"* are governing discriminating application of "exquisite," say in some concrete instance of a complex painting, could in principle convey far more information than explication of the characters by virtue of which the picture may be said to be "large." If the rejoinder be "Yes, but there is still a difference in that virtually every user of a language could apply 'large' correctly (and explicate the basis of its use), whereas in the case of 'exquisite' we can expect much disagreement in application and in explication," then I must ask the questioner to consider that the history of art and of taste provides overwhelming evidence that if we compose a hierarchy of language communities for "exquisite" against appropriate criteria of training and sensitivity, we will find impressive intracommunity agreements with respect both to application and explication.

One can only conclude that the concept of "fact"—or its linguistic counterpart, as e.g., "factual" or "indicative" statement—is sorely in need of reanalysis. Facts must be in some way conceived as differentially charged with value, and whatever else a value may "be," it is a special kind of fact. Value statements in indicative form are not disguised exclamations or imperatives or, as other subjectivistic theories would have it, expressions of interest, wish, or need. Indeed, it is rather more fruitful to regard value utterances in "normative" or "imperative" form as disguised *indicative statements,* in that, at least when made responsibly, they emerge from a context of knowledge or "belief" within the speaker which could be unpacked into the "factual" or "indicative" statements on which the imperative is grounded.

The last point may be worth further examination. Let us concentrate on the case of a "command." When we assert a command, we do this within a context of belief that it will lead to such-and-such consequences for the commander, the commandee, for a third person, for a given group, the "world," etc. Part of that context of belief is a judgment that the intended consequent, or chain thereof, or ultimate consequent, is "good," "bad," "desirable," "undesirable" (often in *specific ways*) with respect to such-and-such or so-and-so. Such a judgment can in principle be unpacked into a sequence of meaningful ("factually" or "indicatively" meaningful, if one prefers) propositions re value properties. The mysterious "leap" from the "is" to the "ought" is no mystery. It is no great epistemological profundity that the rules of English do not permit one to say that a "command" is "verifiable." That it is useful for a language to contain specialized forms which register to a hearer that an action, change of belief, or some such thing is being called for, tells us no profound fact about the universe. As we have suggested, the context of knowledge, belief, expectation, etc., from which a command "issues" can be described via a collectivity of "is" statements, a subclass of which can be said to be indicative of *value properties*. That "is" often signalizes empirically "verifiable" attribution (or predication, etc.), and "ought" obligation (or an "imperative" intent, or imperiousness, sententiousness, arrogance, petulance, prudishness, or passion) is a useful feature of language, but not a regulative principle of the universe.

To repeat, then, the concept of "fact" needs radical revamping: "facts" are suffused with "value"; and "value" diffused in "fact." The last statement is a homespun prolegomenon to a metaphysics. But as a *psychologist,* I can see no other beginning.

Turning now to the relations between values and science—as seen now by the *scientist*—it can be said that the simplisms long accepted by many men of the white cloth exceed in vacuity even the philosophic ones which we have just examined. Thus, it is still something like standard belief that science is concerned exclusively with "neutral" factual relationships, that it seeks "objective" knowledge of invariable associations of observable events, or probable empirical regularities, that it can talk about instrumental relationships or "means-end" relationships, *but can say nothing about ends*. In so far as the standard patter permits reference to "values," their relevance must be allocated, so to say, to the human or social context in which, for some obscene reason, science happens to be embedded. Thus it is permissible (at least on the part of the tender-minded) to suggest that the scientist, as a *citizen,* should be concerned with the relation between scientific knowledge and human welfare, that it is desirable that he take an interest in determining that scientific knowledge be applied to "good" social ends and not evil ones, etc. The *very* daring are even beginning to go so far as to admit that certain moral traits of the *scientist* have a relevance to science—that it is desirable that he have a respect for the "truth," desirable that he not fudge his data.

Perhaps the reader will feel with some indignation that the preceding account is too cynical: is there not, after all, a great clamor now shaping up in scientific circles about such matters as the "responsibility of the scientist"? There in fact is, and I would be the last to think it an unhappy development. But *even* those currently concerned to bring about sharper recognition of the relevance of value factors to science tend to proceed as if the issues can be encapsulated and dispatched in two or three generalizations, or perhaps admonitions. A recent case in point may be found in C. P. Snow's article on "The Moral Un-neutrality of Science" (1961) in which the story comes down pretty much to the fact that scientists respect the truth, and should; that they tend more than most groups to care about people, inclusive of the poor, and should; that they lead relatively cleaner lives with less divorce than do, on average, members of certain other groups, and should. From another of Snow's contributions (1959), we learn that scientists have "the future in their bones." And should.

In rather marked contradistinction to the stereotypes concerning science-value relations, the present position suggests considerations of the following order: Value-property distributions will suffuse all perception, all meaning; such "parameters" of psychological process do not hygienically cancel out when the context becomes one of science. Scientific languages, no matter how restricted, will generate meanings suffused by value properties; indeed, the languages themselves considered as perceptual objects will also "generate" value properties.

Much of science is concerned with the understanding, explication, or causal analysis of value phenomena—or perhaps more properly, phenomena suffused to one or another extent with value properties. If one were to make a global generalization (requiring marked qualification in certain areas), it could be said that as one ascends the scale from the physical sciences through the biological sciences to the social sciences and finally the humanities, one confronts "subject matters" more and more richly permeated with value properties or, more percisely put, these various subject matters may be ordered in terms of differential concentration upon value-property aspects of each. If it be maintained that those who work at the *scientific* levels are *confined* to *factual* statements about the value "aspects" of their subject matter, then I reply that we have shown the conventional usage of "fact" to be either incorrect or systematically ambiguous in the very sense that begs the question. Surely if a scientist discovers a polio vaccine, no semantic prohibition should prevent him from "leaping" from a well-formed and well-evidenced means-end statement to the "ought" injunction that adds a directive rider to the cognitive content. If it be maintained that the scientist is still merely making a conditional statement of the form "if you wish (for some damn fool reason) to remain well

. . ., etc., etc.," then the answer might well be that the state of health is self-recommending by virtue of intrinsic value properties.

Consider now the actual *human context* of science. Or better, the human center. Put the scientist, the actor, back in the picture from which he has been for so long excluded. We have argued that value-determining properties are generated by the neural processes which are the substrate of action; that they must in some sense be thought criterial with respect to the movement-by-movement directionality of action. That we can as yet only speak a metaphorical and vague language about such matters has nothing to do with the force of the evidence that recommends such metaphors. In reaching toward understanding, lawful analysis, "control," if you will, of the phenomena which entice their interest, scientists are reaching toward meanings, toward the maximization of certain value properties immanent within those meanings, and throughout are guided by value-determining properties which are some function of the concurrent "input" and their own internal "processings." The latter will reflect, among other factors, those quasi-permanent "structures" that we also sometimes call "values" in the sense manifested by durable preference-dispositions, etc. Values in this sense are often roughly equated with "tastes," "prizings," "attitudes," sometimes with "needs," etc. However such enduring value systems be conceptualized, they may be seen as organizations which govern the moment-to-moment salience, potency, of differential "clusters" or ranges of "specialized" value properties.

Such durable value dispositions (call them *V*alues) will be heavily implicated in the "options" that a scientist asserts in inquiry, the moment-to-moment decisions that he makes. Are such events rare? There is a way of describing inquiry which sees it, and validly so, as a sequence of human options, a flow of decisions. Yet even the obvious Value foci provided by the optional elements in science tend to be bypassed in standard discussions of science and value. Consider the contingency, at all times, of the scientific enterprise on the "aims" of the scientist, on his predilections with respect to choice of method, both conceptual and empirical, his predilections with respect to mode of problem formulation, his sense of scientific "importance," his perception of the relation between his actions and the standards of his colleagues or the needs of society; his predilections concerning factors in light of which he adjusts his scientific beliefs or assertions to "evidence"; his preferences with respect to modes of theoretical processing, with respect to optimal modes of conduct in the polemical situations of science, and so on and on. Hopefully, many of his options are fixed upon in terms of the "rational" productivity of their consequences in the choices of other men, present and past. Hopefully, they remain contingent in some degree upon such consequences as experienced in his own biography. But such matters are *choices;* they are *decisions.* Nothing should conceal their determination by processes having marked value components (however these be phrased), nor should anything conceal the value aspects of the web of commitment and dedication which interpenetrates all the activities of scientists.

Paul Dirac has recently been widely quoted as having written, "It is more important to have beauty in one's equations than to have them fit experiment." Polanyi has placed strong and consistent emphasis on what he has called the "harmonious character" of a theoretical conception, or set of ideas, in guiding its creation, elaboration, productiveness, and fate. Virtually all major creative figures in the history of theoretical physics and of mathematics—and before these, the Pythagoreans—have said something of the same sort. Indeed, it is a *truism* of the "formal" disciplines generally—logic as well as mathematics—that "elegance" is a prime desideratum. And even logical positivists have included on occasion "elegance"—along with "economy" and the like—as a mark of the "fruitfulness" of theory. Can this vast range of agreement point to something purely adventitious? At this inordinately complex and important level too, then, value is criterial with respect to science.

The present analysis may have seemed at times to be absorbing *everything* in science, all of "fact," into value. Perhaps it has in some sense gone too far in this direction: it is not yet easy to talk about such problems. But judging from the circumstances just mentioned, the present account is in good company. What I should like to urge, though, is that, instructive though it be to acknowledge "beauty," "harmony," "elegance," as criterial with respect to scientific theory, to the processes of thinking which result in theory, this is but the beginning of instruction. "Beauty," "harmony," "elegance," land us back among the most global value-abstractions of aesthetics; they are on a par as well with "good" and "right" in ethics. The burden of this paper has been to urge that the human race cannot forever rest content with so nonspecific and gross a level of analysis of its most meaningful accomplishments, prized artifacts, significant phenomena. The concept of value properties may involve no more than an assertion of faith that finer degrees of specification are possible. Yet in our most fluent dialogues with ourselves and with our friends, when they are fluent, we have proved on countless occasions that finer knowledge is possible.

Bibliography

Ayer, A. J. (1936), *Language, Truth and Logic.* Oxford: Oxford University Press.

Graham, A. C. (1961), *The Problem of Value.* London: Hutchinson University Library.

Hare, R. M. (1963), *Freedom and Reason.* New York and Oxford: Oxford University Press.

Kerner, G. C. (1966), *The Revolution in Ethical Theory.* New York and Oxford: Oxford University Press.

Koch, S. (1954), Clark L. Hull. In *Modern Learning Theory.* New York: Appleton-Century-Crofts, pp. 1-176.

——— (1956), Behavior as "Intrinsically" Regulated: Work Notes towards a Pre-theory of Phenomena Called "Motivational." In *Current Theory and Research in Motivation,* Vol. 4, ed. M. R. Jones. Lincoln: University of Nebraska Press, pp. 42-86.

——— (1959), Epilogue. In *Psychology: A Study of a Science,* Vol. 3, ed. S. Koch. New York: McGraw-Hill, pp. 729-788.

——— (1961), Behaviourism. In *Encyclopaedia Britannica,* 3:326-329.

——— (1964), Psychology and Emerging Conceptions of Knowledge as Unitary. In *Behaviorism and Phenomenology,* ed. T. W. Wann. Chicago: University of Chicago Press.

Miller, G. A., Galanter, E., & Pribram, K. H. (1960), *Plans and the Structure of Behavior.* New York: Holt.

Snow, C. P. (1959), *The Two Cultures and the Scientific Revolution.* New York: Cambridge University Press.

——— (1961), The Moral Un-neutrality of Science. *Science,* 133:256-259.

Stevenson, C. L. (1944), *Ethics and Language.* New Haven: Yale University Press.

von Wright, G. H. (1963), *The Varieties of Goodness.* New York: Humanities Press.

DISCUSSION

DR. KOCH:

One way of putting the terms of my inquiry, which shows more clearly its relation to certain questions discussed here earlier, is to say that it is an exploration of an alternative to the practice long dominant in psychology, as well as in biology, of phrasing behavior, whether descriptively or causally, in terms of adaptation, adjustment, or some such conception. Whatever one thinks of the utility of adaptation in the context of evolutionary theory—and I am not here to judge that question—it is clear, and there seems to have been a current of agreement to this effect, that its value for giving insight into certain aspects of phylogenetic development does not justify and certainly does not necessitate its transposition to the description and analysis of all human activities. Yet most modern psychological theory has explicitly defined its objectives against the framework of organic evolution and indeed founded key concepts upon Darwinian evolutionary theory. Nowhere is this more apparent than in the various subtheories—of instinct, need, drive, etc.—that may be found in formulations as diverse as psychoanalysis, McDougall's "hormic" psychology, and the endless variants of behaviorism.

Take, for an example, a single instance of the last, Clark Hull's neobehaviorist position: as measured by number of investigators influenced, it is probably the most influential of all behaviorist positions. This position was explicitly called by him a "theory of adaptive behavior," and in his writings he time after time identifies the general problem of behavior theory as that of determining the engineering principles which would insure the adaptation to environment of a self-maintaining robot via the reduction of its several needs. Need reduction was the major selective principle in his analysis of learning, and each of the postulates of his theory was presumably an "engineering principle," specifying the dynamics of adaptive behavior.

In my paper I pursue a line of speculation, one purpose of which is to free psychology from the dominance of this adaptational model. (I wouldn't necessarily put it in those terms except for the discussion of Dr. Chance's paper.) That organisms are biologically equipped to be self-maintaining systems, that they have biological arrangements which work toward and mediate survival, both for the individual and the species, I do not deny. This may be an important truth, certainly not a trivial truth, but it is a very general one. I am concerned, so to say, with the content and determinants of the organism's activities during the course of its survival, which after all is the main problem for psychology and of no indifferent interest to a few other human curiosities that may be asserted. I should add that, on *my* analysis, the thought schema represented by concepts like adaptation is far older than evolutionary theory, and is indeed deeply embedded in certain common-sense presuppositions of the West which see all action in an "in-order-to" or instrumental frame. But about this I have written in my paper.

MR. GOLD:

As a defrocked undergraduate I'm sympathetic to your point of view—I was taught the overkill approach to psychology in school. But I'm puzzled as to how far one can really go with the scientific study of taste and such matters. The artist may remind the psychologist of the importance of questions of taste—which lie *beyond* science—but can the psychologist *as such* really do anything with this reminder?

DR. KOCH:

That is a powerful question to which I only wish I could give a final, happy, and exhaustive answer. If I could now dispense a few bottled research careers for graduate students, I would feel peaceful. There *are* modest possibilities of research along these lines. To some extent some of them are already under way, but only to some extent. One could point to a theorist by the name of Gibson—James Gibson of Cornell University—who has been doing some very interesting theoretical and experimental work in recent years. His work is based on the assumption that we've terribly simplified our notion of the stimulating energies that impinge on the organism, as a result of the rather crass phenomenology built into the 19th-century psychophysics, and even the limitations in the physicist's description of the energies to which the organism's sensory surfaces are sensitive. We had come out with certain determinants of aspects of sensory experience that entered into functional relations, were useful for measurement purposes, and so on. This gave us a very simplified and selective description of the sea of stimulation to which we are exposed. Gibson takes the position that one can isolate a large number of *relational* variables in the actual physical stimulus "array," which control detailed and subtle aspects of the perceptual process. There is one in particular—optical texture—which he has worked on and shown in very interesting experiments to have subtle relations with aspects of perception such as size constancy. These experiments can be checked in adequate ways—granting a sensible interpretation of science which permits the belief that observers can report their experience meaningfully, and that the agreement of trained (and relevantly sensitive) observers can have legitimate evidential weight.

Now this is simply an indication of a movement in the direction I have been talking about. Gibson doesn't talk specifically of value properties, but I think he might accept an analysis somewhat similar to this if one were to ask what the implications of his mode of analysis were for such things as I have tried to address. Gibson would perhaps be willing to acknowledge—just as I do—that there are specialized relational invariants in the stimulus array in correspondence with positive and negative value characters in experience, and adient and abient action tendencies of the organism. There would also be strong differences which we need not go into here.

As a more general answer to this question, this approach suggests that there are possibilities for collaboration between psychologists and the artist, the gifted humanist, and so on, toward the end of narrowing down, encroaching upon, such experiential characters as I have called value properties. One doesn't think of this naïvely; one doesn't think of value properties as little segregated entities which some kind of introspective microscope will cause to emerge full-blown. It's a question of increasing the specificity of analysis, past—far past—that achieved by philosophical aesthetics, which has been fairly static for several thousand years. When you come down to it, we haven't gone much past the Greeks, despite a tradition of rather ardent effort by humanists. We want something that gives higher degrees of specificity than rather global concepts like "symmetry," "order," "complexity," "unity in variety," "significant form," and so on. We have to have a faith that this can be done: most of you have noticed that in informal conversations among highly sensitive and competent people concerned with the arts or with other pursuits involving subtle discriminations, much higher orders of specificity *are* often achieved and—if there are comparable levels of training and sensitivity among the discussants—there can be pretty far-reaching agreement.

I can see the possibilities of a certain mode of analysis of art objects (whether these be visual art objects or of any other kind) which could involve a profitable application of certain aspects of psychological method. To begin with, there is a range of procedures called "psychophysical methods" which have generated some very foolish kinds of knowledge, but are nevertheless useful in telling us how to analyze complex perceptual relationships, and we might combine whatever little sophistication is vouchsafed by these with whatever information of a meaningful sort we have about perception, the latter deriving mainly from certain aspects of gestalt psychology. If probing and sensitive protocols in response to art objects were elicited from gifted artists, humanists, etc., under conditions permitting use of these methods, advance *could* occur. Such collaborative research would have to be rather open-ended, but I think that one can anticipate some degree of progress; how much one doesn't know.

But now to take your suggestion, Mr. Gold. You say that the psychologist has been reminded by the humanist of matters like the importance of questions of taste, and that maybe this should remain the relationship. Well, it's not a very symbiotic relationship actually, is it? I mean the psychologist has had many such reminders, and this has done very little good so far as the historical development of psychology is concerned. On the other hand, to me it's a rather austere and dismal circumstance that what is called aesthetics—as practiced by humanists—has remained so static for so long. This certainly has not obviated the possibility of significant assertions of taste—as in great criticism. The play of a fine and informed sensibility can reveal much about the value characters of art objects not accessible to the less qualified—and this without guidance by any technical theory whatsoever. Yet I cannot help feeling that the aridity of traditional aesthetics has limited the depth and specificity of insight that might be attained about aesthetic experience—about the relations of specifiable properties of the art object to specifiable aspects of experience. This may be highly problematic—but perhaps even the humanist and artist could profit a little from a bit of the same kind of empirical curiosity that the psychologist—by the very demands of his subject—should be asserting. But I admit that even for the psychologist such an assertion is a futurity.

PROFESSOR SCOTT:

I'm concerned about the methodological complications of what you say in terms of atomism in talking about value properties. You said you didn't want to make them into entities, but you seemed to talk about analysis in terms of atomistic concepts of pure properties, rather than in terms of the person. It would seem to me at the same time you're saying that judgments have to be made by particular persons. I wonder if there isn't a possible bridge between what you are saying and the Jungian approach, which would say that you talk about images or roles, which are persons. In other words, your value properties might be understood not as separate things but as an expression of either a person or an image of a person, a gestalt, which has many properties related to it, as an element of analysis, rather than an atomistic one.

DR. KOCH:

The second part of your question gets into a realm which I hesitate to discuss. One is dealing with such exceedingly tenuous states of affairs when one begins to think of the bearing of value properties on the Jungian image. I think I'll bow out of that one.

Am I thinking about value properties in atomistic terms? It is part of the nature of language that when you begin to specify, you multiply entities, or seem to because of the requirements of differentiated discourse. I think of value properties as immanent characteristics—extremely embedded relational aspects—most immediately of experience, in the intervening instance ("value-*determining* properties") of the neural processes of which experience is a function, and in the initiating instance ("value-*generating* properties") of the stimulus array. This is the way I think about them.

PROFESSOR POLANYI:

I can see two apparent confirmations of the possibilities which are suggested here. One is in the study of apes painting, in which the categories of aesthetic satisfaction can be identified and also most attractively differentiated or distinguished against drive satisfaction. If you offer a reward to these animals, they immediately start skimping their work; it becomes wholly commercialized and useless.

PROFESSOR KLEIN:

It's been demonstrated.

PROFESSOR POLANYI:

I would also interpret the observation about the restoring effects of dreams in this sense: that the exercise of the imagination is something which is beneficent to the organism and which, I think, is a need very similar to those which produce art and literature. When I first heard the expression "dream deprivation," which Dement coined from his experiments, I immediately thought of the situation in the Soviet Union where obviously the revolution of 1956 was brought about by dream deprivation, by the suppression of the free exercise of true imaginative conflicts.

DR. KOCH:

I'm afraid none of us can say very much about the fine-structure of imaginative process, but I would think of the movement of the imagination as guided on a moment-to-moment basis by value properties. But this statement will have to remain a blank form because the analysis that would give it content is too cumbrous for the occasion—perhaps for any occasion.

PROFESSOR C. DOUGLAS MCGEE:

I feel as if I were a spy from the Society for Cultural Diversity, but I would like to suggest that, as I see it in your paper, the use of the term "value properties" involves a kind of fudge; that is, you slip from "value-determining properties" to "value properties" without indicating where you make this move. If throughout the paper instead of saying value properties you had said "valued properties," you would have emerged with some rather different conclusions. In fact, it is *we* who do the valuing in response to certain properties in the objects. You slip back and forth between the objective characteristics of the object contemplated and our response to it, and this vitiates the conclusions you draw about aesthetics and ethics. What you are really talking about is aesthetics as a descriptive discipline. You are talking about how, in fact, certain kinds of observers respond to certain art objects: you're saying, as Charles Morris tried to do some years back, that we might be able to show in finer and finer and finer terms the objective characteristics in terms of which responses are made. What I'm saying is that the end process of this would at most be a description of characteristics to which classes of respondents responded. This would not touch what has been considered to be the normative aspect of aesthetics at all, unless you want to identify the valued with the valuable. But this, you notice, requires an additional, normative postulate that what such-and-so people value I ought also to value. There are similar issues in ethics. You can talk about the characteristics which are called good, evil, and so on, as discriminated by certain people, that is, about the value-determining properties for their evaluation. The step from there to saying that these are the things that *ought* to be valued is an additional step, and you ought not to fudge the making of that step, by using a term that's ambiguous, between a description of determining characteristics and the response to them.

DR. KOCH:

I'm not impressed with the fact that the step that you accuse me of making is so marked a step, or large a step, as it has tended to be thought to be, in various forms of theory. Because on my analysis, unlike that of Morris, which is a very different analysis, the value properties in experience can be characterized as intrinsic values. They are not contingent on any process of judgment or valuation; indeed, my theory would find it more natural to say that judgment or valuation is contingent on value properties. No specifiable process of valuation takes place. There are immanent attractions, revulsions, and so on, having very specific and differentiated properties in experience. Therefore, what I've been doing is developing an objective theory of value on the basis of what I conceive to be good psychological evidence. And once one has an objective theory of value, one says that intrinsically valuable aspects of experience are related in orderly ways to biological function and to the nature of the stimulating situation—the input situation. Once one can demonstrate that if one controls for observer characteristics, one gets agreements, and that these agreements are not merely results of social learning or some such process, then, it seems to me, the presumably formidable gap between the "is" and the "ought" begins to narrow. I addressed myself to this question in the final part of my paper. I have a feeling I'm going in the right direction in that final section, although I am sure there are one or two analytic philosophers in the world who would not share that feeling.

As for shifting from value-determining properties to value properties—I think if you return to my paper that you will find the usage usually in accord with the context. Sometimes I want to focus attention on the neural value-determining processes of which value properties are a function. Sometimes I focus on value properties. We would make inferences about the characteristics of the value-determining properties from value properties.

DR. KLEIN:

My own field is perception *and* motivation. I'd like to bring the discussion back to the issue of motivation in perception. I sympathize with Dr. Koch's emphasis on value *in* the perceptual process. However, it seems to me that the problem of intrinsic and extrinsic still remains. I think it would be awfully narrow to confine the issue of motivation to the matter of end-seeking definitions of motivation. The extended sense of motivation concerns the question of the significance of behavior, and significance has both an intrinsic and an extrinsic aspect. Significance is given in part by the inherent structure of the perception we're talking about, and this side Dr. Koch properly emphasizes. But significance is also given by a value extrinsic to the perception. For a complete account of the significance of the perception we need both. It's a matter of what Henry Murray once called "synthesism," the matter of putting together discordant elements. For example, Dr. Koch mentioned in passing the issue of doodling. The significance of doodling includes both extrinsic and intrinsic considerations. You cannot account for doodling in terms of any purposive motivational statement alone. This doesn't describe the doodling per se, which has its own structure. But it does add something to the understanding of the significance of doodling to be able to state validly that, say, there is some stylistic pattern in the person's life, some dilemma, being stated in the doodle.

Or take the slip of the tongue. The slip of the tongue has many possible attributes that would tell us of its significance. Among them are statements about motivation, not an end-seeking meaning, but in terms of its significance. One more example: novelty and curiosity behavior. We speak of novelty, and the behaviors associated with curiosity arising from the novelty, as perhaps arising from three possible sources, which give us some sense of its significance. Novelty and curiosity behavior can arise from a fascination with the strange, a need or desire to engage it. Or the same behavior can arise from an intolerance of the strange and the need to degrade it to the familiar. Which of the two is associated with the novelty I think adds to the description of the novelty. And these are extrinsic to the novelty behavior. So I would hate to see the issue of significance, which for me belongs to the question of motivation, ruled out by Dr. Koch's proper emphasis. Traditionally, this issue has been discussed in the form of the difference between purpose and function. Behavior can have a function, and yet not necessarily be purposive in the sense of an end-seeking activity. I still think that we must not shortchange such a consideration.

DR. KOCH:

Dr. Klein, I agree with you. I think there is one tiny ambiguity involved here. It has to do with the sense in which I used "extrinsic" and "intrinsic." I was using "extrinsic" in a very restrictive sense: namely, I was correlating to "extrinsic" a specific disequilibrium/equilibrium-restoral model of motivation. "Intrinsic" I was using in more like the normal meaning of processes that are immanent in an ongoing "unit" of activity or experience. I would say, yes—I am not so berserk as to assume that behavior is an endless flow of unique process syndromes that reflect only the immediately active factors that are governing behavior at that given time. It is, as you know, terribly difficult to distinguish between perception and cognition, cognition and imagination, etc. In perceptual process, obviously, much of the organization and much of that aspect of perception which can be called meaning will be a function of relationships between current input and—here you could choose from a variety of languages—stored residues of previous experience. I think that in these cases, too, value properties are extremely important as selective factors determining the "communication" between the input process and the specific "parts" of the residue system which become activated.

PROFESSOR TAYLOR:

Aren't you still too narrow? I can think of at least three models to add to your two extrinsic ones. There is the one that you're talking about, and there is another intrinsic one, which is not the model of adients or abients to some feature that draws or pushes you away, but simply the explanation that determines that a certain activity is more to be desired. Take an example, in my part of the world, that is, in Canada, it's not safe to go into the woods, for fear you'll be filled with buckshot, in the hunting season. It's not exactly clear why this goes on, but part of it could be explained in terms of the beauties of the wild, which may be a value property.

DR. KOCH:

I seriously think that the intrinsically attractive activities that you're talking about represent in effect the beginning of analysis. On my assumptions, I would like to press analysis as far as I can into a determination of what aspects of this total temporally and spatially deployed input that we're talking about are in effect controlling the adience toward them and the value dimension of experience and behavior at the time.

I suspect, as I tried to say in the case of play and so on, that one can conceivably come up with relational aspects of value experiences in different "domains" which do overlap—though value properties implicated in qualitatively different activities or behavior contexts are unlikely to match each other in all respects. I suspect that the determinants of behavior and experience are of that order. I suspect this in terms of my experience as a human being and in terms of my own capacity to disembed what the leading variables are in my own experience of art, nature, food, and so on. But I can't say a priori that I'm necessarily going to succeed in this reduction to any given point. I think, however, that the human race has been very obstinate in its refusal to press analysis further. I think it should be tried. I'm glad to see the artist, Professor Weismann, nodding his head in agreement. So I think yours is just a special case of my kind of analysis: namely, when my kind of analysis just fails.

DR. STRAUS:

I want to go back to Dr. Klein's point: the larger context of significance. We can only desire what we don't have; we can only desire to be what we are not. Eating a nice steak, if I'm hungry, has certain value properties, but if I'm saturated, it has not. If I return to the dining room after a meal, the smells that attracted me before do so no longer. The lower senses, taste and smell, have in themselves always a characteristic of repelling or attracting. Let me take one example—everyone in the morning looks into the mirror and tries to embellish herself or himself. We prepare the image which we want to present to others. If we are in a bad humor we would say it's vanity. But this vanity is related to the image we want to present to others and which we are not by nature.

Then there would be another level of contrasts. Coming to Brunswick, or to Maine, I've become very much interested in its history. Someone may present this history to me in a way which is lucid and clear, and satisfy better my interest in the historical connections of the fragment which is open to me than someone who tells me a boring story; it's also this way with aesthetic value. With food, it's a revolving process. We are hungry; we eat; we are satisfied; and then nature takes the same course again. But let me say that hearing you talk or seeing a picture for the first time is very different from the experience of, say, a guard in a museum—there is no deeper expression of extreme boredom than can be seen in museum guards. It seems to me property values depend on our own historical situation.

DR. KOCH:

I don't think there is any conflict between what you are saying and what I have said. I did try to indicate that there is an important relationship between certain biogenic deprivation conditions like hunger and value properties. But if you have a model such that you *don't* acknowledge the value properties, but only the biogenic conditions, then you are led into the most crass representation of behavior and experience. For instance, I can conceive of myself as being extraordinarily hungry, but dropping on the floor an insufficiently rare steak. I preferred to phrase the relationship before by saying that the cyclical conditions of the sort that you were discussing (the biogenic deprivations, etc.) tend to make especially salient, in controlling behavior, a certain range of value properties; tend to prime them, tend to make them more or less dominant, so far as the probabilities of behavior and experience are concerned that go on with these conditions. Yet often one will interrupt even such a behavior trend (which is in some loose sense of the word under the control of a biogenic deprivation condition) by virtue of the impact of an intrinsically attractive aspect of experience that just happens to come into play at that particular time—as a result, say, of a change of one's relationship to the environment, or something of the sort. I can conceive of being extraordinarily hungry and setting off for a restaurant and on the way passing an art gallery which is having an exhibit of a painter for whom I have a great fondness and suddenly finding myself in the gallery, not the restaurant.

PROFESSOR CROSSON:

I'd like to raise a question that I think has been suggested partially in other forms to Dr. Koch. He was trying to build two different methods of approach, one of which was descriptive and evaluative in terms of meaning and so on, and the other of which was objective, as suggested by the alternative between elicited behavior and directed action. What struck me was that after having built the bridge, it seemed to me he crossed to the other side and was back where he started. I mean, if it were possible to push further the analysis of aesthetic forms, to the point where we could get some kind of finite list of perceptual qualities which correlated with aesthetic pleasure, then all we would do is find another stimulus-releasing object, drive-satisfying object. The alternatives to that would be an approach toward a description of aesthetic phenomena which would direct itself toward their meaning, rather than to the resolution of an objectively specified set. For example, in aesthetic phenomena, the *meaning* of horizontal lines to man's upright posture.

DR. KOCH:

I see the point you're trying to make. I don't think I'm guilty of this; although how I can make this clear in a short time, or perhaps infinite time, I'm not sure. I invite you to read the part of my paper on aesthetics—where in fact I talk about form versus content, formal versus meaningful aspects of art, and so on. Perhaps I begin to wring too much out of my feeble notion of value properties, but I also talk about *meanings* as characterized by distributions of value properties. I tend to think of meaning in perceptual terms, and presuppose, I'm afraid, an analysis of meaning which I have spelled out at some length in a number of other papers (to confound the problem, some of them unpublished ones). Even if *all* I were looking for is an objectification of relational aspects of the stimulus which control experienced value properties—it should be noted that behaviorists would never ask such a question. I think you're being too kind to behaviorists. In the first instance, experiential value properties are phenomena which their metaphysic—and it still exists despite loud disclaimers for several decades to the effect that the position has a purely "methodological" force—would prevent them from even acknowledging. In the second place, the rather rough grain of their concepts is such that no analogous "phenomena" could ever be phrased in the terms of their conceptual language.

In effect, I don't think that any specifications of value properties that one can achieve are going to conform to any of the recent paradigms of what we mean by that terribly confused concept of the "objective." I do not think we are going to be able to specify them in terms reducible to observable predicates of a "thing language" or any similar reduction base. I think that often—in so far as we achieve consensus with respect to value properties—this will only be within groups of special individuals, who have appropriate qualifications of sensibility and training for making the relevant discriminations. Now this does not conform to any objective paradigm of the sort that you might have had in mind, or certainly that the behaviorist has in mind.

PROFESSOR CROSSON:

I take it that my fundamental assumption was wrong, and that you are really suggesting a quite other kind of psychology, with its own method quite distinct from behaviorism.

DR. KOCH:

Well, I certainly am suggesting a psychology with concepts quite distinct from behaviorism, and methods (in the large) other than those used by behaviorists. I'm not suggesting some wild rejection of the entire history of psychology. There are methods of perceptual analysis—for instance, the congeries of techniques that we refer to as psychophysical method—which can be very helpful in the pursuit of these problems.

DR. STRAUS:

Is not behaviorism based on two fundamental errors? One is that the behaviorist could never apply the principles of behaviorism to himself. Should he try, he would be eliminated as an observer, because *all* events occurring in an experiment would be stimuli acting on *his* brain, and his response would not be identical with the response of the person observed. One must not overlook the fact that in every psychological experiment two brains or two nervous systems are involved—that of the subject observed and that of the observer himself.

The other misidentification, which should be prohibited by law, is the confusion of stimuli and objects. Stimuli arc by definition physical agents and as such are not endowed with secondary qualities. In other words, stimuli cannot be observed. The relationship of an observer to objects of his observation is totally different from that of a nervous system receiving stimuli. Physical agents are transformed into stimuli only after they have reached and acted upon the so-called receptors. Therefore, stimuli are neither identical with objects nor with physical agents in general, but only with those that have been absorbed into an individual nervous system, at one particular time. Stimuli supposedly provoke responses; the response follows the stimulus. But when we speak about a response, we relate a later event back to an earlier one. Since a stimulus necessarily precedes a response, we can never manipulate stimuli in an experiment; they must have already been absorbed in one particular brain, strictly private.

There is no communication possible in terms of stimuli. However, when we administer Rorschach tests, for example, we take it for granted that the same chart is visible to testor and testee, and that both can see each other and communicate with each other. This situation of two persons inspecting one and the same visible object together cannot be translated into the terminology of stimuli and responses. The pencil of light reflected from the chart that stimulates the testee's retinae does not reach the observer. Instead, all the reactions of the patient, including his "responses," would be "stimuli" for the observer. The two brains do not communicate; the two persons do. True, they could not see without light and stimulation; the psychological problem, however, is to acknowledge and to understand how sensory experience transcends the causal relation of nervous system and stimuli.

INDEX

ABOUT THE AUTHORS

M. R. A. CHANCE is a zoologist, and graduated from University College, London, in 1937. He was Lecturer in Experimental Pharmacology at the University of Birmingham (from which he received his D.Sc. in 1958) from 1947 to 1967, when he became Reader in Ethology and head of the Subdepartment of Ethology, Department of Psychiatry. He has published a number of papers on the structure of social behavior of mammals, especially primates.

MARJORIE GRENE received her Ph.D. in philosophy from Radcliffe College in 1935. She has taught philosophy at the University of Chicago, the University of Leeds, and Queens University, Belfast, and is at present Professor of Philosophy at the University of California, Davis. Her recent publications include *A Portrait of Aristotle* (1964), *The Knower and the Known* (1966), and *Approaches to a Philosophical Biology* (1969).

SIGMUND KOCH received his Ph.D. in psychology from Duke University in 1942. He has taught at Clark University, the University of London, and Duke University. In 1953 he became director of the American Psychological Association's study of the status of psychology in the United States, from which issued the seven-volume *Psychology: A Study of a Science* (1959-1963), edited by Dr. Koch. He left Duke in 1964 to become director of the Ford Foundation Program in the Humanities and the Arts. In 1967 he joined The University of Texas at Austin, where he is Stiles Professor in Comparative Studies.

C. F. A. PANTIN received his Sc.D. from Cambridge University in 1933. After a period on the staff of the Marine Biological Association of the United Kingdom, he was later successively Lecturer, Reader, and Professor in the Department of Zoology, Cambridge, where one of his subdepartments concerned animal behavior. He was a Fellow of the Royal Society, President of the Marine Biological Association, and Chairman of Trustees of the British Museum (Natural History). His book, *The Relations between the Sciences,* has been published since his death in 1967.

HELMUTH PLESSNER is Professor Emeritus of Sociology of the University of Göttingen. He is well-known for his work in both philosophy and sociology. Some of his best known books are *Die Stufen des Organischen und der Mensch* (2nd edition, 1965), *Die verspätete Nation* (2nd edition, 1960), and *Lachen und Weinen* (3rd edition, 1961).

MICHAEL POLANYI received his education in Budapest. He was a member of the Kaiser Wilhelm Institute für Physikalische Chemie from 1923 to 1933; in 1933 he became Professor of Physical Chemistry at the University of Manchester, England, and subsequently, from 1948 to 1958, Professor of Social Studies at the same university. He was elected Senior Research Fellow at Merton College, Oxford, in 1959, became an Honorary Foreign Member of the American Academy of Arts and Sciences, Philosophy Section, in 1965, and has been awarded honorary degrees at a number of universities. His publications include *Atomic Reactions* (1932), *Full Employment and Free Trade* (1945), *The Logic of Liberty* (1951), *Personal Knowledge* (1958), *The Study of Man* (1959), and *The Tacit Dimension* (1966).

NEWTON P. STALLKNECHT received his Ph.D. in philosophy from Princeton University in 1930. He was on the faculty of Bowdoin College from 1930 to 1949. He became Chairman of the Department of Philosophy at Indiana University in 1949, and from 1963 to 1968 was Professor of Philosophy and Comparative Literature. He is now Professor of Comparative Literature and Criticism, and Director of the School of Letters. His publications include *Studies in the Philosophy of Creation* (1934), *Strange Seas of Thought, William Wordsworth's Philosophy of Man and Nature* (1945), and, with W. S. Brumbaugh, *The Spirit of Western Philosophy* (1950) and *The Compass of Philosophy* (1954). He was also coeditor and contributor to *Comparative Literature: Method and Perspective* (1961).

Erwin W. Straus received his M. D. from the University of Berlin in 1919. During the 1920's and 1930's he practiced neurology and psychiatry in Berlin, and was Associate Professor at the University of Berlin. He came to the United States in 1938, was Professor of Psychology at Black Mountain College until 1944, and a Research Fellow at Johns Hopkins from 1944 to 1946. He then joined the VA Hospital at Lexington, Kentucky, and was Director of Professional Education and Research until his retirement in 1961. He holds the titles of Clinical Professor in Psychiatry at the University of Kentucky Medical Center and Associate Professor in Psychiatry at the University of Louisville Medical School. His publications include *On Obsession* (1948), *The Primary World of the Senses* (2nd edition, 1956), *Phenomenology: Pure and Applied* (1965), and *Phenomenological Psychology* (1966).

Donald L. Weismann received his Ph.D. in Fine Arts from Ohio State University in 1950. He has taught at Illinois State University, Wayne State University, the University of Kentucky, and, since 1954, at The University of Texas, first as Chairman of the Department of Art and now as University Professor in the Arts and Director of Comparative Studies. Since 1934 he has exhibited paintings and collages nationally and internationally. His two most recent books are *Jelly Was the Word* and *Language and Visual Form.* He has contributed articles to *Midwest Review, Texas Quarterly, New Mexico Quarterly, New Republic, Christian Scholar,* and other journals. In 1966 he was appointed by the President of the United States to a six-year term on the National Council on the Arts.

Eugene P. Wigner was educated in Europe. From 1930 to 1937 he taught at Princeton University and was professor of physics at the University of Wisconsin in 1937-1938. He then returned to Princeton as Thomas D. Jones Professor of Mathematical Physics. He was a member of the General Advisory Committee to the United States Atomic Energy Commission, 1952-1957, 1959-1964, and has been on the physics panel of the National Science Foundation since 1953. He received the Enrico Fermi Award in 1958, the Atoms for Peace Award in 1960, the Max Planck medal in 1961, and the Nobel prize for physics in 1963.